RECONCILABLE DIFFERENCES

HOPE AND HEALING FOR TROUBLED MARRIAGES

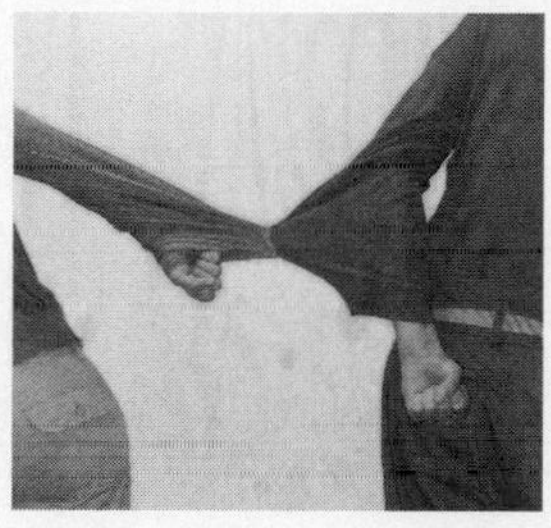

VIRGINIA TODD HOLEMAN

InterVarsity Press
Downers Grove, Illinois

InterVarsity Press
P.O. Box 1400, Downers Grove, IL 60515-1426
World Wide Web: www.ivpress.com
E-mail: mail@ivpress.com

InterVarsity Press® is the book-publishing division of InterVarsity Christian Fellowship/USA®, a student movement active on campus at hundreds of universities, colleges and schools of nursing in the United States of America, and a member movement of the International Fellowship of Evangelical Students. For information about local and regional activities, write Public Relations Dept., InterVarsity Christian Fellowship/USA, 6400 Schroeder Rd., P.O. Box 7895, Madison, WI 53707-7895, or visit the IVCF website at <www.intervarsity.org>.

Design: Cindy Kiple

Images: Colin Hawkins/Getty images

ISBN 0-8308-3219-X

Printed in the United States of America ∞

Library of Congress Cataloging-in-Publication Data

Holeman, Virginia Todd, 1953-
Reconciliable differences : hope and healing for troubled marriages / Virginia Todd Holeman.
p. cm.
Includes bibliographical references
ISBN 0-8308-3219-X (pbk.: alk. paper)
1. Marriage—Religious aspects—Christianity. 2. Reconciliation—Religious aspects—Christianity. I. Title.
BV835.H635 2004
248.8'44—dc22

2004011517

P 19 18 17 16 15 14 13 12 11 10 9 8 7 6 5 4 3 2 1
Y 19 18 17 16 15 14 13 12 11 10 09 08 07 06 05 04

CONTENTS

1. Introduction: The Journey Begins 7

PART 1: COMMITMENTS THAT NURTURE RECONCILIATION

2. Marital Crossroads 33

3. Active Commitment 52

4. Community: Bearing One Another's Burdens 72

PART 2: TASKS THAT ENCOURAGE RECONCILIATION

5. Growing Up and Growing Together 95

6. Seeking Forgiveness 121

7. Extending Forgiveness 147

8. Rebuilding Truth, Trust and Trustworthiness 177

9. Conclusion: We've a Story to Tell 200

Appendix A: Resources for Reconciliation 226

Appendix B: Advice About Reconciliation 231

Glossary 235

References 240

Acknowledgments 248

Subject and Names Index 249

Scripture Index 252

1

INTRODUCTION

The Journey Begins

Intimate relationships are a part of life. If you desire an intimate relationship, you may cling to the hope that you will soon meet "the one" for you. If you are in an intimate relationship, all may seem right with your world. But if you have been wounded by someone who is emotionally close to you, you may wonder whether that relationship will survive the assault—especially when another's rejection, betrayal, disloyalty or addictive behaviors have hurt you severely, repeatedly and unjustly. You may very well echo the words of Psalm 55:

> If an enemy were insulting me,
> I could endure it;
> if a foe were raising himself against me,
> I could hide from him.
> But it is you, a [person] like myself,
> my companion, my close friend,
> with whom I once enjoyed sweet fellowship
> as we walked with the throng at the house of God. (vv. 12-14)

When your relationship is fractured, you may fear that it is beyond repair. Whether that relationship is with a longtime friend, business colleague or other family member, you may wonder about the feasibility of reconciliation. When the betrayer is your spouse, the wound seems even more deadly.

Many wish they could erase what has happened. Victims may want to trust wrongdoers again and, just like the loving father of the prodigal (see Lk 15:20-24), they watch for signs that the ones from whom they are estranged have come to their senses and are returning home. Sorrowful transgressors, longing to undo the damage they have done, may throw themselves on the mercy of the injured party like the prodigal son threw himself on his father's mercy (see Lk 15:11-20).

Unfortunately far too many of us experience just the opposite. Extensive betrayal threatens to destroy our relationship. Repair seems out of the question. Parting is not filled with sweet sorrow. It is fraught with problems, unanticipated consequences and great emotional turmoil. Injured parties, who see perpetrators through the lens of white-hot anger, may hold a grudge and, like Esau, long for revenge (see Gen 27:36-41). Transgressors may want to escape or evade the fallout and, like Jacob, abandon the wounded relationship for years (see Gen 27:42-45).

Distance, suspicion and estrangement replace intimacy, acceptance and belonging. The thought of restoration is appalling, and the idea of termination is appealing. In other words, reconciliation seems like a pipe dream. Can people in severely damaged relationships reconcile? More specifically, can couples in severely damaged marriages reconcile? Consider Tom and Sandy's situation.

Tom and Sandy's Story

Tom and Sandy were high-school sweethearts. They married before they graduated from high school, when Sandy became pregnant. During the next three years, Sandy and Tom added two more children to their family. Sandy says, *"We had all of our children by the time I was twenty-three. . . . Tom got really busy with his job. He was working, providing for the family. And I was busy taking care of the home. I always felt like the man went out and brought home the paycheck, and the wife stayed home and kept the home front. . . . Those first few years were bliss for me."*

Of those years, Tom says, *"I was married, but I didn't really feel the impact. . . . I kept doing my thing."*

Sandy was aware that Tom drank, but she didn't become alarmed by it until he began drinking heavily. Things deteriorated. After a time, Sandy says, *"I went to the bars; I grabbed him up by his shirt collar and dragged him out."*

Tom says, *"I never did stop loving Sandy and the kids. That was never, never a question, but I always felt that I was missing out on something."* As time passed, Tom became an expert alcoholic. He drank all night and worked all day. Sandy discovered that she could control Tom through her biting, sarcastic language. Their lives were rapidly spiraling out of control.

Eventually Sandy convinced Tom to enter treatment. He stopped drinking, about which he says, *"I did that for five years, and in the back of my little mind I knew that after five years I'd drink again."* And he did. After five years of sobriety, Tom told Sandy that he was going to start drinking again. Sandy was actually relieved because now she would have an explanation for Tom's recent depressed behavior. Their former pattern reasserted itself, and family life quickly descended into chaos.

Added to this mix was the fact that their daughters were now teenagers. Tom and his oldest daughter had a particularly combative relationship. If Tom and his daughter weren't fighting, Sandy was browbeating him. He learned that he could avoid all this if he drank enough to send himself into a minor alcoholic stupor. He would pass out on the couch, and there would be "peace" in the home.

Things continued to deteriorate. A few more years passed, and Sandy finally reached the end of her rope. After a particularly nasty episode, she told Tom, *"You need to choose the alcohol or your family."*

Tom replied, *"Well, I'll be out in an hour."* He packed his bags and left.

What Does Reconciliation Look Like?

Sadly, Sandy and Tom's story is not exceptional. I think it's safe to say that all of us know of at least one couple whose relationship has ended because of some painful moral transgression. Abandonment and neglect, addiction, adultery, abuse (physical, emotional, sexual and even spiritual), various types of betrayals, financial irresponsibility, deceitfulness, disrespect—the list goes on. I suspect that many of us know more than just one couple. In some cases you may not be surprised to learn that a spouse has moved out, while in other situations you are shocked. Sandy and Tom, for instance, seemed like the "perfect family" at church. Home was another story entirely. Their situation begs us to ask the questions that shape this book: Can couples reconcile when their marriage has been severely damaged by moral wrongdoing? What roles do forgiveness and repentance play? Do other elements contribute to marital reconciliation in addition to forgiveness and repentance? Do reconciled marriages look alike, or are their contours unique, given the various contexts in which couples find themselves?

Before we dive into these questions, let's begin by defining the principal term of this book: *reconciliation*. Describing reconciliation is not as straightforward as it appears. Often elements of forgiveness are stirred in with the reconciliation batter so that "to forgive" becomes synonymous with "to reconcile," and somehow accountability and change (repentance) are omitted from the recipe altogether. This would be the case if Tom said he was sorry and came back home but nothing changed. Sandy appears to forgive Tom. Tom appears to repent. The couple seems to have reconciled because they are living together again. But if they pick up where they left off (Tom drinking and Sandy berating), is *this* what reconciliation is all about?

What picture comes to your mind when you think about reconciliation? I think images of reconciliation are as varied as the troubles that tear people apart. Maybe you think about the two feuding families in Shakespeare's *Romeo and Juliet* and how the death of their children ended the hostility between them. Perhaps you know a story of reconciliation that occurred on someone's deathbed. You may even consider the wonder of your own reconciliation with God through the cross of Jesus Christ. These few examples reveal that reconciliation can mean different things under different circumstances. Let's look at this more closely.

Sometimes reconciliation is like a cease-fire in which warring parties stop their barrage of negative exchanges. Did your parents ever tell you to tell someone you were sorry? In this case a more powerful external authority imposes reconciliation on the contentious relationship. Or did a serious ideological argument threaten a friendship? To preserve your connection without abandoning your ideals, you may have decided to settle your differences by agreeing to disagree. In these examples, the external fighting ends but the internal tension remains. These unresolved issues may smolder for years under an apparently banked fire, ready to ignite when the conditions are right.

At other times reconciliation implies that you have achieved some degree of friendliness with the person from whom you are estranged. Here we add a positive element to reconciliation. We not only call a cease-fire (end negative exchanges) but also create a treaty (begin positive exchanges). Divorced parents embody this kind of reconciliation when they cooperate around the tasks of parenting their children. In effect they create a space for a special kind of connection. They do not intend to remarry, because many differences between them continue to exist. However, they settle enough of their differences so that they can work together for the sake of their children.

Reconciliation also can imply that you have balanced a relationship account. Deathbed confessions and statements of forgiveness are intended to close the books on some unresolved interpersonal episode and may bring comfort and release to the bereaved. Of course, you don't have to wait until you are dying to reconcile a relationship debt! Replacing a broken item or returning a favor may help to balance overdue accounts. Unfortunately, restocking material goods does not relieve the sense of personal violation that often accompanies such a loss.

Trust is not easily restored. Yet these strategies make up much of what we call reconciliation in our day-to-day life, and they do help us to preserve our relationships. However, they preserve only the *form* of a relationship; they do not change its heart. In other words, they do not bring about the kind of *relationship renewal* that a couple like Sandy and Tom needs in order to have a healthy relationship.

Sadly, Tom and Sandy—and those around them—may be content to settle for "cheap reconciliation." Here beliefs about one another and ways of interacting do not *radically* change. Wrongdoers do not hold themselves fully accountable, nor do they commit themselves to consistent changed behavior over time. Injured parties extend a form of forgiveness but may harbor grudges that persist for years. The problems that threatened to undo the couple are still present either overtly (repeated infractions occur) or covertly (fear or threat of repeated harm is present). "Catastrophe" has been averted, and the status quo has been maintained. However, the status quo is *not* acceptable when emotional betrayal, addictions, or physical and sexual violence damage close relationships. Our picture of reconciliation must therefore go beyond mere preservation.

Recently scholars have begun to write about reconciliation. Family therapist Froma Walsh observes that reconciliation requires "a readiness on the part of each person to take the others seriously, to acknowledge violations to the relationship, and to experience the pain associated with the acknowledgment. Reconciliation is more than righting wrongs; it brings us to a deeper place of trust and commitment" (1998, p. 284).

A definition of reconciliation: Reconciliation is the active commitment to the restoration of love and trustworthiness by both injured party and transgressor so that their relationship may be transformed.

Forgiveness researcher Everett L. Worthington Jr. defines reconciliation as "restoring trust in a relationship in which trust has been damaged" (2001, p. 157). He and his colleague Dewitt Drinkard (2000) have experimented with a psychoeducational program to promote reconciliation in couples. Walsh, Worthington and Drinkard are obviously pointing to more than relationship *preservation*. They have set their sights on relationship *transformation*. With this in mind, I define reconciliation as *the active commitment to the restoration of love and trustworthiness by both injured party and transgressor so that their relationship may be transformed.* Let's look at the four parts of this definition a bit closer.

First, transformation is the ultimate goal of reconciliation. This is more than the cessation of negativity, the introduction of goodwill or the balancing of emotional ledgers, although these may be part of the larger process. Often they are as far as the relationship goes. Full reconciliation, however, involves a metamorphosis of injured party, transgressor *and* their relationship (Holeman, 2000, 2003; Pargament & Rye, 1998). This is especially important in severely damaged relationships like that of Sandy and Tom. Transformation is not a return to the way things used to be. Instead it involves courageous reengagement between victim and wrongdoer to reshape their relationship and to restore truth, trust and love.

It would be helpful at this point to differentiate transformative reconciliation from other types of relationship repair strategies. Transforming reconciliation may include aspects of conflict management, but it is not merely conflict management. Conflict management suggests that there is a solid moral basis on which to build but this base is threatened by the escalating tension between various parties. Moral violations have not entered the picture—at least not yet.

Reconciliation that transforms is also different from *forbearance, accommodation* or *acceptance*. When you extend forbearance to another, you resist avoidance, refrain from revenge and continue to treat the wrongdoer kindly (McCullough, Fincham & Tsang, 2003). If you engage in accommodation strategies, you not only inhibit the impulse to react negatively in return, you also act in a constructive manner (Rusbult, Bissonnette, Arriaga & Cox, 1998). If you adopt acceptance, you embrace annoying mannerisms or behaviors as what is given about your mate, and you release your desire for your mate to change (Jacobson & Christensen, 1996).

These strategies may adequately mend many garden-variety relationship offenses, and they may be successfully employed to calm interpersonal rough waters when differences in personality exist. By suggesting that relationship transformation is the ultimate goal of reconciliation, I am not discounting the unfolding nature of reconciling; conflict management, forbearance, accommodation or acceptance may be needed as couples seek relationship transformation. Neither am I *prescribing* what reconciled relationships will look like when all is said and done. I am saying, however, that transformed relationships look and feel differently from their "pre-reconciled" state. When dissolution seems the most likely response to a moral offense, reconciliation requires vital change.

Second, reconciliation that transforms demands the undivided attention of both parties in the close relationship. While one partner can offer forbearance, accommodation or acceptance and thereby avoid divorce, it takes two to attain transformation. In marriages, relationship transformation is *not* a solo performance. This is one aspect that distinguishes reconciliation from forgiving and repenting. When injured parties forgive transgressors, they replace negative emotions such as bitterness, anger and fear with positive emotions such as compassion, empathy and love. Injured parties can forgive independent of any change in the wrongdoer (Worthington, 2001). When offenders repent, they confess and commit to changed behavior over time. Transgressors can repent even if those they offended reject them. Both victim and victimizer must participate to reconcile.

Third, the restoration of love and trustworthiness is the focus of transforming reconciliation. These are the intangible but very real things that were destroyed by the offending action. And because they are intangible, they are more difficult to repair than a broken lamp or a diminished bank account. Love and trustworthiness are rebuilt over time, just like forgiveness (McCullough et al., 2003; Worthington et al., 2000).

For a couple like Sandy and Tom, it would not be difficult to conceive of them working on reconciliation for about two years before they feel they can breathe easy. This brings us to the fourth aspect of this definition: active commitment. Transforming reconciliation is hard work. Only those with the active commitment to stick with it will survive the early months of doubt, pain, fear and disappointment.

Elizabeth and Alan's Story, Part One

"Hey, girl, can you tell me where Jim lives?" Not the most auspicious opening line, but it was enough. Alan and a buddy were on their way home from a college golf tournament. They had stopped at a gas station to track down a friend, and Elizabeth happened to be the first person they saw. A year later, Alan and Elizabeth began dating. He was a sophomore in college, and she was a high-school senior.

After four chaotic years of dating, Alan thought about ending their relationship. Then Elizabeth told him she was pregnant. The young couple married, but Alan's drinking and his desire for his premarital bachelor lifestyle of golfing troubled their early marital relationship. He sobered up (literally and figuratively) when he didn't make the cut for the Professional Golfers' Association. While Alan moved from one low-level job to another, Elizabeth's income wasn't enough to keep them out of debt. Alan was despondent. One day he just screamed out, *"God, this can't be what you intended for my life. Either take me back or show me the way."* And God did.

A whirlwind of movement and change characterized the next few years. On the surface their marriage seemed to improve, but a hidden threat had entered the picture. Of this time, Elizabeth says, *"I felt endangered because a man had come into my life that I was attracted to and became interested in having an affair with. . . . I knew that if I wasn't careful, something was going to happen. That's when I went to church. I said, 'Going to church will protect me.'"*

Alan and Elizabeth joined a church where they became baptized and committed followers of Jesus Christ. They grew in their faith. Alan decided that he wanted to become a pastor, and he began seminary. In the meantime Elizabeth began a three-year, on-and-off affair. Of the affair, she says, *"It was easy for me to say, 'God's going to forgive me.' But I now realize that just cheapens God's grace. To look at me, everyone would have said, 'She's the perfect example of what a Christian woman/mother/wife should be.' . . . So though it appeared that I was really running headlong toward God with every step I took, I was hightailing it out of there."* Alan had some misgivings about Elizabeth's relationship with her coworker, but because he trusted her, he disregarded his internal warning system. Yet he grew more suspicious.

One day Alan listened to Elizabeth's voice mail. What he heard confirmed his doubts: Elizabeth was having an affair. When she came home from work, Alan confronted her. She denied it until he repeated the content of the voice mail. Alan says, *"I yelled and cussed and screamed and called her a whore. . . . I was just in a state of shock and anger. I remember that I took one of the kitchen chairs and slammed it down. It broke. The spindle broke on it. She said, 'That was my grandma's chair.' I said, 'Screw Grandma's chair. What about my life and my heart?'"*

Recalling this confrontation, Elizabeth says, *"He was furious. . . . I was suicidal. If there had been anything stronger than Tylenol in my house, I probably wouldn't be alive today, because I would have taken it and just faded away because of the pain it was causing him and was going to cause him, and us, and me."* Elizabeth implored him to give her a second chance. Alan halfheartedly agreed, but they wondered if they would make it.

Is Reconciliation an Impossible Journey?

What does it take to restore a damaged relationship, especially a wounded marriage? Common sense tells us that willingness to reconcile rests on such things as who did what to whom, when, for how long and how often. When transgressors' offenses are minor and happen infrequently or when wrongdoers apologize and change, relationship restoration is likely. For example, when someone you care about is late, forgetful or short tempered, you can often overlook or ignore what happened. You may decide that you can tolerate the other's actions. However, when offenses are serious and occur frequently, and transgressors show little remorse or make no effort to permanently change their behavior, reconciliation seems improbable. In fact, maintaining a destructive relationship may be at best unwise and at worst dangerous, particularly in cases of physical, emotional and sexual abuse. While you may long to restore the fractured relationship, returning to the way things were does not challenge the sinful actions of the transgressor in ways that demand change in his or her behaviors and attitudes and that establish relationship safety, accountability and trustworthiness. In the vignettes you have read, both Sandy and Alan faced this exact situation. The behavior of their spouses required confrontation, not coddling.

Sadly, many who desire reconciliation will not achieve it. Good reasons exist that explain why some couples encounter relational "Road Closed" signs, and closed roads can stop us in our tracks. Let me explain.

When I was a teenager, decades before anyone had heard of cell phones, my mother and I regularly shared holiday meals with family friends. One particular Easter, a surprising but not unprecedented snow fell as we worshiped our risen Lord. We emerged from church to find at least six inches of snow on the roads and not a snowplow in sight. Our Easter dinner awaited us.

My mother and I got into the car and began our trip from church to our friend's home, which normally took no more than five minutes. Our friend's neighborhood was built into the side of a mountain, and the only way to get there was to go up a steep hill. We went on our merry way, confident that our car would not let us down. One hour later, within one block of the crest of the hill and almost within sight of our destination, my mother gave up. Too much snow lay on the ground. Too much time had passed. Too much energy had been expended. My mother just wanted to go home. Somehow she managed to turn the car around and began our journey home. That trip, which normally took fifteen minutes, lasted another two hours.

How does this story clarify my picture of closed roads? We need to differentiate between closed roads and roadblocks or detours. Closed roads can bring our journey to an end; alternate routes to our destination do not exist. To take another route means to accept a different destination.

For some, dissolution of a marriage may be the wisest course of action, especially when abuse or repeated and unrepentant betrayals factor into the picture (Lamb, 2002). For others, the decision is taken out of their hands because their partner does not desire reconciliation. One reconciler recognized this fact when she said, *"Both of us really wanted to reconcile, and I believe that's the key to rebuilding anything—both of you have to have a very strong desire. And that's not always the case."*

Worthington (2001) has developed a model of reconciliation based on the image of building a bridge over the great divide that transgressions create between two people. The first plank on the bridge is "decide to reconcile." Worthington notes that there are a number of reasons people may decide *not* to reconcile. For example, they have "clicked off" to one another and are not interested in "clicking on." Maybe they like being apart more than they liked being together, or the work of reconciliation is too daunting and one or both lack the energy to try. The costs of reconciling can also outweigh the benefits.

Worthington points out several aspects of reconciliation that contribute to whether or not you encounter a closed road. First, he states that reconciliation entails risk. We may long for a risk-free relationship, but none exists. When people consider whether or not to reenter a wounded relationship, risk factors are painted in neon letters and should not be ignored.

Second, Worthington observes that reconciliation is not always desirable. He writes, "It may be unhealthy or unsafe to try to reconcile" (2001, p. 163). This is particularly true if you have been subject to abuse or domination of any kind in your relationship. No one should return to an abusive relationship until the abuser has had help and has demonstrated changed behavior over time. Clearly reconciliation is impossible if the wrongdoer is unrepentant, shows no sincere sorrow and has no intention of changing. Injured parties need to recognize that they may want someone to change but they cannot will the offender to want to change (Friedman, 1985).

Third, reconciliation may not be possible. One of the two people might be unavailable (that is, in jail, deceased, very ill and so on) or may have changed his or her life in such a way that reconciliation cannot happen (such as remarried or relocated).

Fourth, reconciliation may not be prudent. An offer of reconciliation may come after too much pain has been dumped into the relationship. The work of reconciliation may exceed the strength and stamina that either the transgressor or the wounded party possesses, or not enough healing has happened for the couple to enter into the process of reconciling.

So Can This Marriage Be Saved?

As a seminary professor and a marriage and family therapist, I know all too well how Christians struggle with the tension between the biblical teaching about reconciliation and the everyday reality of their lives. Because of Christ's life, death and resurrection, we have been reconciled to God. This is the vertical dimension of reconciliation. But biblical reconciliation also has a horizontal dimension. Not only are we reconciled to God, we are also to be reconciled with one another. This sounds great in theory. Research suggests that religious people perceive themselves to be forgiving people (McCullough & Worthington, 1999)—that is, until we have been deeply and unjustly hurt by someone *in particular.* Then our theology and our experience collide. We love being forgiven by God; we question the sanity of forgiving and being reconciled with one another. Through the cross of Christ, God—the divine injured party—endured great pain for the sake of our relationship with him. When we, as human injured parties, contemplate enduring similar pain, we often argue, "It's not fair! I've already been hurt once; now you want me to suffer more pain to save this relationship?" This is where we left Alan and Elizabeth. We will continue their story in chapter two.

Social scientists have amassed an impressive body of research that sheds light on why marriages dissolve (see, for example, Gottman, 1994; Markman, Stanley & Blumberg, 1994) so that counselors today know a lot about what factors contribute to divorce. For example, John Gottman (1994) and his colleagues at the University of Washington have studied thousands of couples in their "marriage lab." They can predict with surprising accuracy which couples are most likely to experience marriage-threatening trouble. Gottman notes that when four specific interaction patterns are present, a couple may eventually head toward the slippery slope of divorce:

- Criticism: "attacking someone's personality or character—rather than a specific behavior—usually with blame" (p. 73). Criticisms are blaming, generalized judgments (for example, "you always" or "you never"), as opposed to complaints that are statements of displeasure or anger about specific behaviors.

- Contempt: "the intention to insult and psychologically abuse [the other person]" (p. 79). Contempt includes insults, name calling, hostile humor, mockery and contemptuous body language (for example, a sneer).
- Defensiveness: statements that deflect blame. Defensive statements can also include denying responsibility, making excuses, whining and cross-complaining.
- Stonewalling: psychologically or physically checking out of the relationship (for example, giving someone the "silent treatment" or "cold shoulder").

Gottman's work focused on predictors of marital dissolution. This is invaluable information for pastors and counselors. We know what danger signs to look for and can devise remediation measures.

I pursued this study because I was interested in a different set of questions. Because I believe that God equips us to do what he calls us to do, I wanted to investigate how real people repair real relationships when they seem irreparable. What motivates reconciliation in severely wounded close relationships? How do couples do it? What do these restored relationships look like? To answer these questions, I asked friends, students and professional colleagues if they knew of anyone who had successfully recovered from a severely damaged relationship. My hope was to collect as many stories as I could from as many different kinds of relationships (siblings, coworkers, friends, spouses, adult children-parents) as I could. I was willing to talk with "whosoever" would share their stories with me, provided both participants were over eighteen years old, they almost lost their relationship because of a wrongdoing, and their relationship was still ongoing.

These inquiries led me to twelve couples from across the United States and Canada who accepted my invitation to talk in depth with me about their marriage.[1] I did not select these couples because of the specific nature of the problem they faced but because they were willing to share their stories with me. Of these twelve couples, only two of the major offenses were committed by wives, and eight of the stories centered on infidelity. Obviously this is not a random sample of marital problems! While I would have wished to find more equal representation of sinning by both genders, and a broader spectrum of offenses, I do believe that the lessons from the lives of these twelve brave couples transcend most types of offenses that married couples might experience.

You may be reading this book as a person who wants to reconcile another type of relationship (such as with a friend, coworker or sibling) and may be wondering if there is anything in here for you. The chapters that follow can help you too, even if these examples are exclusively marital ones. Whether differences exist between how married couples reconcile and how other types of relationships reconcile is a question for future research. Nevertheless, I encourage you to read on and listen to the stories more for the processes in which these couples engaged than for the exact nature of the offenses from which they recovered.

I interviewed each mate separately for an hour and a half to hear the story of what went wrong, and then the three of us met for another ninety-minute conversation as we discussed how they went about the repair process. In several cases I traveled to their home and spent time with them beyond the formal interviews, so I was able to get a sense of their current marital well-being firsthand. These courageous couples gave me permission to audiotape our conversations for further analysis. (I have changed their names and adjusted information to protect their identities.) I analyzed our discussions and searched for common threads that these couples wove into the fabric of their story. The themes that

[1]The call for participants also surfaced six nonmarried individuals who agreed to be interviewed and who were interviewed following the three-interview protocol. I do not include their stories in this work because (1) I was not able to speak with the other person who was involved in the process of reconciling and (2) I desire a larger sample of nonmarried reconciling partners. This will be the work of future research.

emerged and the stories themselves form the heart of this book.[2]

These couples desire two things. First, they want their stories to offer hope that radical relationship transformation can and does happen. They do not view reconciliation through rose-colored glasses. As they began to rebuild their marriages, at least half of the couples had doubted their ability to achieve and maintain significant changes in their relationship, and all of them struggled through many dark days of emotional pain and suffering along the way. They offer their stories as a *description* of what God can do with damaged hearts, not as a *prescription* for what another couple should do. Second, they want to help counselors and pastors work more effectively with people whose relationships are at the brink of disaster. They offer examples of ways in which clergy, counselors and even friends and family can help or hinder reconciliation.

While personal testimonies can inspire, a firmer foundation is needed to delve into the mysteries of reconciliation. When investigating uncharted territory, explorers use two known points (such as stars) to determine their whereabouts. This process is called triangulation. For many, reconciliation is indeed uncharted territory, and we therefore need two fixed points to help us to find our location. Biblical/theological studies and psychological discoveries will serve as my two orienting points. The biblical narrative describes how God's people struggled to reconcile with each other, just as we do today, and presents reconciliation as a major theme of Christ's earthly mission, which is carried on by God's redeemed and reconciled people. Theological discussions embed reconciliation in the context of the Trinity where the life, death and resurrection of Jesus Christ are the model for and the call to reconciliation. Finally, current psychological discussions about forgiving, repenting and reconciling will describe the "how to" for biblical and theological "can and ought to." Let's take a brief look at these orienting points.

---

[2]For those of you who are interested in more specifics about the research methodology of this study, see my 2003 article "Marital Reconciliation: A Long and Winding Road," *Journal of Psychology and Christianity* 22:30-42.

The God of Transformation and Reconciliation

God has been in the transformation business since the beginning of time. Through his word, he transformed a formless, empty darkness into the earth. Through his breath, he transformed the dust of the ground into humanity. Through his promise, he transformed Abram and Sarai into Israel, his chosen people. Through his Son, he transformed his chosen people into the ecclesia—the church.

God has been in the reconciliation business for an equally long period of time. Scripture reveals a loving and merciful God who seeks and desires reconciliation with a people who have become hostile toward him and estranged from him. Whenever God's people betray their covenant relationship with him, he provides a way for them to return and to restore their intimacy with him. For example, Adam and Eve's sin devastated their perfect union and intimacy with God and with one another. Yet God continued to seek them out and provided clothing and a new home for them instead of instantaneous damnation. Although their act of betrayal closed the door to pure communion with their Creator, God transformed this breach into the portal through which Christ would enter the world.

Time and time again God's chosen people rejected the one true God, who delivered them out of Egypt, and they pledged their loyalty to the foreign gods of the land in which they lived. Eventually their disloyalty cost them their homeland and sent them into exile, despite God's repeated pleas to return to him. Yet even in their exile, God continued to speak to them words of hope, restoration and reconciliation through the voice of God's prophets, instead of abandoning them forever.

The triune God paints the picture of transforming reconciliation most boldly through the life, death and resurrection of Jesus Christ. You may even consider reconciliation as a theme of Jesus' life and ministry. Christ comes so that we can be reconciled to God and to one another. His life embodies forgiveness as the pathway to reconciliation. From the story of Adam and Eve, throughout the history of the children of Israel, within the narratives of the New Testament and up until our lives today, this pattern repeats.

Four New Testament passages speak specifically about the reconciling work of the cross of Christ. The cross provides for the reconciliation of the cosmos to God (Col 1:19-23), humanity to God (Rom 5:10-11), groups of people (for example, Jews and Gentiles) to God and to one another (Eph 2:11-22), and members of the body of Christ with one another (Eph 2:11-22; 2 Cor 5:18—6:2). Divine reconciliation destroys the hostility that separates God's people from God and from one another by grappling with the root cause of that enmity: our sin.

Note that God did not create the hostility that separates us from him. *We* did, through our deliberate disloyalty and betrayal of our covenant relationship with God. Our hearts of stone need transformation; God's heart of everlasting love does not. Scripture teaches that the cross of Christ reveals not God's wrath but his unfathomable, eternal and unquenchable love for us (Green & Baker, 2000; Shults & Sandage, 2003). Christ died so that we, who are God's enemies, can now become God's children. His love motivates, sustains and provides the way for this reconciliation. When we are reconciled to God through the life, death and resurrection of Jesus Christ, we are transformed into members of God's reconciled and redeemed people. This isn't a reconciliation that preserves the status quo. It is a reconciliation that intends to transform hearts of stone into hearts overflowing with Christ's love.

Through the cross of Christ, personal transformation and interpersonal reconciliation should go hand in hand. Church historian Martin Marty observes, "In the New Testament . . . forgiveness always leads to reconciliation, and reconciliation results from mutual experiences of forgiveness. They cannot be separated" (1998, p. 11). That is, Scripture links our reconciliation with God to our reconciliation with one another. For example, Paul describes how the cross of Christ destroys the walls of hostility that separate groups of people (see Eph 2:11-22). We see this specifically in Paul's challenge to Philemon to contemplate the implications of his new life in Christ, that is, to be reconciled with

Onesimus, his former slave. According to 2 Corinthians 5, we are reconciled to God through the cross of Christ and we are given the ministry of reconciliation with one another. Please note that in 2 Corinthians, Paul, a brother in Christ, appeals to the church in Corinth to be reconciled to him and to one another. This reconciliation happens within the household of faith.

It will not take you long to recognize a wide gap between the ideal and the real, between the interpersonal transformation that *should* take place in the lives of people who are forgiven and reconciled to God and the transgressions that *do* take place between the same. The parable of the unforgiving servant highlights this dilemma (see Mt 18:23-35). In this parable the king graciously forgives his servant of a debt so large that the servant had no hope of ever repaying it. Upon receiving this unprecedented gift, you might imagine that the servant would be overflowing with gratitude and generosity. Instead we discover that the forgiven servant angrily demands payment of a much lesser debt that a coworker owes him. In other words, we love being forgiven by God and reconciled to God, but we are reluctant, if not resistant, to extending the same gracious gift to someone who we believe "owes us." This presents us with a conundrum. If you concur with me that the biblical bias is reconciliation, then you see that we are in a real predicament when we hurt each other in ways that make biblical reconciliation seem untenable. Psychological discoveries may help us to put feet to this biblical "can and ought to."

Psychological Discoveries

As we enter the twenty-first century, social scientists have turned their attention to a study of those things that enhance our personal and interpersonal lives. This emphasis on positive psychology has launched discussions on things like hope, humility, altruism, gratitude and love. Explorations about seeking forgiveness, extending forgiveness and reconciling would fall under this large umbrella. Groundbreaking investigations have helped us to learn about how people extend forgiveness (see, for example, Enright & Fitzgibbons, 2000; McCullough, Pargament & Thoresen, 2000; Worthington, 1998b). We now know that several things help people to forgive. First, empathy facilitates forgiving. It helps us to walk a mile in the other person's shoes. We can view the hurtful exchange from our perspective *and* from the perspective of the other. Second, humility reminds us that we too have hurt others and are not morally superior to the one who wounded us. Third, reframing allows us to look at the other through a wider lens. Our transgressor is no longer the epitome of pure evil but a human being with strengths and weaknesses, like us.

Researchers are just beginning to look into the dynamics of seeking forgiveness. Psychologist Steve Sandage and his colleagues (2000) have observed that people are more prone to ask for forgiveness as they mature morally. Awareness of the impact of one's actions on another enhances the likelihood of repentance, whereas narcissism (that is, being absorbed with one's own importance) decreases the likelihood. We also know that our moral emotions, especially shame and guilt, play a role in relationship repair (Tangney & Fischer, 1995). We experience shame as an extraordinarily painful negative evaluation of our self in response to an interpersonal situation. We are ashamed of who we are, and we believe that our damaged self is broken beyond repair. In addition, we cannot imagine any way to return to right relationships with those who pointed out our shameful condition. We feel exposed and believe that others think badly about us (whether or not they really do think this way). We feel small and powerless.

Shame motivates us in one of two directions. We want to avoid, hide and escape, or we want to blame others or strike out angrily. Neither of these strategies promotes repentance or engenders forgiveness. On the other hand, we experience guilt as less painful than shame. We feel guilt about particular behaviors without drawing conclusions about our self-worth. In guilt, we feel tension, remorse and regret about what we have done. We can imagine any number of ways to undo the damage, and we have hope that we can also repair the breach in our relationship through these acts of atonement. Guilt motivates us to confess, apologize and make amends. These actions help to call forth forgiveness in the heart of the wounded individual.

The formal scientific study of reconciliation is in an embryonic state. Earlier in this chapter I discussed how other scholars have defined reconciliation, and I offered the definition that shapes this book: reconciliation is the active commitment to the restoration of love and trustworthiness by both injured party and transgressor so that their relationship may be transformed. This interview-based exploration is an early admission into this arena. As the field of reconciliation studies grows and develops, we will know even more about how to do what Scripture says we ought to and can do.

The Journey Ahead

One summer I visited a friend in Colorado and another friend in Washington. My Colorado trip included a visit to the snowfields of the Rocky Mountains, while my Washington excursion took me to the glacier at Mount Rainier. My Colorado friend, Clyde, told me about his disastrous first experience with wilderness trekking. Prior to moving to Colorado, Clyde had often flown to Denver for business. On one of his trips, he had a long wait between the end of his meetings and his flight home, so a friend invited him to go wilderness trekking. They headed into the Rocky Mountains decked in sneakers, shorts and T-shirts. They had neither hats nor sunscreen, food nor water. The sun was out. The hike was long.

Resolute and determined men that they are, they hiked on. They were well off the beaten path when the weather changed. Icy rain replaced the blistering sun. At one point, Clyde slipped into a small stream. Wet shoes and socks do not dry quickly in cold temperatures. The pair were tired, hungry, sunburned and cold. Fortunately their story has a happy ending. Unfortunately Clyde said that he suffered the worst case of sunburn he has ever experienced. He learned a valuable lesson that day: wilderness trekking requires preparation. But what kind?

That's where my trip to Mount Rainier comes in. Having heard my friend's story, I paid careful attention to a list posted in the lodge from which amateur hikers were most likely to embark. This list specified the things that you should pack for a safe experience. The list of "essential items" included hat, sunscreen, change of clothing, matches in a watertight container, portable shelter, flashlight, walking stick, shovel, food and water. You will observe that my friend did not have *any* of these things with him when he set off into the backwoods of the Rocky Mountains. No wonder he got into so much difficulty!

As I pondered the list, I realized how much it had in common with reconciliation. If you are going for a stroll just outside the lodge (as I was), a bottle of water, a cap and some sunscreen will do the trick. But if you are planning on climbing a glacier, you need the essential items listed and more. The effort required to repair wounds and restore relationships covers an equally broad range. Small hurts ("I forgot your birthday") require less energy than large ones ("I betrayed your confidence and I emptied our joint bank account"), and the kinds of hurts that threaten to destroy a relationship require the most energy of all. But what does the essential items list for reconcilers look like?

Based on my study of the interviews with couples, I have developed a list of "essential items" for repairing damaged relationships in general and marital relationships in particular. Part one of this book discusses the commitments required for reconciliation. These include commitment to Christ (chapter two), commitment to reconciliation (chapter three) and commitment to a reconciliation-friendly community (chapter four). Part two describes actions or tasks that facilitate reconciliation. These actions include emotionally growing up (chapter five), repenting (chapter six), forgiving (chapter seven), and restoring truth and trustworthiness (chapter eight). The final chapter (chapter nine) illustrates how a new story emerges as couples discover that their work has paid off. Let me make it clear that I do not consider these eight "easy steps" to reconciliation. Wounded relationships are too unpredictable and the repair process is too messy for something so cut-and-dried. Nevertheless, I do believe that reconciliation takes particular types of commitments and that certain tasks or actions *can* help couples move toward reconciliation.

Some may not need everything on the list in order to successfully rebuild their relationship, and others may discover things that should be added to the list. I have organized the items in a way that makes sense to me. Each chapter can be read independently, and I invite you to start with the chapter(s) that seems most germane to your situation.

Biblical, theological and psychological information is woven into each chapter. My desire is that you will see how psychological research discoveries about forgiving, repenting and reconciling are consistent with God's truth. Throughout each chapter there are suggestions for personal reflection and action that may help you on your own journey on reconciliation road. If you're ready, let's begin.

PART ONE

COMMITMENTS THAT NURTURE RECONCILIATION

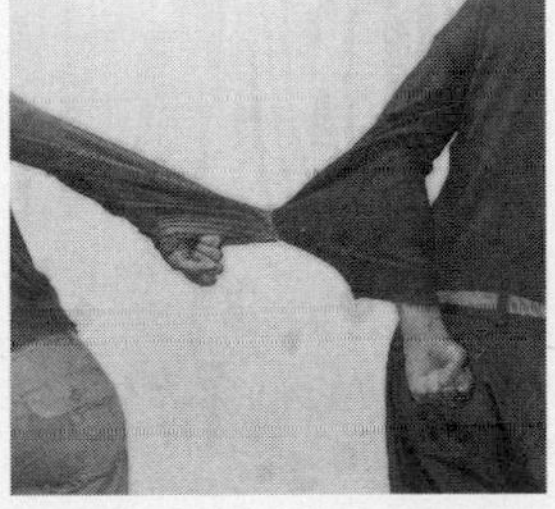

2

MARITAL CROSSROADS

I am directionally challenged. Whereas some people have an innate sense of where north, south, east and west lie, I don't. I am easily disoriented, so I rely on landmarks to help me get my directional bearings. For example, when I lived near Chicago, I knew that Lake Michigan was to the north. When I lived near Cleveland, Lake Erie was my indicator of north. As long as I knew where the lake was, I was fine.

I will never forget the first time I drove home to Cleveland after a visit to Toronto. I'd had a great weekend visiting with friends; however, all good things must come to an end, and I needed to head home. I was in a part of town that was unfamiliar to me. Twilight had fallen, so the map was hard to read. I had counted on my friend to point me in the right direction, and he had said, "Take this street to the Gardiner Expressway and head west on the Queen Elizabeth Way."

I was driving to Cleveland via Buffalo, New York. As I headed toward the Gardiner, my brain froze. In, my mind Buffalo was east of Toronto, not west! *Do I really want to go west in order to go east?* This made absolutely no sense to me. I conjured up memories of the times when my failure to trust my own directional "instincts" doubled my travel time.

I came to the crossroad. I had to decide. *Do I go east or west? Should I take the one that makes sense to me (east) or the one my friend advised (west)?* I decided to trust the instructions of my friend, a Toronto native, even if that direction did not feel right to me. Those of you who are familiar with Toronto may have already identified the source of my dilemma. I had always lived with the lake to the north, but Lake Ontario is to the south of the city. If I had headed east, I would have landed in Montreal, not Buffalo.

Life brings us to similar crossroads. We have confidence in choosing our direction when we are sure of our life landmarks. But when our landmarks are obscured at the crossroad, we become disoriented. How do we know which way to turn? Such is the crossroad we face when one of our relationships is severely damaged by moral betrayals. When that relationship is a marriage, it seems as if the burden of deciding what to do is increased because of the relational, emotional, not to mention legal, aspects involved. Do mates dissolve their marriage or rebuild their relationship? The way ahead is not clear.

Many voices in society offer guidance and advice. But what seems easiest or logical may not be the wise way to go. How do couples choose? What "life marks" will guide them when they face such moral and marital crossroads? I made it home from Toronto because I trusted my friend. When it came to traversing the ribbon of highways that surround Toronto, I knew that my friend had "been there, done that." The reconciling couples I interviewed discovered directional clarity when they submitted their reconciliation crossroad to Jesus Christ—the divine Reconciler who has "been there, done that."

In chapter one I presented the idea of gathering essential items in preparation for wilderness trekking as the guiding metaphor for this book. Chapters two through four will launch our discussion about commitments that support reconciliation. This chapter presents commitment to Jesus Christ as the first essential item that you need as you face this reconciliation crossroad. The love of God—demonstrated in the life, death and resurrection of Jesus Christ—is the model and the motivation for our reconciliation with one another, especially in marriage. The reconcilers who share their stories with us affirm that the power of the cross of Christ *is* the power of interpersonal reconciliation. In this chapter you will see how, in the midst of turmoil and pain, reconcilers gain hope for reconciliation and discover strength to hold on and stamina to move forward as they embody the way of the cross. I will use excerpts from different couples' stories to show you how reconciliation with one another begins with, is motivated by and is sustained by reconciliation with God. Let's see how Sam and Gwen turned away from divorce and turned toward rebuilding when they encountered the master Reconciler, Jesus Christ.

Gwen and Sam's Story, Part One

Gwen, a junior in college, met Sam while he was visiting a mutual friend on her campus. A year and a half later they exchanged their long-distance dating relationship for marriage. Gwen says, *"Our marriage started on dental floss. We saw each other a total of thirteen times before we got married. We got married to our vacation selves, but we met our real selves. The honeymoon was over. I discovered that Sam had a temper."*

When Gwen failed to reach Sam's standard of perfection or when she disagreed with him, he would demean and berate her. Sam says, *"I would finally just attack verbally and defend my position to the point where she was too scared to fight back verbally. It didn't matter whether I was right or wrong. It was the way I talked to her—just a very cutting attitude and tone in my voice."*

As Gwen's fear escalated, her sexual desire evaporated. *"He continued to make [sexual] advances. I continued to give in. But of course I built up an aversion. Before we knew it, it was really bad."*

In spite of this, Sam was extremely proud of his commitment to fidelity. It was the cornerstone of his self-image, and Gwen hung on to that with all her might. She says, *"In our marriage I never had any doubt in my mind that he would consider being unfaithful, even when we were not sexually active after all these years, because I knew him."*

After twelve years of emotional battles and sexual stand-offs, Gwen and Sam felt hopeless about the future of their marriage, and they began talking about divorce. At this time an attractive coworker began to pursue Sam sexually. According to Sam, *"I was getting less and less committed, less and less interested in keeping this thing [marriage] going. And then I met somebody while I was working who was very attractive and extremely aggres-*

sive. . . . Before I knew it, I was loving the attention she was paying me. I was loving the desire she had for me. And it was our office game. . . . Nothing happened but some phone calls. . . . I kept telling her, 'You know, this can't be. I'm not going to let this happen.'"

Alarmed that things *were* getting out of control, Sam talked to Gwen about his problem. She exploded. This launched an argument between them that escalated in intensity over the course of five days. Then Gwen impulsively phoned the coworker's supervisor and reported the woman's behavior. Gwen says, *"I came home and Sam was here, and I told him that I made the phone call. And he went absolutely crazy. He was frightened. He was sobbing. . . . He ran out. . . . I was lying in bed. This was my lowest point because I knew that he wanted to leave me. Maybe before, I thought he loved me, but at that point, I mean, let's give it up. That was the loneliest point of my life. And I prayed, and . . . God and I just talked about it."*

In the meantime Sam was trying to decide what to do. He was enraged that Gwen had called his workplace and terrified that her call might cost him his career. Sam felt that Gwen was trying to strip him of everything he enjoyed. *"I was so unbelievably mad that I left. I threw it in. I thought about suicide. I mean, it was just very depressing. And then the other possibility came up: 'I'll just call the other woman.' And so we talked, and we had sex together, and when we did it, it was like somebody shot me in the heart because I had done it. . . . I had done the one thing I swore I would never do. . . . And after that happened I began to feel dirty. . . . I felt every bit of the sin that I had done; it was all over me."*

Sam was so distraught that he called Gwen and told her everything that had happened. She was devastated. Both Sam and Gwen believed that their marriage was near dead. Gwen had been hanging on because of her belief in Sam's fidelity; now even that hope was gone. With his admission, Sam had put the nail in the coffin of their marriage.

A New Horizon

During a counseling session, a client said to me, "I feel like I am standing on a ledge with my nose pressed against the rock face."

I responded, "Then you may need to turn around. I think your situation may look different if you had a wider horizon."

Sam and Gwen needed a new horizon. When our interpersonal horizon is limited to the human one, painful events in our past and present become the dominant filter through which we view one another. This is where we left Sam and Gwen. One is the transgressor; the other is the injured party. One is powerful; the other is weak. One is dangerous; the other seeks safety. A mountain of pain hides hope for reconciliation. But the human context is not the only context. When we place the painful chapters in our lives within the larger story of Jesus Christ, we discover this new horizon. Marital accounts of betrayal are no longer self-contained narratives. Instead they become a paragraph that is embedded within a greater, magnificent chronicle of love. This new horizon encompasses the love of God, as shown through the life, death and resurrection of Jesus Christ. Gwen and Sam were at a marital crossroad. As we continue their story, you will see how they saw a new horizon and were able to change direction when they submitted their crossroad to the cross.

Sam and Gwen's Story, Part Two

After talking with Gwen, Sam called one of his pastors. This pastor agreed to meet him at their church. Sam says, *"I went in [to the church], and I went on my knees at the altar and I began to pray for forgiveness. I began to pour out all of these things about myself that I'd never considered that I had to take responsibility for. It was very shattering . . . realizing that there are a lot of reasons I am the way I am. But it [was] time for me to stop playing, time for me to recognize what I had done. . . . That was the beginning of the healing of the relationship. I came home that night, and Gwen could see there was something different about me."*

When Sam got home, he got on his knees and asked Gwen for forgiveness. Of this, Sam says, *"I was not going to move back on my own accord; I was going to make sure I had permission. But it had been such an earth-shattering experience for me; I thought at least she should hear me out.*

And I don't know how, but it touched her heart enough for her to let me come back into the home."

Gwen remembers: *"He said that he was so sorry, and he said that he'd asked God's forgiveness and he would ask for mine. . . . He said that he knew I could not just give him a blanket forgiveness but that he hoped that he was committed to us, and he just cried."*

Sam returned home that night with Gwen's permission. The couple made a turn toward reconciliation. They still faced the daunting challenge of repairing their broken relationship and learning how to relate to one another without Sam's verbal abuse and without Gwen's physical and emotional withdrawal, but they had started on their journey. Gwen says, *"We really would be nothing if we hadn't committed ourselves to Christ at this time. We were ready to contact a lawyer; things were going so bad that I was convinced divorce was going to be how I would live. But you know, God had a plan."*

Reconciled to God: The Divine Love Story

What is it about God's story that is so compelling that it changes the course of marriages on the edge of disaster? The pages of Scripture unveil the greatest story of love, betrayal *and* reconciliation that has ever been told. It is God's story. And it can be our story as well. The biblical narrative begins where any good story begins—at the beginning: "In the beginning God . . ." (Gen 1:1). Immediately Scripture introduces us to the primary character in this divine love story, that is, the triune God. Theologian Stanley Grenz (2001) describes the effervescent and abundant love found among the members of the Godhead: Father, Son and Holy Spirit. It is a love characterized by mutual self-giving and receiving and liberally punctuated with graciousness. In classic orthodox theology, the image of the dance is often employed as a metaphor for the loving relationships between Father, Son and Spirit. Without losing their unique identities, they participate in a divine sharing of life that is characterized by perfect mutuality, reciprocity and love.

Then God makes room for us. It is as if creation results from an overflowing abundance of God's relational joy. And because God as Trinity is essentially relational, so we, God's people—created in God's image as relational beings—are capable of deep intimacy with our Creator *and* with one another. In other words, the people of God are welcomed into the sphere of his effervescent and holy love.

Then the unthinkable happens. The beloved human creation—we who are created to receive and give God's perfect love—rejects the divine lover. Alienation and enmity replace perfect intimacy. Sin weaves shame and fear into the human heart. When the apostle Paul later reflects on the nature of sin, he does not picture sin as a series of individual acts. Instead he thinks of sin as a relational problem—"a general disposition of hostility toward God and God's people, a refusal to honor God as God" (Green & Baker, 2000, p. 95). We still carry this "disposition of hostility" within us today. This results in broken relationships with one another and with God.

Our part in the divine story could have rightfully ended there. God could have begun a new story that did not include us. But he didn't, for the love of God continued to overflow for the betraying creature because *God chose to risk and to love*. Subsequently, God the everlasting lover became God the eternal pursuer, who seeks and saves what was lost. The story of Adam and Eve in the Garden of Eden (Gen 1—3) became an example of what has followed for generation upon generation. This message of reconciling love was first spoken to God's people in the Old Testament through the priests and the prophets. It continues in the New Testament through the life of Jesus Christ and reaches its climax on the cross of Calvary—God in human flesh making possible our reconciliation with God.

Jesus came preaching a message of repentance and forgiveness of sins—the good news! He practiced what he preached. His life of obedience honored God as God. He showed us how to live in right relationship with God and with one another. He called us to leave our old ways behind and to embrace the life of a follower. But many found his message hard to hear. He held people accountable for the injustice they inflicted on one another. He challenged people to live differently, to live lives characterized by the same kind of holy love that overflowed from the heart of God. Jesus offered forgiveness and reconciliation with God to those who came to him confessing their sins and committing to living as Jesus lived. His message and mission led to Calvary, where he paid the ultimate price to bring peace between God and sinful humanity: "God demonstrates his own love for us in this: While we were still sinners, Christ died for us" (Rom 5:8).

You read about how Sam changed when he came face to face with the forgiving and reconciling Christ. When he came home, he was not the man he had been hours earlier. He was now part of God's new creation. The apostle Paul writes about our reconciliation with God in 2 Corinthians, making it clear that God is reconciliation's initiator. God is never reconciled to us; we are reconciled to God through the cross of Christ (see 2 Cor 5:18-19). According to New Testament scholar Ralph Martin, "God in Christ has acted in such a way as to restore friendly relations between the world and himself. 'He has reconciled us to himself' means simply 'he has put us in right relations with himself'" (1981, p. 106). We are utterly helpless to *repair* our broken relationship with God. We can only *respond* in faith to what God has accomplished on our behalf out of his everlasting and passionate love for us.

And our lives are transformed as a result. In 2 Corinthians 5:17 Paul describes it this way: "Therefore, if anyone is in Christ, he is a new creation: the old has gone, the new has come." God was transforming Sam into a person who could reflect kingdom values in his marriage. Gwen noticed the difference. Another unfaithful husband, a lifetime alcoholic, also had a life-changing experience with Christ. He said, *"I had to turn my life over to the Lord to start with. If you don't love yourself, you don't love anybody else, and if you don't love the Lord, you do nothing but make a mess. That's what the first part of my life was. I rededicated my life to the Lord, and that's the day we [my wife and I] really started going in the right direction."*

Reconciled to One Another

Paul links our reconciliation with God to our reconciliation with one another. We are transformed, not for our own sake but to become part of God's redeemed people whose lifestyles are characterized by repentance, forgiveness *and* reconciliation. This is not just a tidy theological point that Paul wants to make. Second Corinthians 2:14—7:4 is addressed to the church in Corinth, some of whom had rejected Paul and his gospel message. He pleads with them to leave their hostility behind and to be reconciled with him, as he already was with their ringleader (2 Cor 2:5-11; 7:12). Without a doubt, Paul links reconciliation with God to reconciliation with one another and connects reconciliation with one another to reconciliation with God.

This is what happened for Sam. Seeking reconciliation with Gwen emerged out of his reconciliation with God. Sam made the connection between the two instantaneously. When he sought and received Gwen's forgiveness, they began the arduous journey of restoring their damaged relationship. Indeed, twelve years of verbal abuse and sexual aversion did not change overnight. They had steep paths to climb before they felt secure with their renewed relationship. But they were not on this path alone; the Spirit of the living God accompanied them. Sam says, *"I'm fighting for us. I'm fighting because I know God has written it across my forehead. A number of times he swiped me with a two-by-four in the last couple of years [to show] that he wants us together."*

If you have not embraced the story of the cross of Christ as your own, won't you consider doing that now? You may want to talk to a pastor or Christian counselor in your area about this life-changing relationship with Jesus.

Reflect on your own experience of being reconciled to God through the cross of Christ. How does that reality affect your thoughts, feelings and actions in your current relationships? Have you linked the call to be reconciled with one another to your own reconciliation with God? Remember that this awareness serves as a guidepost when our relationships reach crossroads in uncharted territory. Whether or not you will attain your final destination of being reconciled will depend on many other factors that will be discussed throughout this book. Sam and Gwen are an example of a couple whose journey along reconciliation road was launched by a divine encounter. Other reconcilers, such as Elizabeth and Alan (you met them in chapter one), pursued reconciliation because they believed that it was what Christ modeled for their life. In their case a *renewed* awareness of God's forgiveness motivated their reconciliation.

An Attitude of Gratitude

When we paused their story in chapter one, Alan had just confronted Elizabeth about her affair. She was filled with guilt and shame. He felt deeply betrayed. What could possibly motivate Alan to reconcile with Elizabeth? All the injured parties I spoke with wrestled with this question. Some may pursue reconciliation out of a sense of duty or to avoid criticism. Others may stay married to avoid guilt and shame. While these are reasons people may stay together, they do not create radical transformation of heart and home.

The question boils down to this: what motivates injured parties to extend forgiveness and transgressors to seek forgiveness? Studies have yet to examine repentance as fully as they have studied forgiveness. Nevertheless, researchers have discovered that empathy and humility motivate the deepest levels of extending forgiveness to another (Worthington, 1998a). In other words, people who have been forgiven see forgiving the other as a way to resolve interpersonal dilemmas. We remember what it was like to need forgiveness from somebody we had hurt. We recall our sense of release and relief when that person forgave us. The greater the interpersonal debt we have been forgiven, the greater the model we have for becoming forgivers. As we continue with Alan and Elizabeth's journey, observe the role gratitude plays in Alan's decisions around forgiving Elizabeth.

Elizabeth and Alan's Story, Part Two

Somehow Alan and Elizabeth made it through the first few gut-wrenching months. Alan felt so betrayed by his wife that he wasn't sure he could forgive her. He told his chaplain about his marriage dilemma. Alan remembers: "*The chaplain told me two things: 'Your marriage isn't over yet, and God is not through using you. . . . You can make it through this, and you can have a better marriage than ever before, because it's not dead yet.'*"

Alan heeded the chaplain's advice. He decided that he would give God three years to do something significant with his marriage, because the affair had lasted three years. He says, "*It's not the best kind of attitude to rebuild a marriage, but it's better than nothing. It was based in gratitude to God for rescuing me in my life. So it came from that. It did have a good foundation, although, looking back, it feels arrogant. But at the time, that was enough. . . . The biggest piece of it was God. And that's where we were. It was just not in my power to forgive. I couldn't will it. I wanted to will it, because I didn't like feeling miserable and in pain.*"

For fourteen months, Alan and Elizabeth lived in marital limbo. That's when Alan reluctantly attended a Promise Keepers rally. During one of the talks there, he began to think about the kind of legacy he would be passing on to his son if he divorced Elizabeth. Alan says:

> *God started working on me, and I just had to ask myself the question, "What do I want to pass on to my son?" And in that, more than anything in my life, I wanted to be close to God and I wanted to pass that on to my son. That was a decision that felt first like more of a decision for God than anything. It was just very deep, and it was a very huge moment. This is what my life is about; this is my core identity. . . . I remembered God's forgiveness. I went back and offered forgiveness to Elizabeth, and then she could relax and begin to grieve over what she had done. That was the biggest piece of our forgiveness process.*

The Transforming Power of Forgiving

Two streams of thought can help us to understand Alan's journey of forgiveness. The first stream is theological. The second is psychological. In the prayer Jesus taught his disciples, forgiving—not repenting or even reconciling—is the only activity that is assigned to humanity:[1] "Forgive us our sins, / for we also forgive everyone who sins against us" (Lk 11:4). The meaning we often attribute to Luke 11:4 is this: God will not or cannot forgive me until I have forgiven others. This understanding creates guilt and anguish for those who rightfully struggle to forgive, like Alan. Does this mean they stand in an unforgiven state before God? New Testament scholar Joel B. Green disagrees with this common interpretation. In his commentary on the Gospel of Luke, Green writes that this verse is not

> a relationship of *quid pro quo* between divine and human forgiveness, as though God's forgiveness were dependent on human activity (cf. 6:35; 23:34)! Instead, Jesus grounds the disciples' request for divine forgiveness in their own practices of extending forgiveness. As in previous texts (esp. 6:36), Jesus spins human behavior from the cloth of divine behavior; the embodiment of forgiveness in the practices of Jesus' followers is a *manifestation* and *imitation* of God's own character. (1997, pp. 443-44, emphasis added)

Alan's response to his own forgiven-ness highlights the relationship between our gratitude for God's forgiveness of us and our forgiveness of one another. Theologian Gregory Jones (1995) suggests that the highest motivation for forgiving one another arises out of our deep gratitude to Christ for his forgiveness of our sins. This is the moral in the parable of the merciful king and the unmerciful servant (see Mt 18:23-35). The servant is forgiven a debt that he can never repay. Then he promptly fails to

---

[1]This is not to deny the importance of confessing and repenting in the process of reconciling. Forgiving is part of the process of reconciling, but as I stated in chapter one, forgiving is not synonymous with reconciling.

forgive the debt of a fellow servant. When the other servants report this to the king, he is not happy, and he has the unmerciful servant thrown into prison. What the unmerciful servant lacked is gratitude. Gratitude is released within us when we grasp the *magnitude* of the forgiveness that God extends to us. Referring to this parable, Jones writes, "Those who are forgiven by God must be transformed by that forgiveness into people who embody forgiveness and repentance throughout their lives" (1995, p. 162). We can forgive one another our "few dollars' debt" because God has forgiven our "billion-dollar debt" (see Mt 18:21-35). We forgive because God first forgave us.

Psychologically Alan experienced forgiving as a method of coping that psychologist Ken Pargament calls "transformational coping" (Pargament, 1997; Pargament & Rye, 1998). Pargament and his colleagues suggest that when we face crises, our coping styles fall into one of two camps: either conservational coping or transformational coping. Conservational coping maintains the status quo. We hold on to what we believe about life and relationships, and we do not change our worldview. Conversely, transformational coping reshapes our worldview so that new meaning and significance emerge out of our crisis. Pargament and Rye argue that forgiving is transformational. I would add that repenting and reconciling also are. These practices—forgiving, repenting, reconciling—challenge us to reconsider our values and realign our behavior to reflect our deepest beliefs. As a result we engage in the process of re-creation. Pargament concludes that "a greater purpose in living has been found and a new hub for the individual's energy and affection has been discovered" (1997, p. 157).

Amazing, Sustaining Grace

So far we have explored two ways in which the cross of Christ moved couples toward reconciliation. An initial saving encounter with Jesus spearheaded Sam and Gwen's reconciliation. A renewed awareness of gratitude to God motivated Alan to forgive and reconcile with Elizabeth. There is yet a third way the cross supports interpersonal reconciliation:

through sustaining our efforts to reconcile in the face of discouragement.

Consider Cathy and David. They were committed followers of Jesus Christ and leaders in their church. Anyone who knew them would have said they were a model Christian couple. Cathy discovered David's addiction to Internet pornography while she was doing some work-related research on their home computer. Her training as a professional counselor left her no doubt about the seriousness of what she saw materialize on her computer monitor. Her sense of betrayal ran bone deep when David eventually admitted to her that this activity had been developing for six years. Cathy says,

> *It was just so incredibly out of character and so unfathomable to me that he would be able to sneak and get away with something. I just didn't think he had the capacity to lie. I really didn't. So when I found out that not only was he doing this stuff but he was lying to me about what he was doing, even after he was caught, I felt totally off kilter. I felt like our relationship was totally off. I wondered, "What else don't I know about this person? What else don't I know about how we are as a couple?" It just put all sorts of things in question that had never been in question before.*

Cathy quickly mobilized her support networks. She talked with her pastor and called close friends to be in prayer for her and David. Cathy knew that she wanted to give God a chance to repair their marriage. She says,

> *Part of it is certainly my wanting to give God a chance to do whatever God can do and trusting that God can do anything he puts his mind to. . . . I found through this that there was a bedrock of faith. In counseling I would tell clients, "It's when you're going through the hardest times that you really find out what you've got in terms of faith." And I had to experience my own words and find that, no matter what, God was going to take care of me—I didn't have to rush a decision, because no matter what, God was not going to abandon me or forsake me. I was going to*

be okay. The marriage might not ultimately be okay, but I would be okay. I didn't have to make a decision to escape pain, because God would see me through that. God would take care of that.

Cathy and David began a difficult three-year journey. They attended individual and separate group counseling sessions to help them cope. They didn't want to just preserve their marriage, they wanted to transform it. Through counseling David learned that he had been basing his sense of self on performance. He says,

Out of finally being confronted, and thinking about and talking about my own failures and my own brokenness, I started to see my need for God in a real way . . . seeing how he really does love me and I don't have to do all this other stuff. One of the things I wrote as I was journaling back in the first few years is that if I never do anything, God will be pleased with me just for being his son. . . . That was a real profound thing for me: I don't have to earn this. And I knew all this stuff in my head, but that's not how I was living my life and acting out. I was living my life as if I had to look a certain way to earn my way into the club. . . . That discovery was a real significant thing for me.

Cathy discovered the faithfulness of God in a whole new way:

There was part of me that really wanted to control it and make sure that "this is going to happen and this is going to happen and this is going to happen." But that was always in conflict with "God is in control of this. It was God who brought this to light. And it was by God's grace that I found this out, and it's out in the light now, so why in the world would God abandon me . . . ?" The other thing that was helpful for me during this time, especially the really raw time, was remembering how God got me through other things. Certainly God wasn't going to change his ways. I can't tell you how important it was for me to know that I would be okay no matter what. I think that belief was more important than any other belief that I had—other than my belief in God. It was because of my belief in God I could say, "No matter what, I am going to be okay. I'm going to be okay, 'cause that's God's design for me. As long as I'm working with him, I'm going to be okay." That was a mooring. That was an anchor. Regardless of what else, I knew that.

Reconcilers learn that Christ represents both injured parties and wrongdoers on the cross. As the divine injured party, Jesus represents all victims as he embraces the pain of the cross to open the door for our reconciliation with God.

> According to Christian teaching, the Maker of all things has honored the human race by becoming a member of it, has honored all who suffer horrendous evils by identifying with them through his passion and death. Still more amazing, God will be seen to have honored even the perpetrators of horrors by identifying with their condition, becoming ritually cursed through his death on a tree, taking his stand with the cursed to cancel the power of the curse forever. For Christians, the cross is an outward and visible sign that through such identification, God has nullified the power of horrendous evil to degrade. (Adams, 1999, p. 127)

Isaiah 53:3-4 portrays the innocence of Jesus Christ this way:

> He was despised and rejected by men,
> a man of sorrows, and familiar with suffering.
> Like one from whom men hide their faces
> he was despised, and we esteemed him not.
>
> Surely he took up our infirmities
> and carried our sorrows,
> yet we considered him stricken by God,
> smitten by him, and afflicted.

Yet at the same time, Christ represents wrongdoers (also known as "sinners") because it is for *our* sins that Christ died. Again, the words of Isaiah:

> But he was pierced for our transgressions,

he was crushed for our iniquities;
the punishment that brought us peace was upon him,
and by his wounds we are healed.

We all, like sheep, have gone astray,
each of us has turned to his own way;
and the LORD has laid on him
the iniquity of us all. (53:5-6)

The cross of Christ calls wrongdoers to repentance and injured parties to forgiveness so that as participants in God's redeemed community we may live lives characterized by forgiveness, repentance and reconciliation with one another that arise out of the gratitude we feel for our reconciliation with God. This is a universal theme of the stories of reconciliation told in this book.

If you are a follower of Jesus Christ, take a few moments to remember what it was like for you when you realized the depths of God's love for you. Recall what you thought and felt as you accepted God's forgiveness. How might this truth in your life sustain you as you seek reconciliation with others?

Hard Realities

Before you begin to assume that all reconciliation efforts will end in glorious restoration, think again. Scripture clearly testifies that reconciliation is the heart of God. But Scripture also bears witness to the truth that not all people will be reconciled to God. As Charles Williams says,

> Sin is the name of a certain relationship between [humanity] and God. When it is fixed, if it is, into a final state, he gives it other names; he calls it *hell* and *damnation*. But if [humanity] were to be restored, what was to happen to sin? He had a name for that relationship too; like a second Adam indeed he named the beasts of our nature as they wandered in the ruined Paradise; he called this "forgiveness." (1956, p. 33)

Sadly, not all will enter the kingdom of heaven. Likewise some of our best efforts at reconciliation will fail. In fact, at least half of the interviewed couples had serious reservations about their future together. Their common use of the statement "I didn't know if we would make it" was indicative of this ambivalence. If all of humanity has not and will not respond to the sacrificial and extravagant love of God in Christ by accepting God's invitation to forgiveness and reconciliation manifested in the cross, it may be unrealistic for us to expect that all of our attempts to reconcile will succeed. Reconciliation can be thwarted by a lack of repentance and significant change *or* by a lack of forgiveness. Interpersonal scar tissue may so line the human heart that risking reunion is humanly impossible. What God desires is that we strive to align our hearts with his heart—that is, that we seek what God seeks, which is reconciliation with one another—and that we mourn and grieve when our invitation to reconcile is refused.

At this very point, God redeems our pain and creates a new future for us. It may not be the future we had imagined, but it will be a future blessed by the God of reconciliation. As one writer puts it:

> Divine order is not static but dynamic and evolving. No matter what mess we make, God can clean it up, not only "the easy way" by eliminating it . . . but by recontextualizing it into a more subtle plot. . . . In the Realm of God, the worst that we can suffer, be, or do, is not finally ruinous because God invents a new organizational grid that endows us with amazing meaning. (Adams, 1999, p. 102)

Wrapping Up

Reconciliation was not an afterthought in the divine love story. The anticipated end was *always* reconciliation. The means was *always* repentance and forgiveness. Continually God sought his people and in eternal lovingkindness rekindled his covenant relationship with them. Yet repeatedly, as the pages of Scripture testify, God's people rejected him. They dishonored God by spurning his commands. Their own actions resulted in their alienation from God's presence. They became enemies of

God, and enmity replaced intimacy. Yet God never totally abandoned them. When, through repentance, God's people turned to him, he returned his people from their exile time and time again. God's heart was—and is—the heart of a reconciler. Jesus' ministry on earth was—and is—that of reconciliation.

Take a moment to review the stories in this chapter. What these couples realized was that their personal reconciliation with God called them to *pursue* reconciliation with one another. It was the direction in which they turned. At the onset they had no guarantee that their efforts would be successful. In fact, many factors suggested that their efforts would be futile. Nevertheless they chose the path in which they were to walk based on their commitment to the way of the cross. Please note well: their commitment to Christ did *not* magically solve anything; they had many dark days ahead as they faced multiple decisions that influenced the outcome of their turn toward reconciliation.

Strange as it may seem, these professions of faith in the transforming power of the cross surprised me. I had expected couples to engage in some degree of "church talk"; I am a seminary professor, after all. But what continued to amaze me was the degree to which all the couples affirmed both the power of the cross to turn their hearts toward their mate and the presence of Christ to sustain them along their journey. The consistency of this testimony across all couples caught my attention. My gratitude to God deepened as I heard story after story about how the wonderful love of Jesus was embodied in reconciled marriages. Jesus is in the business of transformation. He invites us to partner with him.

3

ACTIVE COMMITMENT

I have been puzzling over a little quirk of mine. I faithfully exercise several times a week in the early morning. However, some mornings I sleep in rather than work out—even when my gym bag is packed. Why do I do this?

One day I realized that my attitude toward exercise as I fall asleep *(maybe I won't get up with the alarm)* affects my action (or the lack of it) the next morning. If I don't commit myself to answering the alarm clock the night before, then my default mode—which is sleeping in—takes over in the morning. One lazy morning will do no harm, but when a week or more of sluggish mornings pile up, trouble is afoot. This pattern is particularly vexing if I have been out of my normal routine for some time. Have you noticed how little effort is required to get *out* of shape and how much energy is required to get back *into* shape? After a prolonged absence, I find that my first time back in the gym is sheer torture. I am tempted to quit. I don't, however, for two reasons. First, I know that physical deterioration is lurking around the proverbial corner, and I want to avoid that. Second, I feel better when I work out regularly. Therefore I renew my commitment to get out of bed—and then do it!

Relationship maintenance is often like my exercise dilemma. When your relationship is on firm footing, you must still work at it to keep it in shape. If you have one unpleasant interaction in an overall pleasant relationship, you quickly get back on track through strategies such as accommodation, forbearance or acceptance. However, when you have been hurt deeply, you are likely to shift to a self-protective, risk-reducing mode. If your relationship has reached the point where termination seems possible, restoring it will take *active commitment.* You may recall that in chapter one I defined reconciliation as active commitment to the restoration of justice and trustworthiness by both injured party and transgressor so that your relationship may be transformed. This chapter explores the contours of active commitment.

I define active commitment as pledging 100 percent of your thoughts, feelings and actions toward a desired goal. Active commitment is, well, active. It requires some kind of "doing." However, this doing is not aimless. The nature of its activity is shaped by the desired outcome. Active commitment also requires perseverance, that is, stick-to-itiveness, not giving up when the going gets tough. Putting this all together, the active commitment of reconciliation is putting all of your self—your heart, mind and strength—into the process of reconciling.

Active commitment to reconciling is the second essential item to carry with you as you trek through your relational wilderness. In chapter two we discovered that commitment to the cross of Christ provides the model and motivation for reconciling. But unless this commitment finds expression in everyday life, it will remain an intellectual assent to the *idea* of reconciling; "Divine love experienced [has] to become divine love expressed" (Gorman, 2002, p. 155). In this chapter we will explore the ways in which active commitment is expressed when we travel on reconciliation road. First let's take a panoramic look at active commitment. Then we will zoom in on some specifics through the life of Jim and Judy.

The active commitment of reconciliation is putting all of your self—heart, mind and strength—into the process of reconciling.

The Big Picture of Active Commitment

While one person can undo a marriage, both partners must be invested in restoring it. Like the tango, active commitment takes two. All the couples who participated in my study voiced in some way the belief that it required "both of us." You can hear that reflected in the statements that follow.

- *I think both of us had to want to try. . . . Both of us had to want to make it work. When he was trying and I wasn't interested, we got nowhere. When I was trying and he wasn't interested, we got nowhere. But when we both wanted to try at the same time, we made progress.*
- *[We had] a different commitment from what we had ever had before. . . . She was willing to go anywhere I wanted to go, to do anything it took to get our lives back together. That was different. Yes, totally different. We were both working on it. We were both working on something for the better, for the future.*

The "two" needed for marital restoration may not apply if you hope to reconcile with a sibling, a parent, a friend or a business associate. Conversations I had with individuals who wanted to reconcile one of these types of relationships painted a different picture of active commitment. It appeared as if reconciliation in relationships that were not marriages might take only one person. For instance, think of the many adults who reconcile with their parents by forgiving them of inadequate parenting, even when the parents never repented. If you are reading this book with a relationship other than marriage in mind, you will find that many of the principles that I discuss will apply to you. However, you will have to adjust your ideas of what you can expect from the other person. The more fully engaged the other person is with reconciliation, the more similar your journey will be to that of married couples.

Active commitment does not come with a money-back guarantee. What struck me about these couples is that they committed to rebuilding *before* they had proof that their endeavors would be successful. Active commitment shaped their thoughts and actions. You can see this modeled in slightly different ways. One mate said, *"The commitment to the vision to [reconcile] came right at the beginning. We said, 'Okay, we want to make this work. What do we have to do to accomplish that?'"* In this case, commitment to reconciliation launched this couple on a hunt to find strategies that would help them restore their relationship.

In the following comment you will notice that commitment kept another person from throwing in the towel when a way forward was not immediately visible: "*[One of the] toughest moments for us in this rebuilding process was this winter. I went for a walk around the block. I was wondering, 'Is this ever going to get any better?' I came back home and walked into the bedroom, and I said, 'I am not quitting you; I am not giving up.' And [my wife] looked at me and said, 'That's exactly what I needed to hear.' I realized that that's the difference now between what I've been before and what I am now. I'm able to go back in and say, 'I'm going to fight for us.'* "

You may want to think about active commitment as a relational watershed boundary. Watersheds are areas of land that drain into certain lakes or rivers. A watershed boundary is a ridge or high area that determines whether water flows *toward* or *away* from that watershed. Picture your relationship as the watershed. The presence or absence of active commitment shapes the contour of the watershed boundary. It determines the *predominant* direction in which your efforts are flowing. Overall are your efforts flowing toward or away from reconciliation? An offended partner took stock of the directional flow of her mate's attitude toward restoration. Her statement reveals how she saw his efforts flowing toward reconciliation: "*I had someone who was saying, 'I'm forsaking this [adulterous] relationship. I'm committed to you and the kids. I will do whatever it takes.' So I had that ingredient in my lap right up front, and I believed it.*"

Active commitment is crucial when the core of your marriage has been severely damaged. As I mentioned earlier, garden-variety offenses may only call for forbearance, accommodation or acceptance. However, when dissolution seems the most likely response to a moral offense, active commitment is mandatory. Research that explores the relationships between commitment and intimate relationships suggests that if you are "for" your relationship, you are more likely to be forgiving (Finkel, Rusbult, Kumashiro & Hannon, 2002). The commitment-forgiveness relationship relies on partners' intent to persist rather than on the degree of their psychological attachment or on a view that their marriage will last over the long term. This persistence helps couples to keep moving forward when the way ahead is foggy. You can see this illustrated in this comment from an offended wife: "*I really felt caught because I couldn't see that he was learning anything; I felt caught by my commitment. But, of course, external pressure doesn't just pressure you. It also supports you. And that external pressure supported me in a good way.*" Her commitment plus her forgiveness sustained her intent to persist, even when she was not seeing the kind of change in her husband that she wanted to see.

Active commitment doesn't mean doubts won't enter the picture. After all, what is freshest in your relationship memory is the recent pain you have experienced. Active commitment sets the overall trajectory, but it does not remove pain from the rebuilding process, as the following statements testify:

- *The commitment I was making was to the process of restoring. . . . I'm committed to the rocky process: there'll be times of anger, and there'll be times of restoring and feeling, "Okay, I can breathe now, and I can look at your face and not feel like I want to hit it."*
- *There was an immediate decision not to leave, to say, "I want to work and see what we can do to heal this." But it was an ongoing decision too, as I would hit more of my pain. I don't think I had any idea of the kind of rock-and-reel I would do or how long I would do that.*

Active commitment keeps you on track when you face setbacks in the early stages of reconciling, and it can help you to temper doubts until misgivings turn into hope. You can hear this echoed in the following statement of an offended husband: "*One thing I told her that day [when her adultery was disclosed] was 'It may not look like that, but we'll get through this.' I said, 'I will hate you and won't feel like being married, but we'll get through this.' I said that to her, and that was kind of in my back pocket all the time. Sometimes I didn't believe it.*"

Two related expressions of commitment—constraint and dedication—help couples to weather these storms. Later in this chapter, we will discuss how constraint and dedication support reconciliation. Now let us meet Jim and Judy and hear their story.

Jim and Judy's Story, Part One

Judy and Jim met in the seventh grade, but it wasn't until they graduated from high school that love ignited between them. They married two years later. Jim and Judy were perfectly mismatched. Judy was needy. Jim was reliable. Judy says, *"I had been abused all my [childhood]. [As we dated], I watched him very carefully. . . . And he was always very even-keeled. . . . I just needed nice and smooth and happy and quiet."*

Judy was emotionally overreactive. Jim was emotionally underreactive. Jim says, *"I was not ever taught to fight. . . . Even the idea of being angry at your wife was really kind of foreign to me."*

Judy was weak. Jim was strong. Jim says, *"I always felt that I had a better handle on things than she did. . . . And I felt like I couldn't have a crack."*

Judy and Jim were in and out of individual and couples counseling because of her frequent bouts with depression. After twenty years of secrecy, she disclosed her childhood sexual abuse to her counselor and to Jim, and then Judy entered a time of incredible growth. Of that time, she remembers: *"I was so excited. I was going to school. I had a job and I was blossoming. I wasn't always depressed and crying. I was having a great time."*

But Jim entered a time of increasing frustration because Judy's growth did not include sexual intimacy with him. He says, *"It was like separate bedrooms. Abstinence for however long. And I wondered, 'What the heck is this all about?' I was going through a crisis."*

The final blow came when Judy told Jim that she hadn't loved him when she married him. She says, *"I finally wanted all the secrets and everything cleared out."*

Jim recalls, *"That was pretty much of a blow. . . . I don't know why I stuck around except that that's what you did. But my heart really turned to stone at that point."* Jim poured himself into work, but his job was in flux because of organizational restructuring. *"I was at a business meeting and it hit me: I had a job but no career. I have no marriage. And I decided that I was going to have something."* That something turned out to be a secret sexual affair with a coworker with whom he had been flirting for the previous year and a half. Over the course of eighteen months, the affair escalated in its intensity and its consequences.

Jim began counseling during that time as a way to manage his increasing stress. He recounts an aspect of one pivotal session:

> *[My counselor] said, "What are you doing? I'm not telling you what to do, but I am telling you, you're not acting in your own best interests. You're in a dangerous situation. You've got to tell Judy [about the affair]. . . . You need to get this resolved." So I told Judy. It was on Saturday morning. I'd gotten up early and made coffee. I was sitting down waiting for her to come down. She knew by the look on my face that there was something wrong. And she thought I was going to say, "This isn't working. We need to work on it." And I said, "Well, this isn't working and I'm out of here. And this is what I've been doing." Needless to say, that was it.*

Judy picks up the story: "*I said to him, 'If you're going to continue to see her, you have to leave.'* " Jim left that same day. A week after he moved out, Judy consulted a lawyer in case they decided to divorce. Before it was over, Jim had affairs with two women.

Eventually the affairs ended. Jim was alone. He finally faced his marriage. Did he want to stay married to Judy—assuming that she would agree to it—or divorce? He decided that he had never really wanted to divorce her. Of that time, Jim says, "*There were a lot of things going on. That's when I had no girlfriend, and I wasn't on the lookout for another one really. So [I] had no place to go. 'I may as well go back home'—I know that's how it appeared.*"

Judy was willing to consider it. "*Before he moved back in, we started getting together. Could we rebuild enough for him to even move back in? I felt safer, and we had been in therapy together a certain amount of time before he moved back in.*" Five months after Jim moved out, he moved home. According to Judy, "*When we got back together, neither one of us really knew if it was gonna work or not.*"

Active Commitment: Constraint and Dedication

Jim and Judy still face an uphill struggle if they are going to transform their marriage. Two expressions of active commitment—constraint and dedication—will aid them in this process.

Clinical psychologist and marriage researcher Scott Stanley defines constraint as "factors that would be costs if the present course is abandoned" (1998, p. 11). Constraint's motto is "I would leave if I could leave, but I can't." Constraints are part of every marriage. The longer you are married, the more constraints you accumulate (for example, children, a mortgage), and you tend to focus on them when things in your relationship are not going well. Constraint is based on obligation and duty. When you feel constrained, you feel trapped. Any sacrifice you make for the relationship is often grudgingly given. If it is not repaid or rewarded, you may feel resentful. As Stanley says, "Constraint doesn't make for deep commitment" (p. 17).

According to Stanley, constraints "act as barriers to ending a marriage" (p. 20). He identifies seven marriage-maintaining constraints. Where applicable, I have juxtaposed these constraints with statements of people I interviewed.

1. Social pressure: the degree to which family and friends' opinions against divorce matter. "*It didn't occur to me for a while to leave the marriage, because my father would have killed me. It would have embarrassed him.*"

2. Morality of divorce: the degree to which you believe divorce is wrong.

3. Concern for the welfare of the children: the degree to which you believe your children may be harmed by divorce. "*It just wasn't that easy to say, 'See you later, kids,' and divorce [my wife]. If they had not been there . . .*"

4. Concern for the spouse's welfare: the degree to which you care how divorce may negatively affect your spouse.

5. Financial considerations: your perception about how your lifestyle may be diminished by divorce. "*At that point in time, we were very deep in debt. . . . And I knew that, because I was the one with the steady job, I would be shouldered with most of the responsibility and debt. So I would have to say that the financial end of it partly kept me in the mar-*

riage. [I was thinking] 'I am not *taking care of this debt by myself.'"*

6. Termination procedures: the degree of difficulty in termination procedures.

7. Alternative quality: the perceived quality of life after divorce. *"For me to make other choices would have been a total life change. It wouldn't have just been dropping one person and adding another person. Or it wouldn't have just been moving out from my husband's home to a friend's apartment."*

The power of constraints can wax and wane as circumstances change. At the time that Jim moved out of their home, few constraints were active. For example, Jim had timed his departure to coincide with his youngest son's freshman year in college. With both sons out of the house, he felt free to leave Judy. Judy asked their pastor and several church friends to speak with Jim before he left. She hoped that he would respond to social and moral pressure. Jim told the pastor, *"If you feel it necessary to Matthew 18 me, go right ahead, but it ain't gonna work."*

While constraints did not keep Jim from moving out of the house, they did keep him from moving toward divorce. He thought about the financial costs and the difficulty of divorce procedures. According to him, *"Some friends of mine had gotten divorced, and their wives had taken them to the cleaners economically and that was part of it. . . . I had a good job and good retirement, and I could see that going down the tubes. [It] was more trouble to do that than it was to stay together, as bad as it was."* When he imagined life with somebody new, he found that aspects of it were less appealing than what he had had with Judy. *"I remember telling [my counselor] that Judy and I are best friends. Judy and I have all this history, and I really want all this—whatever I perceived I was getting—I want this with Judy."*

Judy established criteria that Jim had to meet before he moved back in and that he had to maintain after he returned. Jim recalls, *"I would say [I moved back in] under scrutiny or under conditions. One of the conditions was that we would work on stuff."* While these conditions provided some measure of accountability for Jim, one concern haunted Judy: was Jim changing because she was making him comply, because of constraint? She believed that he was just there doing it because he thought it was the right thing to do. Constraint is an important part of active commitment, but it doesn't produce marital bliss. Constraint makes transformation possible, but not inevitable. Judy wanted Jim to stay because he was dedicated to her, not because he was constrained from leaving her.

Constraint kept Jim and Judy out of divorce court. If their story had ended here, could we say they had reconciled? In a way, we could. Legally they were still married. Is that as good as it gets? In some situations, yes, especially if one spouse is not willing to change and the other is not willing to raise the ante. Many marriages endure like this for years.

You will recall that reconciliation's goal is relational transformation. This is more than the cessation of hostility, the introduction of goodwill or the balancing of relational ledgers (although these may be a part of the larger process). Reconciliation that transforms requires a metamorphosis of persons and their interactions. Transforming reconciliation is not a return to the ways things used to be. Instead it involves courageous reengagement between injured parties and wrongdoers so that the very heart of their commitment is changed. Constraint makes relationship conservation possible, but only dedication opens the door to relationship transformation.

Think about your degree of commitment to maintaining a healthy relationship or to rebuilding one. Rank your level of commitment on a scale of 1 to 5 with 1 being not at all committed and 5 being totally committed. If your commitment level is lower than you'd like, list the things that are currently keeping you in your marriage. Remember, constraint is not bad! Now think of one thing you can do that would be an investment in your relationship.

Dedication is the second facet of active commitment. Stanley defines dedication as "an internal state of devotion to a person. . . . Dedication conveys the sense of a forward-moving force, a motivation based in thoughtful decisions to follow a certain path and give it your best" (1998, p. 11). Dedication's motto is "I could leave if I wanted to leave, but I choose to stay." Dedication is based on love. In marriages where dedication reigns, couples practice self-giving, other-oriented love—the kind of love modeled by Jesus.

Stanley (Stanley & Markman, 1992) has discovered that placing one's mate and marriage as a high priority is an important part of dedication. Sacrifice for the sake of the relationship is willingly and joyfully given without thought of payback. Dedicated couples trust that the sacrifices each makes for the sake of the relationship will balance out in the end. A reciprocal sense of giving and receiving permeates dedication.

Dedication might look something like this: One couple was on the road to reconciling when they decided to pursue the husband's educational plans. This required them to relocate to a state that was quite distant from the wife's parents' home, and her father developed cancer before their moving day arrived. Each mate's dedication was shown in concrete ways. The wife said:

> *When my dad got sick, my husband was terrific. Before we even left our former home, he came home one day and said, "Here's two plane tickets for you to go home once we move out." We were trying to scrimp and save to come out here [for graduate education]. My husband had said to me, "I will wait a year to go to school so you can be here for your dad." And I said, "Something tells me that God still wants us to go. That even with my dad being sick, I should not stay." I think that had we stayed, I would have spent every free moment with my dad. I would have still worked every Friday, Saturday and Sunday night. Monday afternoons I would have driven to my mom and dad's, and on Thursday I probably would have come back home.*

This wife believes that how they managed her father's illness contributed to their restoration. A different choice (not to relocate) might have created more difficulties for them. Their renewed dedication to one another and to the well-being of their marriage helped them to sort through competing family needs. The husband's willingness to forgo school for a year and his purchase of two roundtrip tickets showed his dedication to her. Her willingness to choose her husband over her father demonstrated her dedication to her husband. The point that I want to make is not the outcome (she went rather than stayed) but the process. In other words, she *wanted* (dedication) to be with her husband when she did not *have to* (constraint) be there. He *freely released* her (dedication) to go when he could have *insisted* (constraint) that she stay.

Consider the balance between constraint and dedication in your relationship. What steps can you take to increase your dedication to your spouse? How might you value the constraints in ways that also support reconciliation?

How do you move from "have to" to "want to"? The transition from constraint to dedication is a gradual process that requires your full attention. All of the interviewed couples went through a lengthy time of trial and uncertainty—the no-man's-land of active commitment—before dedication emerged. One offended wife described it like this: *"Sometimes it was not even making a commitment, I mean, when we felt like we couldn't go any further. Not even making a commitment to continue on but just a commitment to stand still. 'Don't make any decisions. Don't do anything. Let's stand still and see what else we need to do.' . . . We didn't try to talk about progressing forward. It was just 'get through the day [laughs] and get through the night.'"*

As you slowly but surely reestablish safety and trust in your relationship, you can begin to experience the closeness and openness of dedication. Each couple individualized their portrait of a safe and trusting relationship. By this I mean couples tailored the requests—or demands—that they made on one another and their relationship in ways that fit the type of betrayal they had experienced. Where there was alcoholism, mates participated in Alcoholics Anonymous or Overcomers Anonymous. Where there was adultery, partners were accountable for their time and activities. Where there were communication troubles, spouses learned new ways to speak and listen to one another. Couples were well on the road toward dedication when they noticed that doubt had been transformed into hope. Let's continue Judy and Jim's story to see how constraint and dedication transformed their relationship.

Jim and Judy, Part Two

Jim and Judy were no longer separated. But they weren't experiencing the oneness of dedication either. Judy says,

> *When he moved back in, I also knew that it might not work. I felt like if he stayed in therapy and he kept doing what he needed to do, he could figure out that he didn't love me anymore and then we'd split up; that was a possibility. But we had so much history together. I felt there was more probability that it would work than that it wouldn't, but it would be really hard. . . . He was really not coming back because he was still in love with me. He was coming back because he thought it was the right thing to do, I think. I was saying, "You can't come back until I figure out if it's me you want [dedication] or you're just doing this to be a good person [constraint]."*

Jim recalls it this way: "*It was a line drawn in the sand, and either we were going to be different or I guess we weren't going to be together.*"

Judy adds, "*We knew that [our marriage] wasn't going to go anyplace the way it used to be. Neither one of us was going to accept the way it used to be.*"

Jim and Judy embraced the active commitment required to restore their relationship. Jim remembers the subsequent year like this: "*Well, it was hard. I was still angry about a lot of stuff and she was angry. She was hurt and I was hurt. And trust had just gone out the window for her with me. So, as my behavior was more trustworthy and more consistent and so forth, I was doing what I thought was the right thing, but she was still questioning it. And I would get angry over that. 'I'm here. I've decided. Can't you see that?' And she'd say, 'Well, it still doesn't feel like that.'*"

Judy adds this thought: "*I didn't know if I would be able to stay with him, because I didn't respect him a lot.*"

Through active commitment, Jim and Judy experienced a difference that made a difference. Judy recalls,

> *Over the following year, I watched him do all these things in his own best interest—not for me, but for him. I found myself gaining a real admiration for him and a different kind of respect than I'd had before. I think that was the next step for me. That's when I really thought, "Well, okay, I probably can do this now." I watched him steadily improve. I watched him go to church when he didn't want to. He was embarrassed. I watched him do all the things that I asked him to do. We moved back together in February, and in the following February, on Valentine's Day, we went out to dinner with our best friends, and I told him at that dinner, "I want you to know that I didn't think that I could ever respect you again. But I really admire you for what you've done in the last year and for what you've put out and done for me, what was in your best interest, in our best interest." . . . And [I told him] that I really respected him a lot. . . . It was really cool [tearful].*

Jim describes their relationship at that moment in this way: "*Out of the dust . . . rising like a phoenix.*" Jim and Judy realized that their relationship was being transformed.

Before moving on to the next section, let's sum up a few things about active commitment, constraint and dedication. Many couples initiate reconciliation with faint hope for success. This hope is challenged by realistic doubts, and those doubts are challenged through active commitment. Constraint helps couples weather the fits and starts of rebuilding safety, love and trustworthiness. As couples start to experience change, hope begins to blossom and dedication begins to bloom. Couples move from a pessimistic view of their ability to restore their relationship to an optimistic one. They go from having one good day in a month of bad days to having one bad day in a month of good ones. Constraint helps couples to hold on to and value that one good day, and dedication helps them to neutralize the effects of that one bad day. Constraint and dedication are two complementary facets of active commitment. Moving from constraint to dedication takes more than wishing on a star. It takes hard work. That is the focus of our next section.

Active Commitment: Training, Not Trying

In his book *The Life You've Always Wanted,* John Ortberg (1997) has you, the reader, imagine that you have been offered the chance of a lifetime. The United States Olympic Committee has selected *you* to run the marathon for the United States in the next Olympics. This future goal captures your imagination. As you cross the finish line, you hear the crowd roar, "USA, USA!" You see yourself receive the gold medal. You feel tears well in your eyes as you hear the national anthem. Then reality strikes.

> The farthest you have ever run is from the couch to the refrigerator. . . . Right now you cannot run a marathon. More to the point, you cannot run a marathon even *if you try really, really hard.* Trying hard can accomplish only so much. If you are serious about seizing this chance of a lifetime, you will have to enter into a life of training. You must arrange your life around certain practices that will enable you to do what you cannot do now by will power alone. When it comes to running a marathon, you must train, not merely try. (pp. 45-46)

The couples I talked with had *tried* to have good marriages. They did what came naturally, and in the process they developed some bad relationship habits. These habits eroded the boundaries that protected their relationship, and the rest, as they say, is history. Fortunately they heeded the wake-up call of their marital crisis. They realized that if they were going to have the marriage they always wanted, they would have to do more than try to rebuild; they would have to enter a life of training so they could participate in the marathon that is greater than that found in the Olympics—the marathon of a marriage that crosses life's finish line.

You may recall that I defined active commitment as putting all of your self—your heart, mind and strength—into the process of reconciling. Constraint and dedication are the first two facets of active commitment and define the nature of *commitment.* Training, the third facet, describes characteristics of *active.* Training to reconcile requires focus. It demands radical lifestyle change. It calls you to develop new skills and to relearn old ones. It involves obtaining necessary equipment. Let's look at each of these areas.

Focus. To train for the Olympics, athletes focus 100 percent of their attention and energy on preparing for their event. They eliminate distractions. They turn toward developing their skills and away from things that may hinder them. When couples train to reconcile, they turn inward toward one another. Restoring their marriage becomes their top priority. In the next series of statements, you can observe the different ways couples made this turn inward.

- *[We focused] in on the two of us being the pivotal point of the family. We'd invested so much time in the children in the past that the relationship between the two parents wasn't there. It was more like we were two caregivers to the kids and we just happened to live in the same house. . . . She realized that I was an important part of the situation too, not just for childcare. . . . We worked on . . . the path in our relationship, clearing a path between ourselves.*

- *[I watched] him make the change that the church was not number one anymore but his family became number one. Our marriage became more important to him than it ever had to me, and I could see that being demonstrated on a daily basis.*

- *We had turned from being outward to turning toward ourselves, to turn inward and become a couple and develop boundaries. Once those boundaries were developed, we could move on as a couple and then see what that was about.*

The turn inward required that these couples change how they spent their time. They were aiming at "quantity time," not just "quality time." One couple took this aspect of reconciling very seriously. He says, *"She was willing to go anywhere I wanted to go, to do anything it took to get our lives back together."*

She says, *"For instance, we go to the store. If I don't want to go, I'll go anyway and sit in the car and read a book while he runs in, or the other way around."*

Turning toward each other instead of away is an important principle for making marriage work, according to marriage researcher John Gottman: "Partners who characteristically turn toward each other rather than away are putting money in the bank. They are building up emotional savings that can serve as a cushion when times get rough. . . . Turning toward your spouse in little ways is also the key to a long-lasting romance" (1999, pp. 80, 81).

Gottman cautions that couples with stable marriages are likely to forget to attend to the small, everyday ways of turning toward one another. If this is important for mates with stable marriages, it is essential for reconciliation. The following comment from the interviews reflects this: *"The restoration process is not a big leap. It's baby steps. Somehow the little day-to-day decisions are so crucial. Whether or not to show love at a particular point. Whether or not to even touch my husband's hand in church—little things like that. To allow him to kiss me at a certain point, even though at that particular moment I was envisioning him with someone else. . . . Those are very, very critical points."*

Radical lifestyle change. Olympic athletes make radical changes in their lifestyles to sustain focused training. Many competitors leave friends and family to train with a specific coach at a distant location. Their entire day is structured around preparation for their Olympic event. Reconcilers-in-training do the same thing. In the next set of statements you will notice how reconciliation became the central organizing principle in the lives of these reconciling couples.

- *Everything was subordinated [to reconciliation] . . . where we went on vacation, whether we were going to do something with somebody else. We were much more likely to check with the other and say, "Can I do . . . this right now?" . . . as opposed to "I'm going out with so-and-so tonight and I'll be home about 11:00."*

- *The crisis point hits and you realize that radical surgery is needed rather than just some incremental change. There's continuous change. There's discontinuous change. And there's radical change. I was working off continuous change, whereas what we needed was radical change.*

One couple moved from a large metropolitan area, where secrets were easy to keep, to a small village, where everyone knew everyone else's business. Another couple left a small family chapel and joined a larger suburban church so they could avoid his family's constant disapproval of their decision to reconcile. Couples attended seminars on family life. They read books. They sought counseling. All of this for the sake of reconciliation. These illustrate ways in which reconciliation became their central organizing principle.

Retraining and retooling. At least three things may keep athletes from competing in top-level competitions like the Olympics. Some athletes do not reach their full potential because they develop bad habits that impede their performance. Others lack advanced skills. Their skills are below those of top athletes in their field. Finally, others do not obtain the new and improved equipment that helps their competition run faster and jump higher.

The reconciling couples I talked with fit all three categories. As I mentioned before, all had developed bad relationship habits that needed to be unlearned. One of the chief offenses was poor communication skills. Most couples sought the help of a relationship coach (also known as a counselor) to help them learn how to talk to one another in relationship-enhancing ways. (In the next chapter I will say more about the role counselors may play in reconciliation.)

Another problem was secrecy, or the lack of forthright and difficult conversations. Training to reconcile meant that couples talked, and talked, and talked to one another with honesty. Some partners created their own training routine. For example, one pair spent every Sunday for seven weeks going through a Bible study together. Another couple found

How does your daily life reflect the fact that you are in training for reconciliation? What training regimen have you established to promote reconciliation? Have you identified the places where your relationship skills need serious attention? If so, what are you doing about it? Have you examined all areas of your life to accentuate those aspects that nurture rebuilding and to eliminate those aspects that tend to nullify your efforts?

joy in reading out loud to one another at night. They developed a five-step pattern of praying, reading, dialoguing, praying and loving. Some couples attended conferences. Others devoured books on how to strengthen relationships or how to recover from affairs. (You will find a list of books and activities in appendix B.)

Just as Olympic athletes train to perfect their current skills or to master more difficult feats, so the couples trained to develop new relationship skills or vastly improve the ones they had. Practice not only made perfect; it also made permanent. These reconcilers unlearned harmful, habitual ways of relating to one another and developed new habits. This took persistence and perseverance. It took active commitment. They set their sights on their destination—reconciling—and then asked, "What do we need to do to reach the goal we want to attain?"

Active Commitment: Running the Race

The attitude of active commitment reminds me very much of the biblical passage Hebrews 12:1-3, in which the author adopts a training metaphor to describe the Christian life.

> Therefore, since we are surrounded by such a great cloud of witnesses, let us throw off everything that hinders and the sin that so easily entangles, and let us run with perseverance the race marked out for us. Let us fix our eyes on Jesus, the author and perfecter of our faith, who for the joy set before him endured the cross, scorning its shame, and sat down at the right hand of the throne of God.

> Consider him who endured such opposition from sinful men, so that you will not grow weary and lose heart.

The image is that of a race. The challenge is to run *with perseverance.* The implication is that the race is not easy and that resolve—active commitment—is required to complete it. The "race marked out" for the interviewed couples was reconciliation. In this race, the important factor is to cross the finish line. All who cross are winners; rank is irrelevant. The passage in Hebrews also reflects what our reconcilers testify to: that one of the keys to running with perseverance is to "fix our eyes on Jesus," whose model of perseverance is one we are called to imitate. As we consider him, we will not "grow weary and lose heart."

I'll let Judy have the last word in this chapter. When I asked her why she and Jim had been able to reclaim their marriage, she responded with the following words:

> *I think it might be just who we are as people at the core, and then the rest of it is God's work. I think that God has that for everybody that wants it, but if you don't allow him to do that, then you don't get it, and you go your own selfish way and take off. . . . I think, basically, that we have allowed the Lord to do the work that we needed to do and to continue to do. . . . And I mostly feel this burden to tell you, to tell other people, that it can work. But it's really hard, and you both have to be really committed to doing it. And actually you have to be really committed to the Lord to do it. Because he's the only one that can change our hearts and minds and take us outside of ourselves enough to get past some of the mental tricks that we play.*

4

COMMUNITY

Bearing One Another's Burdens

When I was a girl, I enjoyed watching Tarzan movies starring Johnny Weissmuller. Inevitably somebody fell into quicksand. When the victim was a villain, the quicksand pulled him under (villains tended to be males). When the victim was a hero, someone—like Tarzan—came along and pulled the hero out.

As you challenge dysfunctional relationship patterns on the journey of reconciliation, you quickly discover that escaping your history of interpersonal pain is as difficult as extracting yourself from quicksand if no additional leverage is available. Researchers Ken Pargament and Mark Rye make an interesting observation about forgiveness and a concept called *social facilitation:* "[An] implicit, but often overlooked, ingredient of forgiving is social facilitation. Much of what we know about the process of forgiving comes from studies in which we have tried to facilitate forgiveness through education, encouragement, and therapy. It is reasonable to ask whether forgiveness, in the transformational sense used here, can take place outside of a facilitative context. Radical change isn't easy" (1998, p. 64).

The education, encouragement and therapy strategies mentioned above take place in an interpersonal or community (broadly defined) context where a potential forgiver meets individually with a personal counselor or in groups with a facilitator. This line of research has helped psychologists to unlock some of the processes behind forgiving. (I will discuss many of their findings in chapter six.) If Pargament and Rye are correct, a facilitative context may provide the leverage you need to escape relationship quicksand.

When the path to reconciliation becomes difficult, others help to "strengthen the feeble hands, / steady the knees that give way" (Is 35:3). The apostle Paul put it like this: "Carry each other's burdens, and in this way you will fulfill the law of Christ" (Gal 6:2). Consider the range of roles that friends, acquaintances and others can play. The following statements highlight how another's intervention or advice can launch someone on her or his journey of reconciliation:

- *I was just waiting for my income tax to come in and I was going to move out. . . . [My wife] asked one of her friends to come over and talk to me. So a local couple came over, and neither one of them is an alcoholic. But Jeff shared about his dad who was an alcoholic, openly and honestly—probably for about four hours. And, you know, lo and behold, the next thing I knew we were on our way to a treatment center.*

- *[I] confronted [my husband] over the phone. . . . I think I said, "Someone's been viewing pornography on the computer." And I left a silence, and it stayed silent. That was my answer. . . . I think first he said it wasn't him. Then pretty quickly he said, "Well, yeah, I only did it a couple times." And that's when I said, "We need to talk about that." I knew he was lying. I just knew in my heart at that moment that he was lying that it was just a couple of times. . . . I rallied all my resources. I sure did that real fast. I called a friend to be praying for me. Then I called [my] pastor . . . and made an appointment to go and talk to him that day, and told him there was a crisis.*

- *I was at [Lucy and Bill's]. These are longtime friends of ours. I just spilled to them my frustration and my not knowing what to do and so on. And they, in their typical fashion, were very gentle and kind but . . . affirmed that I needed to keep working at it [the marriage] and that they would be in prayer.*

- *I moved out [of my home], but there were two guys in the church who said to me, "Look, we really don't like what you're doing, but we really love you. So let's stay connected somehow." And one guy helped me move to all these different places because [someone] was following me around. In fact . . . I rented a place in his basement for a month. He was an easygoing guy, and [he and] his wife were just loving. They were friends as a couple, you know. They really didn't like what was going on, but they supported me as an individual. And then another guy who was an elder in the church and really hadn't had a whole lot of contact with me before—he was involved in the counseling ministry—he and I got together probably weekly or every other week for dinner. It was the same story: "I don't like what you're doing, but I like you. Come on over for dinner and let's talk." So we really stayed connected. And that, really, was amazing. I couldn't believe these two guys would do that and would say, "I love you. I don't like what you're doing, but . . ."*

This chapter will conclude our discussion of the commitments that support reconciliation. Now that we've discussed commitment to Christ and commitment to the work of reconciling, we'll explore how commitment to a reconciliation-friendly community facilitates reconciliation. First we will zoom out for a panoramic view of community. Then we'll zoom in to see particular portraits of community in action through Leo and Darla's story.

Who Is Your Community?

How do you define community? I can think of several definitions. Community can refer to the place where you live. It can also be a group of people who hold a common interest, such as a community of bird watchers. Moreover, ethnic and gender groups identify themselves as communities, such as the African American community.

Family therapist William Doherty offers another perspective on community that will be helpful to our discussion about reconciliation. He defines community as "people who are stakeholders in [one another's] lives, stakeholders in [one another's] marriage, stakeholders in [one another's] well-being with whom that's reciprocated" (Sandage, 1999, p. 358). From this perspective your community consists of people who invest in your life and in whose life you invest. Stakeholders may include family, friends and colleagues with whom you interact on a regular basis, such as the friends in the preceding statements. We will return to the relationship between stakeholders and reconciliation shortly, but first, I'd like to talk about the church.

For the people of God, the church is a special category of community within which practices of forgiveness, repentance and reconciliation may take place. You may be familiar with New Testament metaphors that describe the interdependent nature of this community. We are members of the body of Christ (1 Cor 12:12-26). We are part of a new creation (2 Cor 5:17). We are brothers and sisters in the family of God (1 Jn 3:1-3). We are "a chosen people, a royal priesthood, a holy nation, a people belonging to God" (1 Pet 2:9). In the biblical world, it is "the web of human covenants and commitments that enable just and loving relationships" (Augsburger, 1996, p. 148). However, covenants and commitments make just and loving relationships possible but not inevitable. Along with interpersonal communion comes the probability of interpersonal conflict. In God's loving mercy, he established practices of repentance and forgiveness as ways for his people to restore communion with him and with one another. According to church historian Martin Marty,

Identify the stakeholders in your community who can come alongside you in the process of reconciliation. Stakeholders can pray for you and mentor you.

> Forgiveness in the Hebrew Scriptures occurred within and affected the whole community. . . . Christians took over that concept in the ekklesia, the "called out" community of the forgiven and forgivers. Thus, in ways hard to recall in the modern world, where purely in-

> dividualist expression of Christianity is so common, the New Testament words about forgiveness were perceived as issuing from, in, and to the believing community. Thus, the community's distinguishing character was derived from the ethos of God, of God in Christ, and of God the Holy Spirit. (1998, p. 22)

Why is community important to reconciliation? Community sets the moral and ethical *content* out of which decisions about how to handle interpersonal betrayal flow, and community provides the *context* for reconciling. First, stories that shape our ethical beliefs and behaviors come from community. According to psychologist David Augsburger, "One's communal narrative, or history, records significant persons, events, and actions in the past and points toward character, occurrences, and options for the future. . . . In pledging our lives to a particular community story, we choose the meaning of our existence!" (1996, p. 118).

Which community stories provide the foundation for your beliefs and practices about reconciliation? A friend of mine grew up as a missionary kid in the jungles of Peru. He told me that among the tribes with which his parents worked, the modus operandi for resolving interpersonal offenses was revenge, including murder. As the good news of the gospel took root in this tribe, a new ethic emerged from the story of the cross. As the community was shaped by the story of God's self-sacrificial, nonretaliatory love modeled by Jesus Christ, forgiveness, repentance and reconciliation replaced revenge.

Second, community provides reconciliation's context. Practices of reconciliation, or the lack of them, affect the communities to which we belong (that is, family, church, workplace and so on). For example, in Genesis we read about individuals who were entitled to retribution, but who chose to forgo retaliation in favor of reconciliation. The reconciliation of Jacob and Esau (Gen 27—36) and Joseph and his brothers (Gen 37—50) reunited not only the offender and the offended but also entire families.

The impact of reconciliation on the community is continued in the New Testament. In the parable of the prodigal son (see Lk 15:11-32), the younger son shamed his father in the eyes of the community when he asked for his inheritance and liquidated his gain. This same son returned home, repentant and broken, seeking a place in his father's household as no more than a servant. The community would have expected this son to bear the responsibility of restoring his father's honor. Instead the father ran toward his son and publicly embraced him (undignified!) and bestowed on him signs of restored sonship (undeserved!). To celebrate this homecoming, the father held a *community* gala, not a private family party. The community witnessed the son's dishonoring of his father and the father's bestowal of honor on his son.

Locate the community that shapes the moral stories on which you are basing your decision. For example, do your stories come from your family, your church, the media? How reconciliation-friendly are the communities in which you participate and the stories that emerge from these communities?

Community provides a different kind of context for reconciliation in other New Testament passages. In the parable of the unmerciful servant (see Mt 18:23-35), the community (of servants) observed how one of their own failed to show compassion to another slave after his own unrepayable debt to the king was forgiven. The fellow servants were distressed by this and reported it to the king. Note also that in Philemon 2 Paul addressed his plea for reconciliation between Philemon and Onesimus to "the church that meets in your home."

When we are members of God's community, the divine story becomes the defining narrative for our lives, and we grow into the ethical comportment derived from God's story. But this is often easier said than done. Applying the primacy of reconciling to our individual lives today often requires more than personal commitment, as critical as that is. It also requires community participation. We find the leverage that we need to reconcile within the context provided by community stakeholders. In the remainder of this chapter, we will explore community as reconciliation's facilitative context through Leo and Darla's story.

Leo and Darla's Story

Darla and Leo met when they were in elementary school. Of this, Leo says, "*We were in the second- and third-grade classes, and we fell in love early in our lives . . . during the eleventh grade.*"

Darla adds, "*We knew from about a month into our dating relationship that we wanted to be married. We could see each other as lifetime partners.*"

Leo continues, "*There was no doubt in our minds. Our relationship was founded on love.*"

Leo was committed to sexual purity before marriage, but Darla says, "*I was expecting more . . . and kind of set things up in our college days when he spent the night. And it was just one encounter and I was pregnant and we were married.*"

Leo clarifies: "*We knew beforehand [that we wanted to marry]; the pregnancy kind of sped things up and moved things right along.*"

Unfortunately they did not live happily ever after. Darla soon realized that "*we were not relating sexually. My needs were a whole lot higher than his needs. And we discussed it as much as we could at age nineteen. It was very frustrating for me . . . just trying to communicate that to him, sometimes in a loving way, sometimes in a not-so-loving way. That was the start of our marriage relationship. As years went on we had good times and bad times as far as our sexual relationship went. But as far as our day-to-day lives . . . it was the job. It was the kids. We really didn't focus on 'how are you doing?' 'What's going on with you today?'*"

Leo's perspective is a little different. "*Whenever we'd had to deal with something that was deep, I would become uncomfortable. I would become fidgety. I would not want to deal with whatever it was. . . . I wanted everything to appear . . . smooth and pretty and nice and lovely. So I didn't allow myself to get involved in any kind of conversation that would trouble the waters.*"

For the first twelve years of marriage, Darla and Leo were busy working and raising their three children. They did not discuss the emotional gap between them. Their emotional and conversational intimacy did not improve after Leo accepted a call to the ministry. Darla says, *"Life got even busier. That was like having five hundred babies sometimes, because [it] was a new church and most of the members were new believers. It was quite a distraction from family life. We rarely ever had a family dinner together. We never rode to church together. It was me and the kids. [Leo] went on earlier because he had more responsibilities. Family events? It was rare that my husband was there, because there was always something going on in the church. We were going to get that quality time somewhere, somehow, but it never happened."*

Nine years of ministry passed. Darla reflects on that time: *"There were some things that my husband was telling me about his needs, but because I was too busy, it wasn't easy for me to meet those needs. It would require almost a character change."* Leo wanted affirmation; Darla gave him criticism. Leo wanted to hear what he had done right; Darla told him what he had done wrong.

Gradually Leo became aware that Loretta, a church member, was sexually attracted to him. He had taken pride in keeping his guard up when it came to relating to women, but according to Leo this woman *"worked on my mind. I began to entertain thoughts of taking that a step further. And I found myself really beginning to think about a physical relationship with her."* He knew it was wrong, but Loretta helped soothe his conscience. *"She helped to calm things by saying to me, 'You know, no one will ever know,' because we both had so much to lose."* Loretta provided all the affirmation Leo wanted. *"I was getting fuller and fuller because she fed and fed. . . . It made me feel good."*

Loretta eventually became the church's administrative assistant. They continued the affair on and off for three and a half years. However, eight hours a day of Loretta was too much for Leo. *"It was a constant reminder of my sin. It was just upsetting that this person worked so close with me on a daily basis. I felt as though she had something hanging over my head."* What had begun as a tantalizing secret turned into a private hell. *"I was tired. This woman had this thing over my head, and I was tired of myself. I was tired of living that lie with someone. I just didn't want anyone owning me. In a manner of speaking, I belonged to her . . . and I didn't want to belong to her."*

One day, that all changed. *"I was out [of the church office] for a bit that Monday morning. When I came in, she invited me into the senior pastor's office. When the three of us were sitting in his office, she shared with him what had taken place between us. . . . My whole world came crashing down. There was nothing I could do but just admit it. I was tired of living that lie with someone. I just did not want anyone owning me. I didn't want to belong to anyone other than my wife."*

Meanwhile Darla was at home, troubled by a sense that something bad was going to happen. Leo came into the house and said, *"We have to talk,"* then confessed.

Darla says,

> *I remember my arms and legs just tingling. I didn't know what I was supposed to do at this point. . . . So I picked up my keys off the counter and said, "I think I'm supposed to go running out of the house or something." I just couldn't cry; it was too unreal. It felt like a dream, and I got in the car. I drove down the road. I remember thinking in my mind, "I can't look at my house because it's on the ground." Like it burned or something has happened to it. I recall driving fast. . . . "There's no reason for me to live past this point." . . . My next thought was to drive through a very busy intersection and if God saves me . . . then I'm supposed to live, and if he doesn't then I'm supposed to die.*

The next thing Darla knew, she had pulled into a gas station. She called Leo and told him to meet her at the church, where they could talk with the senior pastor about Leo's infidelity.

As Darla waited for Leo to arrive at the church office, compassion for him began to stir in her heart. Darla recalls, *"He walked in the office. I said, 'Here's my husband, poor thing . . .' This is not out loud [laughs]. I'm sure they would have taken me away in a white jacket or something. I thought somehow through all this excitement I would finally get a chance to see the real Leo. I also knew at the same time . . . his heart for the ministry and the people. He just poured out his life into their lives. I just knew that this was his heart. And I knew that he would no longer be a part of that community."*

The meeting was brief. The pastor reviewed with Darla and Leo what they already knew. According to the church's bylaws, Leo would be dismissed from the church staff immediately with no severance pay, and his family could no longer participate in the life of the church. Darla says, "*I didn't know what was up ahead. I couldn't see anything at all. What do you do now that you've lost your job? You've lost your church home. Everything that we were so busy about is now gone. We walked to the parking lot, and we got into the car. He sat in the driver's seat, and I sat in the passenger's seat. We just sat there and stared into space. That was when I turned to him and motioned for a hug. And we hugged. And I whispered in his ear, 'We're going to get through this.'*"

Leo was amazed. "*She was going to make an effort. She was going to try at least to stand by me. It was something I wasn't expecting.*"

Leo and Darla endured a long, sleepless night. Leo realized, "*I didn't know what to do. It's the lowest I've ever been in my life. I thought, 'What am I going to do? I've lost my job, my ministry. I've lost my membership to the church. I've lost my money. No income.'*"

Panic seized Darla's heart—literally and figuratively. She recalls, "*I was taken to the hospital complaining of chest pains. Just being emotionally overwhelmed is more of what the issue was. That's when the pain gripped me incredibly. I just cried and screamed. I knew I was going to stay in my marriage, but how do you do that?*"

WITH A LITTLE HELP FROM MY FRIENDS

If it takes a village to raise a child, then it takes a community to repair a marriage. Augsburger writes, "We cannot heal ourselves; healing is either actualized, mediated, or surrogated within community" (1996, p. 97). I find it fascinating that none of the couples I interviewed isolated themselves and emerged reconciled. All of these couples selectively reached out to others to find strength and help on their journey toward reconciliation. Because these reconcilers were participants in the community of believers, they often looked to that community for support.

According to New Testament scholar Michael Gorman, the apostle Paul uses the Greek word *parakleis* to represent "everyday Christian encouragement" (2002, p. 198), and this type of encouragement is to be a hallmark of Christian community. Gorman proposes that the community should practice Galatians 5:6 ("The only thing that counts is faith expressing itself through love") as they bear one another's burdens. This burden-bearing love is selfless, other-centered, edifying and nonretaliatory. Gorman writes, "For Paul, then, grace experienced must become grace shared in concrete service . . . to others in need. The grace shared must have the same form as the grace experienced—abundant, sacrificial, concerned for the good of the other" (p. 244).

What kind of support is helpful to reconcilers? In what ways can community help to carry the burden of reconciliation? Three metaphors will help us answer these questions. First, community can become a reservoir of hope. Second, community can provide support and stability, like walking sticks that help hikers over rough terrain. Finally, community is like a guide who helps travelers reach their destination safely.

Community of Hope

Many couples launch into the seas of reconciliation with little but hope against hope. Just as kindling must be carefully fanned into flame, so must these faint sparks of hope. Community can serve that function. It can be a reservoir of hope in a dry land. How does community support hope? The work of psychologist C. R. Snyder sheds light on this important function. Snyder, Scott Michael and Jennifer Cheavens (1999) suggest that we conceptualize hope in terms of how people think about goals, rather than in terms of an emotion. If attainment of a goal is 100 percent certain, then you don't need hope. However, if some uncertainty exists about your ability to obtain your goal, hope-oriented thinking comes into play. To experience hope, people need to see a *way* to reach their goal (pathway thinking) and have the *will* to do it (agency thinking). Snyder's research shows that people with higher hope generate many different pathways to reach their goal (Snyder, 2000; Snyder, Rand & Sigmon, 2002). When obstacles occur, higher-hope individuals look for alternatives. Higher-hope people also believe that they will be able to successfully reach their goal, just like *The Little Engine That Could,* whose mantra "I think I can" helped him deliver a train full of toys (Piper, 1954). Snyder and associates (1999) suggest that others can nurture pathway and agency thinking.

Pathway thinking. Pathway thinking generates a variety of ways to reach your goal. However, if you don't know where to start, you may have a difficult time thinking of alternatives. Or you may not be able to think as clearly during a crisis as you do at other times. Darla's plaintive plea *"I knew I was going to stay in my marriage, but how do you do that?"* reflects this conundrum. She had a goal, but she didn't know how to get there.

Community members can help you think of ways to reach your goal. Darla reached out for help. In the excerpt of her interview that follows, you can see how her phone call to a friend who was also a pastor's wife (the president of the local pastors' wives association) cultivated pathway thinking.

> *She comforted me by telling me that I was not alone. She prayed for me, and then she gave me a list of resources . . . places to call . . . things to start thinking about. She gave me some stories of women who had recovered from this. She just gave me a lot of hope. She said, "Okay, sweetie, this is what you need to do. Let me tell you. Okay, I want you to call Gail MacDonald. Her husband has written books and he's been down this road. You do that. Okay?" I said, "Yes, I will." She said, "I've got this wonderful retreat center that I'm gonna pray that you and your husband go to—Marble Retreat Center. It's crisis counseling for ministry couples only. I'm going to call them and see that you guys get a scholarship." And she just started giving me a list of things to do.*

By asking for help, Darla discovered a wealth of resources. She now had the makings of an action plan.

Asking for help is sometimes difficult to do, especially in individualistic cultures like that in the United States. Many of the stories in our culture hold the self-made person or the rugged individual in high esteem. As a result you may associate asking for help with weakness. You may believe that you are supposed to pull yourself up by our own bootstraps. You may be embarrassed by the nature of the issue with which you need help. And you may fear that others will condemn you rather than comfort you. These beliefs may rob you of much-needed hope and help if they're left unchallenged. Certainly you need to use discretion in deciding how much of your story you tell and to whom you tell it; fear of rejection and judgment often has its basis in reality. Rather than isolating yourself, however, carefully consider who the safe people are in your community and contact them.

Agency thinking. Agency thinking is hope's "I think I can." You believe that you are *able* to do what you need to do to reach your goal, and you *want* to do it. Often the stories of others who have mastered challenges similar to ours can inspire agency thinking. We say to ourselves, *If they can do it, so can I.*

Two days after Leo's private confession in the pastor's office, he made a public confession in the Wednesday evening service. Darla came and stood beside him on the platform as a sign of their solidarity as he confessed his actions to the people. After the service, he and Darla stood in a receiving line to bid farewell to the church. Darla recalls the moment: *"Many people had words of encouragement, and there were tears. There were also many women and men who whispered in my ear, 'I know where you are.' And as I heard that, I just began to think not that this is okay but that people have survived and perhaps I will."*

"Perhaps I will." Agency thinking in the making!

Social Support

Community is like a hiker's walking stick, which provides support when the going gets rough. For one offended wife, social support came from *"people who were able to keep us from feeling . . . alone or crazy."* The benefits of social support are well documented in research. The general conclusion is that social support is good for your psychological well-being, improves overall coping and protects you from potentially adverse effects of stressful situations. Several categories of social support are readily apparent (Cohen & Willis, 1985). For example, others can affirm that we are lovable and valuable. One couple found this kind of support in two cardboard boxes full of cards people sent to them. Sometimes community members can be sources of information that help us to cope better. A case in point is a chaplain who encouraged an offended husband to press toward reconciliation. This husband says, *"The chaplain pointed me to resources, and that was so helpful."*

Friends can also come alongside us as companions on our journey. These fellow travelers do not need to be physically present. An offended wife describes the emotional support she received from friends who no longer lived near them but who *"knew that we really struggled. They would just touch base with us and allow us to share whatever we needed to share. I always got the sense that they were always there."*

Others can also provide concrete assistance and material resources, as happened for Darla and Leo. One church family immediately hired Leo to work for them. Another couple supplemented Darla and Leo's income. Darla remarks that *"this couple came around us, created activities for our children, literally took care of our finances for us. Their approach to us was 'We need to take this away from you right now, so you can focus on your relationship.'"*

Sometimes social support comes from unlikely sources. One couple found that their preschool children played this role. The offended husband recalled that the two older children *"drew little pictures with the family all together. [The pictures were] positive reinforcement. I knew inside what I wanted to have happen, but little things like that helped me to go the right direction."*

Support Groups

We have seen how reconcilers received help from others whose lives intertwined with their own because of family, friendship or church connections. However, these naturally occurring communities were not the only type of community that offered help and hope. Many reconcilers benefited from the support of groups. Groups came in many different shapes and sizes. These reconciling couples attended marriage conferences and marriage enrichment weekends. They joined Bible Study Fellowship or a small group at their local church, or met informally with a few others on a regular basis. Three couples participated in some kind of recovery group, such as Alcoholics Anonymous.

What groups are open to you that are reconciliation-friendly? What level of participation might further your reconciliation?

Groups can help to instill a sense of hopefulness and provide useful information to its members. Group participation also lets us know that we are not alone with our struggles (Yalom, 1985). One offended wife sums up her support group experience in this way: *"It was hope-giving to me because I'd see people that are newer along the path and I could see where I had come, how God has met my needs and how our relationship is getting better. And so I could be a support to someone but also offer some hope: 'I'm still here. This didn't destroy me. God will not let this destroy you.'"*

Moreover, you can practice new skills in a group setting and receive feedback on how you come across to others. This helps you to become aware of your blind spots. Darla and Leo attended a structured group where they learned new communication skills and a nonstructured group that provided ongoing peer support. Darla comments, *"The [retreat] group broke down into small groups after the weekend, and we continued to meet with them. I think it was maybe twice a month or something like that. It was just nice to see the other couples progressing. Some weren't, but most were progressing after the weekend. It felt like, hey, this is going to take us to the top."*

Community and Bumps in the Road

So far, this chapter has focused on ways in which community can come alongside couples who desire to reconcile. But what role does community play when reconciliation is not possible? In chapter one I noted instances when the road to reconciliation may be closed. The community can be a source of support and strength as you rebuild your life without your partner. For example, community members can help single parents shoulder the task of raising their children when the nonresidential parent is uninvolved. When lives no longer fit into preconceived ideas of how life (and God) should work, continued participation in the people of God can be the lifeline that keeps your head above the swirling seas of doubt and despair.

This point is particularly salient if the "other" with whom you cannot reconcile is a brother or sister in Christ. Augsburger draws on the work of theologian Carl Reinhold Bråkenhielm (1993) when he writes,

> The participation in the larger moral community that [injured party and transgressor] share is reaffirmed by forgiveness, and this may be the appropriate level for the parties in the future. The breakdown of an intense personal relationship will require profound forgiveness from both sides, and the outcome of the conciliation may be the return to civility in the moral context of the larger community that embraces them *without* the resumption of the special relationship that existed before the rupture. . . . When the resumption of the covenant and commitment is not possible, each can commit the self to seek respect for the well-being of the other with an attitude of goodwill that restores an appropriate moral relationship *within the larger moral community.* This too is positive forgiveness although the bonding has been severed and the union no longer exists. (1996, p. 20, emphasis added)

Bråkenhielm recognizes that times exist when brothers and sisters in Christ will choose not to reconcile with one another. He then looks to the "larger moral community" as the location within which estranged people can operate on a basis of civility toward one another for the sake of the body. In this way, as members of God's redeemed community, repentant transgressors and forgiving injured parties can see each other through the eyes of Christ, even if they do not maintain contact with each other.

Community Failures

Unfortunately, community can be a hindrance to reconciliation instead of a help. Failures in community result when reconcilers expect support from community friends but do not receive it. Sometimes support is absent because others do not agree with the decision to reconcile. One offended wife paid this kind of price: *"I cognitively knew that the decision to choose to stay and rebuild placed me next to the 'infidel' rather than separate and divorced. And I realized the sacrifice I would be making, lacking church support because I was choosing to stay and rebuild. . . . Had I chosen to separate or kick him out, the church would have rallied around—brought meals, taken care of kids. They would have done anything. I got none of that because I was staying with him, and nobody knew how to deal with the pastor whose wife was standing with him."*

The lack of response may be attributable in part to the shock that the church as a whole was experiencing. The man in this case, a pastor, not only had betrayed his wife, he also had betrayed his congregation. It is possible that church members did not know how to sort through their own sense of betrayal and anger in contrast to the wife's loyalty. That the couple immediately moved out of town after the husband resigned from his pastorate also may have contributed to the wife's impression that the church was not supporting her.

Another offended wife expressed dismay because her church fellowship rallied around her husband as he worked through his sexual addiction, but seemed to ignore her. *"I have a lot of sadness that when we would see people who knew what we were going through, they would go to my husband and say, 'How are you doing?' I'd be standing right there, but no one would say, 'And how are you doing?' I felt invisible. I felt like my wound wasn't visible. I felt like saying, 'I was the injured party here!'"*

Community failures are painful. Reconcilers hope for support and find none, or worse, find condemnation. Few congregations have a formal policy to follow when relationship failures surface in their midst. Often partners in wounded relationships are labeled as "the good one" and "the bad one." Decisions on who is virtuous and who is the villain are made based on incomplete information. In reality, the situation is often far from clear-cut, and few outside the marriage know the whole story of what went on within it.

Many friends feel caught in the middle. *If I support the transgressor, will I appear disloyal to the injured one? If I befriend the wrongdoer, will I appear to condone the wrong done?* Resolving this dilemma is not easy, especially if one of the estranged parties demands exclusive loyalty from friends. Moreover, many friends want to be helpful but do not know how. For fear of losing the friendship, a friend may hesitate to challenge someone to remain in a relationship rather than bail out. And sometimes friendly advice turns out to be not so friendly after all. Injured parties whose friends expect them to "get over it" quickly experience some of the saddest encounters. Long-term friendships are lost because the friend is not a reconciliation ally in the way that is needed.

Failures by clergy also contributed to reconciliation detours. Many pastors do (and did) offer competent guidance, spiritual direction or counsel to troubled marriages. However, the reconcilers I interviewed experienced a few unhelpful ministers. Leo and Darla expected help from the church leaders but discovered that this was not going to be forthcoming. Darla remembers that as *"the saddest part of the whole thing."* Another couple reports that their pastor had no idea how to help them—not even a referral! Conversely, one offender was caught in the backlash of clergy countertransference. When this contrite offender sought help, the pastor affirmed the spouse's right to leave. The repentant partner concluded that this pastor *"basically wanted me to feel bad. I didn't know that he had had a bad divorce himself . . . so he could not be objective in a situation if he got totally drawn into it. [He] took my mate's defense, and there was absolutely no counsel I was going to get from him at that point."*

Professional Counselor as a Guide

In earlier sections you saw how community members fanned hope into flame by nurturing agency and pathway thinking. You also saw how individuals and groups provided social support to reconcilers. In this section we explore how professional counselors support couples' reconciliation. While individuals and groups are supportive like a hiker's walking stick, professional and pastoral counselors assume the role of professional guide. With the exception of two couples who immersed themselves in recovery communities, all the interviewed couples sought professional counseling.

You may think I am stretching the definition of community a bit when I apply it to the one-on-one relationship that forms between a counselor and a client. And I suppose I am. But if you will allow me wiggle room, you will see how these therapeutic relationships are valuable to reconcilers. Counselors form a special category of community stakeholders because two variables make the counseling relationship unique. First, the personal life of the counselor does not intertwine with reconcilers' in the way the lives of other community members do. Counselors work to minimize dual relationships. Reconcilers employ counselors as temporary, professional guides on their journey. Second, the focus of the relationship is unidirectional, not mutual or interdependent. The counselor is there to help the couple save their marriage, not vice versa. The confidentiality and intensity of the counseling relationship, plus the skill of a competent counselor, make for fertile soil in which old relationship habits can be unlearned and new habits developed.

Among our reconcilers, no school of therapy emerged as the "winner." Couples saw counselors who worked from different theoretical perspectives. Several individuals dealt with issues from the past, while others focused only on their present and future. Many learned new relationship and communication skills. However, three therapeutic factors wove their way through all comments about the nature of these couples' relationships with their counselors. First, counselors promoted hope by helping couples develop agency and pathway thinking. Snyder and colleagues (1999) suggest that this may be one way to explain why different approaches to counseling work for people with the same problem. The strategies may differ, but successful therapies support the development of different ways to reach goals (pathway thinking) and support clients' desire to get there (agency thinking).

Second, reconcilers developed a solid working relationship with their counselors. Reconcilers felt respected by their counselors. One husband put it like this: *"My counselor changed my life. He is the first man I talked with who treated me with respect. I don't even know how to describe these feelings. I felt genuinely appreciated for who I was and genuinely listened to by a man for the first time in my life. [My counselor] was wonderful. He held me accountable. He made a wonderful difference in my life."*

Reconcilers also felt that their counselors were on their side and understood their perspective. As one offended party said, *"The first thing the [counselor] said to me was, 'Wow, you must be in a lot of pain.' And that really fit me. I thought, 'Gosh, here's somebody I can talk with about that.' There was such pressure to 'buck up and get on with life' around everywhere that that was very good to hear that."*

Finally, counselors shared the couples' goal of saving their marriage. One clinician was fired after spending several sessions trying to convince one of the reconciling couples to buy herbal medicines instead of dealing with their marriage. Another was fired because he was following his own agenda for the couple instead of their agenda: *"I was getting frustrated with him because of that group he put me in where everybody said I should get divorced. And he had been divorced, so he knew this was the answer. But no, it was not the end to which I was working. 'I'd appreciate it if you'd work with me toward the end that I'm working toward.'"*

In what ways might professional counseling help you move closer to reconciliation? Often pastors can refer you to reputable counselors in your area. Professional counseling organizations such as the American Association of Christian Counselors (<www.aacc.net>) and the Christian Association for Psychological Studies (<www.caps.net>) have websites through which you can find a counselor in your area.

Some Closing Thoughts

So far we have explored three essential items for the journey toward reconciliation. First, we saw how commitment to Jesus Christ provides a model and motive for reconciling. Second, we looked at couples' commitment to the process of reconciling and saw how couples turned inward while they concentrated on repairing their relationship. Couples sought those activities, persons or events that would help them reconcile, and they removed from their lives anything that opposed reconciliation.

In this chapter we discussed a third essential item: the facilitating role of community. Community is a source of great strength for reconcilers, but unfortunately it can also be a source of great pain. Reconcilers reached out to their community, but they used discretion about whom they told what details to. As you continue to think about your own communities, consider whether or not they are reconciliation-friendly and how you can draw on the strength of those groups that will support your journey toward reconciliation.

PART TWO

TASKS THAT ENCOURAGE RECONCILIATION

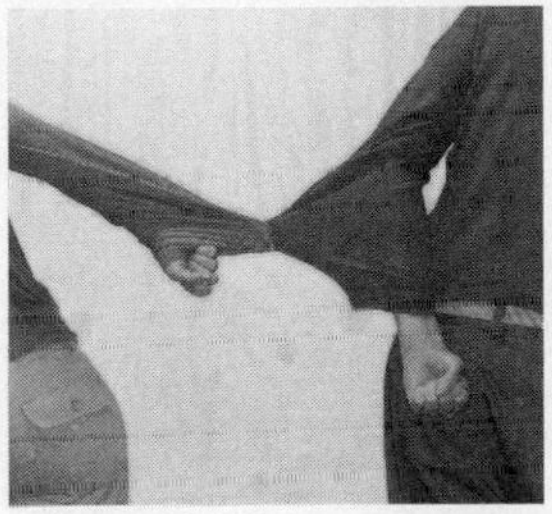

5

GROWING UP AND GROWING TOGETHER

I confess. I'm a Trekkie, a fan of all things Star Trek. (I'll say more about confession in chapter six.) In episode 221 of *Star Trek: The Next Generation,* the Enterprise is transporting Ambassador Briam and his cargo, an unusual cocoon, to meet Alrik of Valt. The contents of the cocoon, a gift to Alrik, will end centuries of conflict between these two worlds.

An accident in the cargo bay dissolves the cocoon, revealing its contents: a woman, Kamala. In addition to her beauty and empathic talents, Kamala possesses another special feature: she is genetically designed to mold her personality and preferences to her future mate. In essence, she erases what is uniquely her to become what flawlessly matches another. In the eyes of her people, this renders her the perfect mate. "I am for you, Alrik of Valt."

What do you think? Would you like a mate like Kamala? Your relationship would be conflict-free because your partner would never argue with you or request that you do something you don't want to do. This person would have only those thoughts, feelings or interests that please you. In this case, the two become one—you.

If we are honest with ourselves, many of us picture the "two becoming one" marriage principle this way. You may find the concept appealing, but the truth is, it does not work. Marriage researcher John Gottman reports that our belief that "compatibility is the foundation of stable marriages" is a myth: "My research shows that much more important than having compatible views is *how* couples work out their differences" (1994, pp. 23-24).

You do not marry your clone. You marry a person who is made in the image of God like you but who is *unlike* you in many vital ways. You marry the person who eventually activates all of your unfinished business from your family of origin and who in this way challenges you to finish growing up.

Take heart. This discomfort and anxiety goes both ways. According to marriage and sex therapist David Schnarch, this is a normal process in healthy marriages (Schnarch, 1997, 2002). What transforms this process from function to dysfunction is when couples try to escape this tension instead of working with it. Then they hit the wall Schnarch calls "gridlock."

This was the gridlock that the marriages you are reading about hit, and hit big time. Initial attempts to deal with their mounting relationship anxiety included strategies such as trying to control the partner, resentfully giving in to the partner, or emotionally or physically withdrawing from the relationship (Schnarch, 1997, 2002). These same strategies eventually escalated into the problems that threatened the very life of the marriage (that is, affairs, alcoholism, emotional abuse and so on).

How can couples cope with this normal relational anxiety without allowing it to threaten their marriage? Family therapists—such as Murray Bowen (Kerr & Bowen, 1988), Edwin Friedman (1985), Harriet Lerner (1989) and David Schnarch (1997, 2002)—see the solution to this problem in the process of emotionally and relationally growing up, or to use the psychological term, differentiation of self. Reconcilers discovered that their marriage plummeted toward divorce in their attempts to dodge growing up. But when they embraced this challenge by confronting themselves and becoming more differentiated (Schnarch, 1997), they began to chart a new course for their marriage.

In chapters two through four you read about the essential commitments that support marital reconciliation. You saw that commitment to Christ, commitment to the hard work of reconciling and participation in a reconciliation-friendly community provide a firm foundation for the work of reconciliation. Now we turn our attention to specific tasks that comprise the work of reconciliation. In upcoming chapters you will learn about the roles that repenting, forgiving and rebuilding truth and trustworthiness play in helping couples to transform their wounded relationships into vibrant marriages.

In this chapter you will learn about differentiation of self, self-soothing and self-responsibility. This emphasis on "self" may raise red flags for some readers because of its association with selfishness or self-centeredness. As you read further, however, you will discover that *finding* your self is a key to being able to truly *give* yourself fully to others—just the opposite of selfishness or self-centeredness. After the story of Tom and Marge, I will discuss these three important building blocks of reconciliation: differentiation of self, self-soothing and self-responsibility.

Marge and Tom's Story

Marge, a single parent with three small boys, met Tom two years after her divorce from her physically abusive first husband. Although Marge and Tom had grown up in the same small town, they did not know each other. *"I'm ten years older than he is,"* Marge explains. *"We worked in the same facility, and that's how we met. We had known each other's family before we had actually known each other. He was very thoughtful and sweet, and I was ready for somebody to be nice to me."*

Six months later they married. Along with being thoughtful, Tom was an alcoholic. *"A wonderfully sweet, big-hearted drunk was my husband,"* says Marge. Not surprisingly, their marriage was turbulent from the start. They often fought over money.

Tom says, *"I promised her anything to get her to do anything I wanted her to do, like help me buy something. . . . So that's the way it worked."*

Marge agrees with Tom's assessment. *"If he wants something, he wants it today. And I would [say], 'Okay, I'll cosign with you if you'll quit drinking.' He would agree. That's easy. . . . Scratch that promise. And this is how I used money, but all that we did was get ourselves in over our heads."*

Marge believed it was her calling in life to straighten Tom up. She saw herself as "*perfect in every way. I thought I was going to fix this man if I killed him doing it. I was bound and determined to make this marriage work, and the only way to do it was for him to shape up and fit the mold of what a husband was supposed to be. I would be doing him a favor if I were able to fix him.*"

Tom had a different opinion. "*I thought all she wanted me to do was to let her control me. And I didn't want to give up control. 'I don't care what you think' was my reaction. 'I do what I want to and you can like it or lump it.' I'd tell her a lie in a heartbeat and prop it up with another one.*"

For fifteen years Tom drank and Marge nagged. Marge reflects on this: "*Tom was a precious, precious person, and there could have been good times. But when he was sober, I was explaining to him how terrible he had been on his previous drink.*"

Finally things came to a head. Tom recalls, "*We got in a big argument one evening when I was drinking. She and her momma went somewhere, and while they were [gone] I just packed my stuff up and left.*"

Three days later Marge filed for divorce. She recounts that time: "'*There's no telling what-all kinds of foolish things he's going to do.' The first of the week I went and filed for divorce; I needed to protect myself [financially] because he was very visibly irresponsible. I don't know whether he really wanted a divorce or just wanted to be free. It was never discussed after that day because I had just made up my mind to go ahead and get it done.*"

Tom adds, "*Actually all I wanted to be able [to do was] drink and not have to put up with any hassles. And I always got a hassle when I was drinking. 'I don't need this. I don't need to put up with this nagging all the time when I'm drinking, because I want to do what I want to do. I don't care about anything else.*'"

The divorce was granted. Marge and Tom saw each other two times during the following year. Life was very difficult for Marge. She was lonely. She was in debt. She threw herself into her job and her grandchildren. Marge tried to tell herself, "'*This is enough for anybody.' It was not. I think it was because my relationship had ended so unsuccessfully.*"

On the other hand, Tom says he "*stayed drunk a year. I got up every morning, drank three beers on the way to work, went home, went out to the store at dinner and got a six-pack and drank it and came back to work and worked the rest of the afternoon, and after work I'd go to the club right outside the gate and stay till closing time."*

In the meantime, Marge's four-year-old granddaughter was praying for her grandfather to come home. Marge remembers one pivotal event vividly, when her granddaughter *"started praying for her poppy . . . that [God] would bring her poppy home. The little church we were attending at the time had a function where all the past members and so forth came, and Tom called and asked if he could go to the gathering and the dinner."*

Tom picks up the story:

> *I was over at my mother's. Then Momma was talking about Marge. She said, "You know, all you've got to do is call her if you want to go to church with her." I said, "Well, I don't know. She might not let me." And Momma said, "Well, why don't you call her and find out?" So I called over [there]. I said, "Marge, can I go to church with you?" And she said, "Yes."*
>
> *I went to church with her, and I rededicated my life to the Lord that day. That's the day things really started going in the right direction. I lived with my mother and daddy, and we [Marge and I] got to where we were riding back and forth to work together, and we just dated, and then we got married. We got married on the same anniversary we had.*

Although they had resumed their relationship, they were not out of the woods. Tom was still trying to live in two worlds. He explains, *"I tried to have a beer with the boys at work at dinner, then come home and be a nice guy."*

Marge still believed it was her calling in life to fix Tom. Soon they had resumed their old pattern: Tom drank and Marge nagged. Tom took the first chance that came along to escape from Marge's "help." Three months after their remarriage, Tom volunteered to go overseas to work for four months. Marge recalls, *"He was working sixteen hours a day, sending all of his money home, and I was a married person but with freedom to do anything I wanted to do. I was able to catch up all of his bills that he had messed up while he was gone. Oh, it was just really good. This was not an unpleasant time for me at all. I had just what I needed—a husband in a box."*

Six months after Tom returned to the States, he went on a three-day drinking binge. He remembers it this way:

> *I got drunk, three days. And because I knew I had blown it, I knew it [the marriage] was over with, but I didn't care. But when I decided to come home and talk, it took me two hours to drive three hundred yards from where I was, where I had to sit down and get myself together and do what I had to do. . . . I asked the Lord, "Just take the desire for alcohol away from me." And from that day forth I never had a desire for it.*
>
> *I had to go through the treatment center because that's what my kids and my wife expected me to do. You have to fight alcoholism the way they say do it—you know, the AA thing. I did that, and she didn't call, she didn't come, she didn't contact me until I got out. Then when I got out, I went over to my mother and daddy's (they live a half a mile from here) and stayed with them.*

Tom and Marge continued to work on their relationship during this time. Tom says, *"Marge and I drove back and forth to work every day together, and then at night we went to AA meetings."*

Then one day Marge and Tom were visiting a new church. In the vestibule Marge saw an advertisement for *"a Bible-based, Christian-taught twelve-step program, and the advertisement was, 'Are you sick and tired of being sick and tired?' I said, 'O Lord, yes I am.' We attended that class together."* That was the turning point in their marriage.

Differentiation of Self: Finding Your Self Without Losing the Other

In the beginning, the interviewed partners had been clear about how *their mates* needed to change, but not how *they* needed to change. Let a comment from Marge serve as example: *"My husband was an alcoholic, and I was perfect in every way."* However, when partners gained insight into their *own* needed change, their journey toward reconciliation took another step forward. You can hear this change in what Marge says: *"I had to look at myself, and it's not easy to look at yourself. The pain that I had inflicted on my husband and my kids had to be dealt with. I had a mouth that was like a dragon. A cutting, cutting tongue. It didn't bother me a bit to lash out. In thinking that I was helping by . . . scolding, I was cutting to ribbons. My constant nagging gave him license to drink again. And I never saw any of that."* What Marge "saw" eventually were ways that she contributed to the pain in her marriage. These were things that she *could* control and change.

While the particulars varied from couple to couple, one common denominator remained. Everybody had to grow up. This was the process of going "on to maturity" (Heb 6:1). In its context, this verse refers to maturing in the teachings about Christ, taking spiritual meat instead of spiritual milk. According to the writer of Hebrews, "Solid food is for the mature, who by constant use have trained themselves to distinguish good from evil" (Heb 5:14). Sometimes discerning good from evil *appeared* straightforward, as the first quotation in this section indicated. Tom was evil (an alcoholic). Marge was good (perfect in every way). However, Jesus had a different perspective: "Why do you look at the speck of sawdust in your brother's [spouse's] eye and pay no attention to the plank in your own eye?" (Mt 7:3). Recognizing and confronting the "evil" in yourself requires discernment, and according to Hebrews 5:14, discernment emerges from maturity. Family therapists call this plank-removing and "going on to maturity" the process of *self-differentiation*.

How does differentiation of self work? If you are working toward being self-differentiated, you will want to focus on five characteristics: a clear knowledge of who you are in relation to others, the ability to see yourself and others as uniquely created by God, the ability to tell the difference between what you think and what you feel, a lack of fear of engulfment or abandonment, and a tolerance of pain for the sake of growth.

Knowledge of who you are in relation to others. First, when you are an "I," you are clear about what you think, feel, want and desire, and you are able to let others—especially those with whom you are the closest—have their own thoughts, feelings, wants and desires without your feeling threatened (that is, angry at them for being different) or diminished (that is, angry at yourself for being different). "People who are clear about who they are and what they believe are able to value and listen to others' opinions and feelings without losing their own position" (Schnarch, 1997, p. 174).

Let's revisit a statement from Tom that models how this does *not* look. In this next quotation you can hear how Tom was not able to listen to Marge's perspective without engaging in a form of manipulation. *"We always talked, but it was always one-sided. 'We' were going to do it 'my way.' . . . And I promised her anything to get her to do anything I wanted her to do, like help me buy something."*

As you grow in differentiation, you do not feel compelled to disassociate important parts of your self from yourself in order to make someone else comfortable (that is, less anxious). Nor do you demand that the other person disassociate important parts of his or her self in order to keep you nonanxious (Friedman, 1985). "Our goal will be to have relationships with both men and women that do not operate at the expense of the self and to have a self that does not operate at the expense of the other" (Lerner, 1989, p. 4).

As Tom became more of a "self," he also became more of a partner with Marge, as you can see in his statement: *"Now if something comes up [that] we want to do, we sit down and talk about it. And we'll make a rational decision about it."* Anxiety is a central emotion in this process (Friedman, 1985; Kerr & Bowen, 1988; Schnarch, 1997, 2002). Later in this chapter I'll say more about anxiety and our management of it as a facet of differentiation of self. The important thing to remember now is that self-defined people are clear about who they are *and* can relate intimately with others without losing themselves or overshadowing the other in the process.

To develop this aspect of differentiation, you may consider making a list of what you believe, want, value and desire. Identify those aspects that your partner would endorse and those aspects that your partner would not endorse. Encourage your mate to make a similar list; then plan a time to have a good discussion about your lists. The point of the conversation is not to win your mate over but to deepen your understanding of yourself and your partner. Pay careful attention to the items that call forth anxiety in you. Then spend some time in prayer and meditation. What is it about those items or your exchange at that point that generated anxiety? What fears are aroused? Are those fears realistic or unfounded? You may want to consider sharing these insights with your partner, pastor, good friend or counselor.

Ability to see yourself and others as uniquely created by God. When you are an "I," you value yourself for your own made-in-the-image-of-God uniqueness, and you value others for theirs. Tom's words capture the essence of this. This first statement reflects how Tom used to think about himself. Hear how he devalued himself.

> *I was never bright. I was the oddball in school. I was always the one everybody pulled the jokes on. You know, there's always one in the school that gets the brunt of everything. That's what I was and I was never smart. All I wanted to be able [to do was] drink and not have to put up with any hassle. I was no good to my wife. I was no good to my family. And I sure was no good for my job.*

We could engage in speculation about why and how Tom drew these conclusions about himself. Many of our guesses would be accurate. Regardless of the reasons for a poor view of one's self, differentiation requires one to take firm hold of oneself and to examine the truth about one's gifts and graces. This second statement from Tom shows the change in his picture of himself.

> *Through this Overcomers Ministry I learned how to love myself and have some pride in myself, and I had never had any pride, had never loved myself. If you don't love yourself, you don't love anybody else. And [if] you don't love the Lord, you don't do nothing but make a mess. Okay, that's what the first part of my life was.*

Marge began to define herself by looking honestly at herself. In this statement you can hear how Marge disentangled herself from Tom without distancing herself from him.

This process started when I was in my forties. I had to get literally born again, and I'm not talking about salvation. I'm saying a new person had to be created here. When we found this [Overcomers Anonymous] twelve-step program, we wanted to work on ourselves. We knew that we needed work as individuals. I knew that was what I needed, because I was definitely sick and tired of being sick and tired.

As Marge found herself, she discovered that she could love Tom more deeply than she ever had before, without needing to control him.

I know now that without Tom I could be a complete person. This was not true when we were divorced. I was lonesome; I was miserable. . . . I felt like I had failed, and I had guilt feelings because I had failed. I had been given this project to fix him and had not done it. With or without him, I'm complete. I like it better with him [laughs]. . . . I think that's where we've gotten to, and this is why we complement each other. I learned to love my husband for what he was. What I had planned for him to be was some person that I wouldn't even have liked. I had to get to the point where I could see him for who he is and decide if I liked this person or not. And I do. . . . I may have accepted [myself] for what I am, for who I am. I'm country through and through and like it that way.

This aspect of differentiation of self asks you to take a courageous self-inventory. One way to do this is to list the things you do well. The challenge at this stage for many people is to silence their internal critic, that little voice inside their head that offers only negative comments about self and skills. If necessary, ban that infernal voice from speaking! In other words, no "yeah but-ing" allowed. If you find it impossible to make a list, seek the support of a pastor, counselor or friend to help you see yourself as one uniquely created in the image of God and specially gifted.

Ability to tell the difference between thinking and feeling. Third, when you are an "I," you can tell the difference between your thinking and your feeling, and you can decide which of these important functions will take the lead during intense (that is, anxious) interpersonal exchanges. Regarding your thinking, you can think (relatively) clearly during hard conversations and remain emotionally engaged. Your feelings do not hijack your thinking.

However, you do not become just a talking head. You do not use well-oiled logic to browbeat your mate into giving in to you, nor do you use it to push your mate away from you. In fact, when asked how you feel, you can express that, using appropriate variations of feeling words such as *mad, sad, glad* or *afraid,* rather than saying more about what you *think.* Regarding your feelings, you do not need to shut them off, nor do you allow them to rage out of control. You do not use your emotions to browbeat your mate into submission, nor do you use them to push your mate away. In fact, you can have intense emotions, but you regulate their intensity so that you can continue to discuss important things with your spouse. Tom recalls a recent exchange between Marge and him that illustrates this aspect of differentiation of self: *"We didn't fuss and we didn't fight about it. We dealt with it like two sensible human beings. . . . Ten years ago we would have fought like cats and dogs."*

This is a particularly challenging aspect of self-differentiation because thinking is rewarded in individualistic cultures while feeling is underrated, dismissed and devalued. If you tend to think too much and feel too little, you may want to pay attention to how your physical body reacts during intense exchanges. Emotions show up as body responses. Once you identify your body's cue, see if you can put a label to that feeling. If necessary, start with the basics *(mad, sad, glad and afraid).* Next, figure out its intensity (high, medium, low). Finally, find a word that describes it. For example, can you name a low-intensity sad feeling or a high-intensity mad feeling?[1] If you tend to feel too much and think too late, you also want to pay attention to your body. Your aim, however, is to become aware that your emotional freight train is picking up steam,

---

[1]Such as *blue* or *furious.* You may have thought of other words, but these were the two that first came to my mind.

so that you can lessen your intensity. You may need to take some deep, calming breaths. Or take a short break from an exchange in order to rein in your feelings. Your goal is to release a level of feeling that is just right for the context in which you find yourself, not to repress or deny what you feel.

Freedom from fear of engulfment or abandonment. Fourth, when you are an "I," you fear neither engulfment nor abandonment by significant others (Guerin, Fogarty, Fay & Kautto, 1996; Kerr & Bowen, 1988). People without much sense of self react to significant others out of a fear of separation *(don't leave me or I'll die!)* or a fear of absorption *(go away; you're smothering me!)*. When left unchecked, these fears create a dance of closeness and distance, and—much like the "pushmi-pullyu" in *The Voyages of Dr. Doolittle*—couples who master this dance become emotionally fused. However, when you are an "I," you can tolerate the anxiety of being left or being close without feeling as if you are losing your self. According to David Schnarch, you do not react to changes in closeness on your mate's part (his or her wanting more of you or less of you) by taking over, giving in or withdrawing. When such anxiety is triggered, you "hold on to yourself," in Schnarch's words (1997, 2002), staying clear about who you are. You can see this process in the following statement from Marge:

> *I think I always expected somebody to do me wrong, so I was constantly telling them how good I was and how evil they were. I can see the change in me came about very gradually, because it was a hard thing for me to give up this defense mechanism. I am very emotional and I had become this way. I know it was a work of God, but I had to let all the defenses down. It's a very scary thing to do. But if you can't get through my defenses then you can't get through to me. I had to let go of all of the defenses, and God was there. . . . As it turned out, it was a pretty good thing.*

Facing fear of abandonment or absorption is well worth the effort, because it frees you to more fully and more freely engage with others.

When your mate seeks to be closer or asks for more breathing room, instead of impulsively running away or holding on to your mate more tightly, try to "stand still." Now ask yourself the following question: *Will I really cease to exist if the other moves closer (fear of absorption) or asks for more space (fear of abandonment)?* Your aim is to arrive at an appropriate response to your spouse, not a knee-jerk reaction. I use the word *appropriate* because some individuals do indeed ask for more closeness than you want to give or seek more space than is suitable for the relationship. You may find it helpful to ask yourself, *What are my choices?* during these moments and pay attention to what you say to yourself about what will happen to you if you let the other person come closer or move away.

Ability to tolerate pain for the sake of growth. Fifth, when you are an "I," you tolerate pain for the sake of growth (Friedman, 1985; Schnarch, 1997, 2002). As one injured spouse said, "*The whole point of getting better isn't just seeking pain relief. It's healing a relationship.*" Relationships are messy. Rebuilding damaged relationships is painful. But so is not rebuilding! Our choice is not between a pain-free path and a pain-full path, although freedom from pain is what we wish for.

Notice in the following statement how one offending husband, a pastor, tried to avoid the consequences that would befall him if his wife found out about his affair: "*We were in this building program. I'd get the building paid off, and I would look for another church somewhere else. We'll move out of there and everything would be okay. This was so bizarre. It was the only viable option that I wanted to choose. I certainly didn't want to choose truth telling at that point.*"

In truth, our choice is between *two* pain-filled paths. The question you must answer is this: Which path (with its pain) will help you reach your relationship goals? According to family therapist Edwin Friedman, "The more that family members are motivated to achieve goals, the less their pain will bother them" (1985, p. 48). Pain is often the very thing that motivates you to change and, hopefully, to grow. Richard Dobbins, one of my first professors in counseling, taught me that pain is the only sure motivator of change.[2] Dr. Dobbins often said in class, "When the pain of change is greater than the pain of staying the same, people stay the same. When the pain of change is less than the pain of staying the same, people change."

Tom described an event that was a point of personal growth for him. Marge's sister was diagnosed with cancer shortly after Marge and Tom had moved back together. That day Tom dropped Marge off at her sister's house, which smelled strongly of beer. Tempted, Tom drove to a gas station to buy beer, but instead of making the purchase he returned to his car and left. This was the first time Tom realized that he could trust *himself* not to drink because *he* was making that choice, not because he was afraid of Marge's reaction.

Pain is *not* the enemy (although you may find that hard to believe). Avoiding pain in order to avoid growing is the enemy. Therefore you boldly *challenge yourself* to increase your own threshold for pain for the sake of growth (Friedman, 1985; Schnarch 1997, 2002). You can do this unilaterally, without your partner's consent. There is a catch, however: by increasing your own threshold for pain (that is, relationship anxiety), you also challenge your partner (directly or indirectly) to increase his or her own pain threshold. For example, personal growth for you may mean not rescuing your partner, as has been your habit. Trust me, your partner will not like it! Nevertheless, you tolerate your mate's displeasure with you (that is, being angry with you) for your sake and for his or hers. If you happen to be a people pleaser, you have your work cut out for you.

Perhaps a look at some theological concepts related to differentiation will be helpful at this point. Theologians such as Jürgen Moltmann (1981), Wolfhart Pannenberg (1991) and Stanley Grenz (2001) apply the concept of differentiation to the Trinity. These theologians see the Trinity as "a community and fellowship among three equal persons" (Grenz, 2001, p. 45). The Father, the Son and the Holy Spirit are complete persons who are intimately connected with one another and who mutually relate to one an-

[2]Richard Dobbins, EMERGE Ministries, 900 Mull Avenue, Akron, Ohio 44313.

other. They are three "selves" *and* they are "persons-in-relationship." Historically, the term *perichoresis* refers to the Trinity's interdependent, mutual relationality. *Perichoresis* is like a divine dance in which each member of the Trinity fully participates as Father, Son or Spirit, yet makes room for the other without being diminished as a result. The dance requires each member of the Trinity; otherwise it would be incomplete. With creation, the Trinity makes room for humanity to join the dance, not as a peer with the Trinity but as a full participant nonetheless, with movements that complement those of God. Here is a paradox: each member of the Trinity is complete, and yet each member's identity is incomplete until it is linked relationally with the others.

Even if differentiation of self takes time, it is important to start somewhere. Here are a few suggestions:

Make a list of the things you believe, feel or want. Identify those aspects that you tend to give away when you become anxious. Create an action plan for how you will hold on to those parts of yourself in the future.

Think about your important relationships. Do you tend to overfunction (like Marge) or underfunction (like Tom)? Do you pursue your partner when you get anxious (like Marge) or distance yourself (like Tom)? Identify one thing that you can do to change this pattern.

From this brief discussion of the Trinity we can surmise that self-differentiation is not about individualism, although it *is* about individuality. Differentiation balances, or perhaps I should say marries, autonomy and intimacy without sacrificing individuality or communion. It requires a whole and complete "I" and a whole and complete "you," intimately related to one another through mutual and reciprocal community and fellowship. Simply put, differentiation of self is "the capacity to be an 'I' while remaining connected" to our significant others (Friedman, 1985, p. 27).

You may be growing anxious. Doesn't this contradict traditional Christian teaching about denying oneself? What about Jesus' words in

Luke 9:23-25: "If anyone would come after me, he must deny himself and take up his cross daily and follow me. For whoever wants to save his life will lose it, but whoever loses his life for me will save it. What good is it for a man to gain the whole world, and yet lose or forfeit his very self?" And Philippians 2:5-7: "Your attitude should be the same as that of Christ Jesus: / Who, being in very nature God, / did not consider equality with God something to be grasped, / but *made himself nothing,* / taking the very nature of a servant, / being made in human likeness."

To address this valid concern, two things will be helpful: exploring what differentiation of self is *not* and examining the meaning of these texts. Let's look at what self-differentiation is not. It is not selfishness. Selfish people often function at the expense of others by expecting others to meet their needs. It is also not self-centeredness. Self-centered people also function at the expense of others by eliminating their own awareness of the needs and perspectives of others. Self-differentiation is also not self-annihilation. People without a self get a self by borrowing somebody else's (Kerr & Bowen, 1988). People with a borrowed self do not know what they think, feel or desire. They only know what they think *you* think they should think, feel or desire in order to keep you nonanxious and in the relationship.

A perfect example of a borrowed self is Julia Roberts's character in *Runaway Bride,* whose favorite way to eat eggs is *exactly* like that of each one of her fiancés, none of whom like their eggs the same way. She never knew how *she* liked to eat eggs! Christians can easily see the problems with being selfish or self-centered. However, we often trip over self-annihilation. Scripture clearly talks about denying self and living our life in ways that seek the well-being of others. What we want to deny is our selfishness and our self-centeredness, not our uniquely created-in-the-image-of-God self. Let's now look at the Scriptures noted above.

Luke 9:23-25 does indeed talk about denying self. But what exactly does that mean? We regularly interpret this passage through the eyes of our individualistic culture, so denying self often becomes the equivalent of having no self at all. New Testament scholar Joel B. Green offers a helpful perspective on these verses:

> Discipleship entails radical self-denial, daily crossbearing and accompanying Jesus. Because of the degree to which individuals in Roman antiquity were embedded in networks of kinship, the call to denial cannot be understood along strictly individualistic terms. Rather, to deny oneself was to set aside the relationships, the extended family of origin and inner circle of friends, by which one made up one's identity. By "radical" self-denial, then, is meant *openness to constructing a wholly new identity* not based on ethnic origins (cf. 3:7-9) or relationships of mutual obligation (e.g., 6:27-38), but *in the new community* that is centered on God and resolutely faithful to Jesus' message. Taking up the cross in its Roman context would have referred literally to the victim's carrying the crossbeam of the cross from the site of sentencing to the place of crucifixion. Within Luke's narrative, however, this act has been transformed into a metaphor by the addition of the phrase "day by day," signifying that one is to live on a daily basis as though one has been sentenced to death by crucifixion. In this sense dead to the world that opposes God's purpose, disciples are free to live according to the values of the kingdom of God proclaimed in Jesus' ministry. (1997, pp. 372-73, emphasis added)

Our Western culture today does not operate based on kinship ties as in Jesus' day, when honor and status (antiquity's equivalent to self-esteem) came from one's familial association and social status. You can see that, in this passage, self-denial was the giving up of allegiance to worldly ways (family and social ties) to gain honor and status and replacing them with the status-renouncing way of the cross of Christ. I deny those things that hamper my sense of myself as one who bears the image of God, committed to living according to the values of God's kingdom within the context of the people of God. Therefore, by losing my self, I find my self perfectly reflected in the eyes of Jesus Christ, the one who loves me perfectly. As Bonnie Crandall, one of my counseling colleagues, says, "You discover that you are a child of God and a person of worth."

Philippians 2:5-11 sheds further light on this topic, as it helps us to see Christ's model of self-emptying. New Testament scholar Michael Gorman (2002) observes that, to create this passage, Paul adopted and expanded on a hymn used within the early church to teach the Philippians about Christ-modeled interpersonal relationships.

> Your attitude should be the same as that of Christ Jesus: / Who, being in very nature God, / did not consider equality with God something to be grasped, / but made himself nothing, / taking the very nature of a servant, / being made in human likeness. / And being found in appearance as a man, / he humbled himself / and became obedient to death— / even death on a cross! / Therefore God exalted him to the highest place / and gave him the name that is above every name, / that at the name of Jesus every knee should bow, / in heaven and on earth and under the earth, / and every tongue confess that Jesus Christ is Lord, / to the glory of God the Father.

Christ Jesus, the second member of the Trinity, was entitled to all the rights, privileges and honor due to God. However, he voluntarily set aside those status and honor markers to become human. Truly Christ's self-denial was not about individualism; it was about a shift in self-in-relationship. It involved a drastic change in the nature of his relationship within the Trinity (Jesus "did not consider equality with God something to be grasped"), and with humanity ("taking on the very nature of a servant, being made in human likeness"). In Roman society at that time, a slave was about as much of a nonperson as you could get. Slaves had no rights, no autonomy and no connectedness other than the ties of property to an owner. Jesus Christ emptied himself of a self-in-intimate-divine-relationship-with-God and became a self-in-relation-to-humanity. He denied himself, but not of a *self* in the absolute sense as we might think of it, but as a self of divine status, power and privilege, and became a self-in-humanity.

However, this self-denying did not diminish Jesus. No one who annihilates his self or her self could speak with the kind of authority and command the kind of attention that Jesus did. He was anything but a people pleaser! Because Jesus knew who he was (a child of God and a person of worth, if you will), he was able to give himself for the sake of humanity. He became a slave, as the world would see it, but not a slave to *human* commands. He became a slave who freely chose to obey the will of God, the Father. Jesus taught the disciples to pray, "Your [God's] will be done" (Mt 6:10), and then he lived it (see Lk 22:22). Jesus was very clear about himself (Jn 10:18; 13:1). He was able to draw some people emotionally near (disciples) and keep others at a distance (Pharisees). He loved us without being engulfed by us. Also, he was willing to let us reject him and despise him. He tolerated the pain of the cross for the sake of our reconciliation with God. As you can see, Christ's model of self-denial is consistent with differentiation of self.

The following statement from Marge shows how she began to become clearer about herself as a child of God and a person of worth: *"As I started looking through the twelve steps, I thought, 'Man, I'm not out of control.' Then I thought, 'Yes you are, because you have never really accepted Jesus as Lord of your life.' I had not. I was lord of my life. And if I hadn't turned my life over to God, then I had not really ever given Tom any of my life. I don't even know how long the process took for me to realize that in order to have any perfection it would have to be the Lord's perfection, because I certainly didn't have any."*

Being a self is not for cowards. Most of us would prefer to remain immature hedonists rather than become mature adults, especially when relationships get hard. When you are a self, you *can* sacrifice for the sake of your relationship without feeling you are losing parts of yourself. For Christians, self-differentiation requires courage, integrity and a deepening relationship with Jesus, who himself is our model of differentiation. According to psychologist Harriet Lerner,

> At the simplest level, "being a self" means we can be pretty much who we are in relationships rather than what others wish, need, and

> expect us to be. It also means that we can allow others to do the same. It means we do not participate in relationships at the expense of the "I" (as women are encouraged to do) and we do not bolster the "I" at the expense of the other (as men are encouraged to do). As simple as this may sound, its translation into action is enormously complex. In fact, any sustained move in the direction of "more self" is a difficult challenge and not without risk. (1989, pp. 21-22)

Family therapist Philip Guerin and his colleagues (1996) would offer the following advice about how to grow in differentiation:

Observe how you interact with others. To whom or what do you turn when you begin to get anxious?

People move in one of three directions: toward, away or stand still. Which direction is your favorite when you become anxious? What would be one thing you could do to change that?

If you do make a change, observe how others respond to you. Be prepared for the pressure to change back to the way things were.

Remember, differentiation of self is essentially the process of being who you are in all of your uniqueness *while* you are emotionally available to or connected with significant others. By definition this means that we will encounter anxiety. The next facet of growing up centers on how we cope with that relational anxiety.

Self-Soothing: Embracing Your Anxiety Without Losing Your Mind

In the above quotations, not only can you hear how Marge and Tom became clearer about who they are, you can hear that they took ownership for their own emotional well-being. These reconcilers discovered that learning to manage their own anxiety is essential to differentiation of self. According to marriage and sex therapist David Schnarch (2002), self-soothing is the ability to comfort yourself. Family therapist Edwin Friedman (1985) refers to this as being a "nonanxious presence." Self-soothing is the ability to regulate your own intense feelings when a significant relationship becomes loaded with anxiety. It is a behavior (reducing your own anxiety) and an attitude (yourself as responsible for reducing your own anxiety).

Few emotions are as contagious as anxiety. It can run through relationships faster than the flu runs through families. However, according to family therapists such as Murray Bowen, Edwin Friedman, Harriet Lerner and David Schnarch, anxiety is a regular and normal part of relationships. By anxiety I am not referring to panic attacks or other anxiety disorders, such as posttraumatic stress disorder. Instead I am referring to that knot in the pit of your stomach that you feel whenever you suspect that your conversation with your spouse is going to get difficult. It's the tension in your neck and shoulders that develops when you know that your proposed plan of action will not please your partner and you want your partner to like it. It's the dry mouth you experience when your mate gives you "that look." Your attention is focused on the other person and your own powerlessness. On the other hand, Schnarch writes,

> self-soothing involves turning inward and accessing your own resources to regain your emotional balance and feeling comfortable in your body. Your breathing is unlabored, your heart slows to its normal rate; your shoulders are relaxed, no longer hunched to ward off an anticipated blow. Self-soothing is your ability to comfort yourself, lick your own wounds, and care for yourself without excessive indulgence or deprivation. (1997, p. 170)

Perhaps self-soothing is a new concept to you. That's not surprising. Most of us do not come into adulthood with the belief that we are responsible for tending to our own anxiety. Instead we adopt this formula: "I'm anxious. You change." Or we adhere to its twin: "You're anxious. I'll change." One wife had the following observation about her husband's prereconciliation behavior toward her: *"He did a lot of things not to make me upset. If I were to get upset, that would upset him. He'd feel like less than a husband, and so he felt, 'Okay, this is going to upset her, so I won't do it.'"*

Marriage and sex therapist David Schnarch (2002, p. 136) recommends the following strategies to help you begin to learn how to self-soothe.

When you start to lose your grip on yourself, stop talking and focus on your breathing. Lower your volume, unclench your teeth and talk in a softer tone of voice.

Try not to take your partner's behavior (or lack of change) personally. This is another "opportunity" to let go of your reflected sense of self.

If you can't regulate your emotions, control your behavior. Don't shoot your mouth off or make things worse. When you start saying, "Maybe I shouldn't say this, but—" take your own advice.

Stop your negative mental tapes. Stop telling yourself, "I can't believe this."

Notice how his sole goal was to avoid upsetting his wife. The result was not peace but emotional distance.

In a second example, a husband describes the process by which he would absorb his wife's emotions as his own: *"If she was having a bad day, I'd have a bad day. If she was happy, I'd be happy. Or if she was unhappy, I'd be stoic. I tracked her a lot, not feeling comfortable with having emotions of my own or emotions that were different from hers."*

Does "I'm anxious, you change" work? Certainly. However, your emotional well-being now depends on someone else, which leaves you insecure and hypervigilant to changes in the other. You now have to control that person to maintain your peace of mind. On the other hand, when you learn to self-soothe, or "comfort yourself" in Schnarch's words, you take your anxiety by the hand and refuse to let it dictate how you will respond to others who are important to you. The wife of an alcoholic described her application of self-soothing like this: *"Once I started finding peace within myself . . . I didn't react to his every move. I could say, '[Honey], you know what? I'm having a great, great day, and if you want to go poop on someone else's day go [ahead]. . . . You're not going to poop on my day.'"*

Being a nonanxious presence (Friedman, 1985)—developing the skill of self-soothing (Schnarch, 1997, 2002)—takes time and practice. (You will find Schnarch's suggestions about how to self-soothe in the sidebar on page 116.) With this skill in place, you can appropriately confront your partner, put forward your perspective and listen to his or hers. Self-soothing is not like the tango. It doesn't take two. It only takes one—you! Schnarch writes,

> Self-soothing involves meeting two core challenges of selfhood: (a) not losing yourself to the pressures and demands of others, and (b) developing your capacity for self-centering (stabilizing your own emotions and fears). Sometimes we miss the chance to become self-*centering* and self-soothing because we fear becoming self-*centered*—selfish, self-preoccupied, and indifferent to others. . . . Our ability to maintain ourselves in close emotional proximity to our partners doesn't lead to self-interest at their expense. Differentiation helps us tolerate the tension in recognizing our partners as separate individuals with competing preferences, needs, and agendas. (1997, p. 173)

Self-Responsibility: Accepting Responsibility Without Blaming Your Mate

The final element in finding your self is self-responsibility. Family therapist Philip Guerin and colleagues define self-responsibility as that skill which allows us "to work at seeing the parts of ourselves that contribute significantly to our own pain and our relationship discomfort. . . . [It] is the ability to see a relationship problem as a result not only of the other person's limitation but also of one's own" (1996, p. 43). Self-responsibility is, in a sense, the antidote to the problem of judging that Jesus identifies in Matthew 7:3-5. Self-responsibility requires that we intentionally examine ourselves for the log in our own eye rather than focus on the speck of sawdust in the other's eye. Lerner puts it like this: Self-responsibility "requires us to give up our nonproductive efforts to change or fix the other party (which is not possible) and to put as much energy into working on the self" (1989, p. 207). You can see this type of self-responsibility in the following comment from Marge: *"For the first time in this program [Overcomers Anonymous], [I] accepted my role and my despair and what I had done—how I had set myself up to fail. I [had] put all the responsibility for [my] and my children's well-being on Tom's shoulders, and Tom's shoulders were made of feathers. That was me doing that. I saw not just what I had done—that's no good—but I saw what I could do about it for me."*

Self-responsibility gets you out of the blame game—a responsibility-avoiding strategy that is as old as the Garden of Eden (Gen 3:8-13)—because self-responsibility transfers a person from a state of helpless blaming to one of action. You will feel helpless as long as you focus on how the *other* person should change. However, when you focus on self-responsibility, you identify your contribution to the relationship problem, and you *can* work on that. Once Marge saw her own part in their marital puzzle, she was able to act rather than just react. This element of taking charge of your self is also modeled in the two statements below. Notice how the role of helpless victims changed as these individuals developed self-responsibility.

- *I was having to admit my neediness, my need to please, my desire to please regardless of the consequences to myself. So I was having to admit all that stuff and say [to myself], "This is counterproductive," not to mention sick. To me, sick is one thing, but counterproductive—that does it. "If it doesn't work, I'm going to stop doing this." And that helped.*
- *That started me on personal responsibility as a part of what I could change and looking to myself. I was very victim-focused before that. I had been an only child growing up in the 1950s, when your mother baked you cookies. For a male of that generation, it's a pretty cushy life, and I didn't have much responsibility. . . . So finally, in this time of therapy, I started being forced to own some personal responsibility.*

Of course some people, such as children, truly are victims and have limited or no options for changing circumstances. Others, such as adult victims of physical or emotional abuse, may wrongly believe that they are responsible for their perpetrator's actions. It is beyond the purpose of this chapter to fully discuss domestic violence or child abuse. However, many survivors of all kinds of abuse begin their personal transformation with the recognition that they are *not* responsible for the other's action. Personal growth often follows.

Make a list of all aspects of your relationship problem and identify who is responsible for each aspect. Be careful to look for the log in your eye and not the sawdust in your partner's. If you are having trouble identifying your piece of the puzzle, you may want to talk with a pastor, a mental health professional or a friend who will be very honest with you. When you have noted those aspects of things that are yours, take responsibility for them.

Self-responsibility also does not mean self-blame. You do not assume responsibility for *all* the troubles in your relationship. You take responsibility for your part of the relationship pain—no more and no less. If you take full blame, you rob your mate of an opportunity to grow up. The apostle Paul recognized our tendency to assume too much responsibility: "If it is possible, *as far as it depends on you,* live at peace with everyone" (Rom 12:18). Notice how this verse encourages us to act responsibly *toward* others but to assume responsibility *for ourselves.* When you act responsibly toward others, you act as a person of integrity (self-define). For example, you keep your promises. When you take responsibility for yourself, you manage your own intensity (self-soothe), and you are aware of how your emotions and their resulting behavior affect others (self-responsibility). Too often we want to assume responsibility for others and abdicate responsibility for ourselves. This is the opposite of maturity, because "part of being a grown-up entails developing ease at stepping up and assuming responsibility for one's own emotions and the relationship behavior that the emotions drive" (Guerin et al., 1996, p. 43).

For years Tom ignored the impact of his drinking on his family. He could do this because Marge had assumed it. When Marge stopped nagging, she created the opportunity for Tom to look at himself. When Tom assumed responsibility for his drinking, he began to take self-responsibility. Tom says, *"I could find anywhere to go to get away from her. Now if I go somewhere, if she doesn't want to go, she knows it's okay for me to go by myself 'cause I'll come back like I left—sober. That's the trust. . . . It's better now than it's ever been."*

Some Closing Thoughts

Learning how to be a grown-up is a life project—a marathon, not a sprint. Each stage in family life brings new opportunities to self-define, to self-soothe and to take self-responsibility. As you bring a more clearly defined self to your marriage, you will be able to experience deeper levels of intimacy (Friedman, 1985; Lerner, 1989; Schnarch 1997, 2002). Many individuals find that a counselor can assist them in these processes.

One word of caution is appropriate before I close this chapter. While self-differentiation means you will change, it does not guarantee that the other will change. As I indicated earlier, your differentiation of self is an *invitation* for change in your partner, not a demand. Your partner has the choice to change or to remain the same. You then have to choose your response to that. Among the reconcilers you are reading about, both partners accepted the challenge to change.

6

SEEKING FORGIVENESS

I love whipped cream! When I was four years old, my love of whipped cream got me into trouble. My mother had recently purchased a can of it, and it was calling my name from its home inside the refrigerator. Being an obedient child, I came whenever my name was called, and this time was no exception. I had to do some creative problem-solving because I couldn't quite reach the handle to open the refrigerator door. The freezer portion of our refrigerator was on the bottom. If I slid a kitchen chair over to the refrigerator, I could climb onto the chair, open the refrigerator door, stand on top of the freezer door and claim my prize. And I did. I enjoyed the smooth, sweet taste of whipped cream straight from the can.

My plan had worked perfectly! That is, until I had to get down. I had been fearless climbing up but was terrified to climb down. From where I stood, the seat of the kitchen chair might as well have been a mile away. I was stuck. This was not good. My strategy required secrecy, not discovery.

As I pondered my options, my grandmother came into the kitchen to investigate my whereabouts. Needless to say, I was caught. When confronted about my culinary escapade, I quickly replied that it wasn't me who did it but my imaginary nemesis, who got me into all sorts of trouble as a preschooler.

See how easily I—at the tender age of four—sidestepped accountability by shifting blame away from myself? Confessing and repenting is the hardest thing for many of us to do. Perhaps we want to avoid the consequences of our misdeeds. Maybe our pride gets in our way or we are paralyzed by shame. We may not agree with our accuser that what we did was wrong.

Avoidance of accountability isn't new. The Old Testament tells of a number of people who tried to get off the proverbial hook. For example, Adam and Eve played the blame game (Gen 3). Cain feigned ignorance (Gen 4). Jacob got out of town (Gen 27). King David tried a cover-up (2 Sam 11). "Image-management" strategies like these are often automatic reactions. While they may help us save face or escape punishment, our relationships ultimately pay the price, because failure to admit our misdeeds hinders reconciliation. If we are intent on restoring love and trust to our damaged relationships, we need a different approach. Though we might choose blame, cover-up, deceit or evading responsibility, Scripture calls for another strategy: repentance.

Before moving ahead, let's take a moment to review where we have been and to plot out where we are heading. The first part of this book explored commitments that sustain reconciliation, that is, commitment to Christ, to the work of reconciling and to a reconciliation-friendly community. The previous chapter on growing up (self-differentiation, self-soothing, self-responsibility) introduced the second part of this book, which examines a variety of actions or tasks that promote reconciliation. In upcoming chapters we will consider forgiving and restoring truth and trustworthiness. This chapter looks at the role of repentance.

What Is Repentance?

What kinds of things do you associate with repentance? Do you think of the closing altar call at a revival? Perhaps you imagine a person on a street corner with a sandwich board on which is written, "Repent! The end is near!" *Repentance* is a good, old-fashioned church word that saintly grandparents would have heard every Sunday but that may sound odd to our twenty-first-century ears. You may recall that John the Baptist came "preaching a baptism of repentance for the forgiveness of sins" (Mk 1:4). Matthew presents this sound bite from Jesus' preaching: "Repent, for the kingdom of heaven is near" (Mt 4:17). When the Pharisees questioned Jesus about his association with sinful tax collectors (a category of people who were definitely off-limits to righteous Jews in first-century Palestine), Jesus replied, "I have not come to call the righteous, but sinners to repentance" (Lk 5:32). Whatever images you associate with repentance, it is an important action for Christians, because repenting is our appropriate response to God's gracious offer of forgiveness.

Within the context of our interpersonal relationships, repentance refers to a decisive *turning away* from thoughts, words and deeds that have betrayed love and trust, and a wholehearted *turning toward* attitudes and activities that can restore love and trust to the relationship.

Repentance is often coupled with confession. The two are related but not synonymous. Minimally, confession involves admitting your wrongdoing to another. "Admission of guilt" is a technically correct definition of confession, but it is insufficient when confession occurs within the context of reconciliation. Theologian Thomas Oden (1992) suggests that a good confession is sincere, definite, unconditional and clear. You can confess without repenting, but you cannot repent without confession (explicit or implicit). I will say more about confession later in this chapter.

What, then, is repentance? Repentance is often pictured as a 180-degree turn—a drastic move in the opposite direction. Within the context of our relationship with God, repentance refers to the radical *turning away* from anything that impedes one's *turning toward* a committed relationship with God (Green, McKnight & Marshall, 1992). In the Gospels, "Repentance involves acknowledgment of one's sinfulness . . . as well as a new and holy pattern of daily behavior in relation to others. . . . Thus it is clear that repentance . . . does not simply consist in a 'change of mind,' but in a transformation of the entire person" (p. 670). Within the context of our interpersonal relationships, repentance refers to a decisive *turning away* from thoughts, words and deeds that have betrayed love and trust, and a wholehearted *turning toward* attitudes and activities that can restore love and trust to the relationship. Repentance acknowledges the wrongdoing, accepts responsibility, expresses sorrow and regret, recognizes the impact of the injury on the other, pledges changed behavior and follows through (Augsburger, 1996). When you repent, your orientation changes. Repentance involves a transformation of self and, by extension, a transformation of how the self views the other.

What brings about interpersonal repentance? Scripture reveals at least four prompts. First, painful circumstances can motivate repentance. In the parable of the prodigal son, Luke reports that the younger son came to his senses when he found himself slopping hogs and dining on their bill of fare, an unsavory situation for a good Jew (see Lk 15:14-17). Second, the injured party can confront the wrongdoer, as encouraged by Jesus in Matthew 18:15-17. Third, the wrongdoer can approach the injured party with the intent to make amends, as noted in Matthew 5:23-24. Finally, an intermediary can intervene, as the loving father did when he tried to encourage his truculent and put-out older son to join him in celebrating the homecoming of his prodigal younger brother (see Lk 15:25-32). All four contexts were found within the reconciliation stories retold in this book. Repentance is not easy. In fact, it is a humbling experience. But it is one that can advance our journey toward reconciliation, as you will see in Anne and Rick's story.

Rick and Anne's Story

Anne and Rick married when he was twenty and she was twenty-one. Four years later, Anne had a four-month affair with a coworker. Of this, she says, *"I knew it was wrong. And I realized—like all of a sudden one day the light came on—'I can't do this.'"*

By that time Rick had moved out. Anne continues, *"It took about a week, I guess, for us to talk it out, and we decided we'd get back together. We went through a few visits of counseling and decided to put it behind us and go on."*

Rick adds, *"I still loved her. I knew what she did was bad and all that. I didn't have any trouble getting over it, and I didn't bring it up."*

Within a few years the couple embarked on their *"quest for children,"* as Rick put it. Fertility treatments boiled their sex life down to basic mechanics. Anne gave birth to their first child, and Rick began working out of their home to be with the baby. About this nontraditional family arrangement Rick says, *"Her job paid better, had better benefits. I had experience with children where she didn't [chuckle]. I knew how to change a diaper. I had to teach her how to change a diaper."*

Twenty-two months later Anne gave birth to their second child. Twenty-two months after the birth of their second child, Anne gave birth to their third child. Rick and Anne's emotional connection with one another evaporated, and their sex life disappeared as childcare consumed them. Anne thought, *"'I have no right to complain after what I prayed for' [children]. I just thought, 'Well, this is reality. I'm never going to have that romance thing. We had that before we were married, and all that's gone now. We're parents now with children. He's the father. I'm the mother.'"*

Rick continued in his role as stay-at-home dad. Anne returned to her job. She particularly enjoyed her interaction with her customers. One customer made a point of engaging her in conversation, about which Anne says, *"We were about the same age. Our children were the same age. We had a lot to talk about. He was very, very easy to talk to."* This customer initiated a personal relationship with Anne.

Rick warned her. *"I kept telling her it wasn't right. 'You're asking for trouble. You just don't need to go there.' . . . I was trying to pursue her, to make her want to spend more time with me and interact with me, and that really didn't work."*

While Rick was trying to grow closer to Anne, she was becoming more entangled with her customer. Anne says, *"I felt like I was alive again. After all those years of being weary, all of a sudden I had energy. I had a reason to get up, because each day I would see him."*

Rick convinced Anne, however, to terminate her relationship with this man. She stopped "seeing" him, but she didn't stop phoning him. Eventually she began to meet with him. In response to his suggestions, Anne entertained the idea that they could have an affair. *"I just thought this would be a one-time thing. 'I've got three kids. I've got a job. I can't let this affect my marriage.'"* Their affair continued for a year and a half in spite of Rick's efforts to get Anne to end the relationship.

Rick finally told Anne that she needed to change how she did her job. He believed that this would help Anne end her relationship with the other man. She complied, but six months later Rick exploded when he caught Anne on the phone with the man. Rick pleaded, *"He's bad news, Anne. He's bad. He's going to ruin our marriage. He's going to affect our kids."*

Anne wanted to end the affair, but she didn't think she could. *"I knew adultery was wrong. I* knew *that I was going to suffer the consequences, but in the heat of the moment I was so in love with him that I thought I could stand the consequences."*

The conflict escalated. During one tumultuous argument, when Rick was trying to calm her down by getting her to sit in a chair, Anne fell and was bruised. Things continued to deteriorate. Rick finally called the police. The police encouraged Anne to file a restraining order. Rick left the house. Later, Rick called Anne and said, *"I'm filing for divorce."*

Through their lawyers, Rick and Anne worked out an arrangement where they would take turns living in the house during the week with the children. Anne moved into her lover's apartment. Within a few weeks he dumped her. Anne's response: *"'What?! After I trashed my life for you, you know, it's over!' So it hit me like a ton of bricks. I couldn't believe [it]. I thought, 'Well, looking back, what did I ever expect?' And I called Rick . . . and I said, 'I don't want to live this way anymore.' I didn't tell him that my lover had ended it. I just said, 'I don't want to live this way anymore. I want to get our family back together.' He had a fit; he didn't want any part in it."*

During this unsettled time, Anne and Rick had continued to see a counselor. Through a series of conversations and counseling sessions, Rick agreed to return to being home full time. He clearly told Anne that he was doing this only for the sake of the children. Whether they could reclaim their marriage was still in serious question.

A Call to Repentance

Rick and Anne's situation reminds me of the maxim "Fool me once, shame on you. Fool me twice, shame on me." Many of us can imagine giving someone another chance after a one-time affair (as Rick did earlier in the marriage). Fewer of us can picture doing that after a second affair. How wise do you think it is for Rick to consider reconciliation with Anne? What do you think it will take to turn what may appear to be an imprudent decision into a sensible one?

It seems to me that the answers to these questions rest with Anne. Assuming that Rick is open to rebuilding their relationship, she must now prove her commitment to the marriage. In other words, how serious is Anne about repenting? You may recall that earlier in the chapter I defined interpersonal repentance as a decisive *turning away* from thoughts, words and deeds that have betrayed love and trust, and a wholehearted *turning toward* attitudes and activities that can restore love and trust to the relationship. You may also recall that repentance incorporates confession, but it is much more than saying "I'm sorry." In the remainder of the chapter, I will describe a model of repentance that Anne followed and that may help you in your own efforts to reconcile.

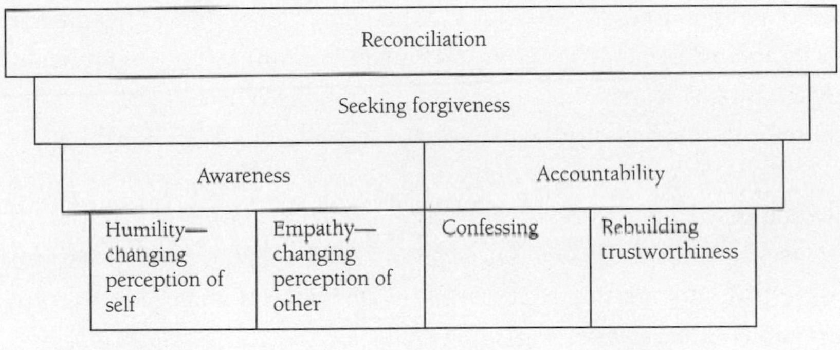

Figure 6.1. A model of repentance

Figure 6.1 gives you a picture of repentance. Repentance is something that happens *within* a transgressor's heart (the internal process of awareness) and something that is transacted *between* transgressors and the ones they have hurt (the interactive process of accountability). In some instances, such as when the injured party is deceased, unwilling (too angry, holding a grudge) or unable (too soon, dealing with consequences from the offense) to grant forgiveness, transgressors repent unilaterally. But most of the time, repentance takes place within the context of the wounded relationship.

Although repenters cannot demand that injured parties forgive them, forgiveness researchers believe that repentance may nurture forgiveness (Exline & Baumeister, 2000). If you peek ahead to figure 7.2 on page 162 in chapter seven, you'll have a preview of where I am heading: toward forgiveness and repentance working together for reconciliation. In chapter seven I will discuss a model of forgiveness developed by family therapist Terry Hargrave (1994, 2001). The portrait of repentance I offer here is a mirror image of Hargrave's model of forgiveness. After you read this chapter and the next, I hope you will have a clearer picture of how repentance and forgiveness can work together to promote reconciliation.

I picture repentance unfolding in two major movements. I have labeled one movement "awareness" and the other "accountability." Awareness involves a change in perception about self, other and the hurtful event. It is akin to the prodigal son's "coming to his senses." Awareness is developed through humility and empathy. Humility and empathy describe processes that happen *within* transgressors. These moral emotions have been associated with granting forgiveness (Sandage, Worthington, Hight & Berry, 2000; Worthington, 1998a), and I believe they play an important role in repentance as well.

Through humility, offenders develop a more accurate picture of themselves. Humble offenders see the sinfulness within themselves that contributed to their relationship's downfall. This insight prompts transgressors to relinquish self-serving, self-centered and defensive ways of thinking. When transgressors experience humility, a moral switch is thrown that shifts offensive actions from "acceptable" to "unacceptable." Humble wrongdoers experience guilt, which prompts them to seek forgiveness. Humility can increase differentiation of self, and differentiation of self can enhance humility (see chapter five).

Empathy is like a huge "aha" about the injured party. When offenders develop empathy for injured parties, they come to *understand and credit* the experiences, feelings and thoughts of those they hurt. In other words, they look at their relationship through the eyes of the injured party. Empathy helps a transgressor realize that his or her mate's view of reality deserves close attention. Through empathy, a wrongdoer takes the injured party's perspective and begins to identify with her or him emotionally.

The second movement of repentance is accountability. Accountability means accepting responsibility for the impact of the offensive action and seeking to repair the damage. It is akin to the prodigal son's rising, going and confessing to his father (see Lk 15:20-21). Accountability is established through confessing and rebuilding trustworthiness. Confessing and rebuilding trustworthiness describe processes that happen *between* offenders and the ones they have offended. These transactional processes have also been associated with forgiveness (Exline & Baumeister, 2000) and capture our intuitive understanding of repentance.

Authentic apology is the hallmark of confession. It is an outpouring of a broken and contrite heart. Offenders take full responsibility for the impact of their actions without offering excuses or justifications.

Rebuilding trustworthiness involves the offender's accomplishment of acts of repair that serve to reestablish her or his trustworthiness and restore love. Often injured parties prescribe actions that they must see in order to rebuild the wounded relationship (Kelley & Waldron, 2003). Differentiation of self helps transgressors to sustain repair attempts.

I will refer to these aspects (humility, empathy, confession, rebuilding trustworthiness) as the four stations of repentance after Hargrave's stations of forgiveness (see chapter seven). The use of the term *station* is intended to minimize the likelihood of thinking about these functions as steps that one must follow in a given order. That is to say, sometimes transgressors enact changed behavior (accountability) and then a deeper understanding emerges (awareness). Conversely, others begin to see themselves and their partners differently (awareness), and then these new insights motivate new ways of behaving (accountability). Let's look at this model of repentance more closely.

AWARENESS

When transgressors develop awareness, they see themselves, their partner and the offense differently. The offense is no longer acceptable or defensible behavior, because transgressors can now see themselves through the eyes of the ones they wounded. Humility and empathy emerge when offenders put away self-centered, self-serving and defensive postures. What motivates awareness? Sometimes a change in circumstances flips the moral switch so that the offensive behavior loses its reward or injured parties promise to cut off contact. At other times wrongdoers may just "wake up" to a new understanding.

These promptings for change may be the result of God's prevenient grace in offenders' lives. According to theologian Thomas Oden, prevenient grace is grace that goes before believers and paves the way for God's will to unfold in their lives. It "awakens responsiveness . . . [and] operates before the will can cooperate" (1992, p. 51). Once the will is awakened, the transgressor has a choice to continue or to stop his or her offending actions. In the case of transgressors, God's grace stirs up their awareness of their sinfulness *and* empowers them to want to change.

Awareness not only ignites a change in orientation (a turn away from the offense), it also includes a change in perspective (a turning toward the victim). Social psychologists notice that offenders and victims see the offense and its impact differently. Compared to victims, transgressors are likely to emphasize times when they apologized and minimize any harm they may have done (Baumeister, Stillwell & Wotman, 1990). Wrongdoers are also more likely to downplay or leave out aspects that could motivate them to accept blame or seek forgiveness (Stillwell & Baumeister, 1997). Social psychologist Roy Baumeister (1997) calls this difference in perception "the magnitude gap." When wrongdoers repent, they close the gap by learning to see themselves and their actions through the eyes of the injured party. The two stations of awareness—humility and empathy—facilitate these processes.

Humility. Humility is the first station of repentance. It is not a very popular concept, even though it is a virtue strongly associated with the

Christian life. Many of us equate humility with humiliation. When we feel humiliated, we feel covered with shame. We experience a painful loss of self-esteem, a loss of face and a sense of shame. One injured wife reported that she was *"covered with shame"* because of her husband's emotional affair with one of their coworkers. His persistent attention to this other woman over the course of several years *"fouled the workplace."* She lost face (Shults & Sandage, 2003) and found facing her coworkers very painful. You will shortly see how shame proneness (unlike guilt proneness) short-circuits repentance.

Humility, on the other hand, includes looking at one's self soberly (see Rom 12:3), that is, having a modest sense of one's own importance. It involves *realistically* acknowledging both strengths and shortcomings (Shults & Sandage, 2003). It is not the same thing as low self-esteem or shame proneness (Emmons, 2000; Tangney, 2002). Hargrave suggests that within the context of marriage, humility helps partners recognize that they "have limitations, problems, and inadequacies that can, and should, be improved" (2000, p. 55). Hargrave continues:

> Humility helps spouses not to think of themselves more highly than they do their spouses. It helps them to be realistic and honest about the limitations, personalities, and characteristics that have shaped their individual personalities and need improvement. This prompts spouses to be willing to work on themselves and adds a hopefulness to their relationship. (p. 57)

Prior to the emergence of humility, transgressors justify their actions, minimize the damage they have done and respond defensively to anyone who questions them. These responses block confessing and seeking forgiveness. Offenders' awareness of their sinfulness takes on new dimensions when humility dawns on them. Secret or hurtful actions that were once tolerated are tolerated no longer. An attitude of humility helps transgressors to "start looking at themselves [and] shift the focus away from their partners" (Hargrave, 2000, p. 57). Humble offenders admit their mistakes, accept the consequences of their hurtful actions, seek the counsel of others to help them change and maintain teachable spirits.

What prompts this change of heart? I wish I could say that noble or spiritual motives always move transgressors. However, more often than not, a shift in the cost-benefit ratio or a sudden confrontation may begin to stir humility in a transgressor's heart. The prodigal son came to his senses when he was broke, at the point of starvation and employed slopping hogs. This was nothing at all like the "wild living" that he had experienced before the famine hit (see Lk 15:13-14). His posture upon his return home signified his humble attitude (Nouwen, 1992).

In Anne's case, her lover dumped her and she wanted to go home. As I said, humility is not necessarily born out of an upright heart, but it can facilitate the development of one. Differentiation of self (see chapter five) may also contribute to this process. You may recall that growth in self-definition requires one to take responsibility for one's actions and to *self*-regulate. This means wrongdoers wake themselves up to their wrongdoing rather than wait for the injured party to "cue them" that something is amiss. Transgressors who grow in self-differentiation do not expect their mate to become their moral police officer.

Humility can activate the transgressor's guilt, and this helps to transform a heart of indifference into a heart of compassion for the injured party. Social psychologist June Tangney (1995) contends that shame and guilt influence repentance in different ways. She describes shame as an extraordinarily painful negative evaluation of the global self in response to an interpersonal transaction. Shame concludes that "*I* am defective and there is *no way* to fix what is wrong." This is not an accurate picture of the self. Shame-prone persons tend to avoid, hide, escape or strike out with defensive anger. They are also more likely to deny any personal responsibility by blaming the injured party ("You made me do this"), or they may abandon the relationship entirely. These behaviors are inconsistent with humility.

On the other hand, Tangney (1995) reports that guilt is experienced as less painful than shame and encourages evaluation of specific actions without the self's becoming enmeshed with a negative evaluation. Guilt concludes, "I *did* something wrong and there *is* a way to fix it." Guilt-prone persons experience tension, remorse and regret, emotions that support repair attempts (Arriaga & Rusbult, 1998). Research by Roy Baumeister, Arlene Stillwell and Todd Heatherton (1994, 1995) demonstrates that guilt motivates people to act in ways that will maintain and benefit their relationship. It helps the relationship recover from transgressions by allocating the emotional distress more fairly. When transgressors feel guilty about their misbehavior, they are (1) more likely to confess, (2) more likely to show that they value the injured party and (3) less likely to appeal to mitigating circumstances or self-justifications. These behaviors are consistent with humility. This type of insight provides leverage that transgressors (and injured parties) need in order to change habits of thought or interaction that damage their marriage.

In what ways might shame constrain you from repenting? In what ways might guilt support your repentance? Make a list of your relationship strengths and weaknesses. Remember that humility tries to take an accurate picture of the self, not a fuzzy one.

You can see this pattern at work in the following statement from Anne: *"I just tried to do everything at the house so he wouldn't have to, because I felt like all those years that he stayed home, . . . he lost his masculinity or something, and it wasn't right for him to have to do domestic stuff around the house. So I tried extra hard to work and pick up the kids and do little things at home and get the kids up in the morning and get them ready so he would have as little to do as possible."*

Empathy. Empathy is the second station of repentance. Empathy is the ability to adopt another person's perspective. It includes cognitive perspective-taking ("I see what you are saying" or "I can understand how you feel that way") and empathic concern for the feelings of another person. Empathy that promotes awareness and fosters repentance may elicit strong feelings in transgressors, such as sadness, fear, anger, guilt and shame (Witvliet, Ludwig & Bauer, 2002). Empathy can answer the following questions: "What if something strange happened, and you were suddenly transformed into your partner? Knowing how you treated [him or her], how would you feel? What would it be like being in an intimate partnership with you?" (Jory, Anderson & Greer, 1997, p. 408).

Some people are just naturally more empathic than others (dispositional empathy). Others can adopt another's perspective in particular circumstances (situation-specific empathy). You can hear Anne's empathy for Rick when she says, *"I wish my husband hadn't had to pay the price, because he didn't deserve it. He was a good husband. He was doing the best he could. He was good to me, but I pushed him to the limit. He took a lot more than most men would."*

What is needed for repentance, I think, is the ability to view the situation from the injured party's perspective (situation-specific empathy). Studies on forgiveness show a positive relationship between forgiveness and empathic appreciation for an injured party's perspective and emotional experience. It seems as if a similar process may support repentance. Psychologist Steven Sandage and colleagues (2000) have learned that seeking forgiveness is restrained when transgressors are self-absorbed or display narcissistic tendencies—characteristics that are not strongly associated with empathy or humility. Anne shows empathy for her family when she says, *"When I saw what my behavior was going to lead to and what my life was going to be like and what my children's life was going to be like, it was a great motivation to stop and to change."*

Remember the magnitude gap? Empathy narrows the gap as wrongdoers validate injured parties' emotional experiences and perspectives. I once counseled a couple on the brink of divorce, and one of the major turning points in their therapy occurred when the husband finally understood that his anger terrified his wife. Up until that point, he had insisted that his rage was not frightening because (1) it didn't frighten him and (2) it was mild compared to how his parents expressed anger during his childhood and youth. Prior to that session, the magnitude gap was as wide as the Grand Canyon. During that session, the husband had a great "aha"; he realized that his wife's viewpoint was valid. Previously, *his* experience was the only one that defined reality in their marriage. Now he saw that she experienced him differently from the way he experienced himself.

After that session, he asked his wife to tell him about the most painful exchanges that still stood between them. He listened to her rendition of his life, without comment but with empathy. His wife reported to me that tears ran down his cheeks as his empathy deepened. He asked her to forgive him for each of those events. He committed himself to change—and did.

Describe the transgression from the perspective of the injured party. Be sure to include how the injured party might think and feel.

Pretend you are your partner. Knowing what you know about how you betrayed your mate, what would it be like being in an intimate partnership with you?

Ask your spouse to tell you her or his version of what transpired between you. Listen without being defensive. In other words, do not refute or correct your partner's story. Live with that version for a while. How might this new perspective help you see things differently?

Accountability

The other movement in repentance is accountability. If awareness describes change that happens *within* transgressors' thoughts and feelings, then accountability depicts change that happens *between* offenders and those they have offended. Accountability is the contemporary version of Jesus' command to "go and sin no more" (see Jn 8:11). David Augsburger writes, "Love may be unconditional, forgiveness is not. There may be no demands as conditions for seeing the other as worthful and precious, but many demands for trusting, risking, and joining in relationship" (1996, p. 16). Through confession and concrete, consistently changed behavior, accountability rebuilds trust and restores love.

In healthy relationships, mutual accountability structures the benefits and burdens, the entitlements and responsibilities of marital partnerships. On the other hand, when transgressions rip this accountability structure to shreds, partners engage in boundary setting for one another (Jory et al., 1997). Several wrongdoers noted that their mate was "in the driver's seat" during the early months of their efforts to rebuild their relationship. By this they meant that their partner was establishing criteria and standards that they had to meet in order to demonstrate trustworthiness. Repentant wrongdoers choose to be accountable to these boundaries, showing respect for their mate, their future and themselves. They increase their level of self-differentiation by embracing responsibility, which requires self-awareness, self-soothing and self-responsibility (see chapter five). The two stations of accountability are confessing and rebuilding trustworthiness. Let's examine each of these in turn.

Confessing. Confessing is the third station of repentance. It involves admission of guilt and sorrow about what happened and about what is happening. Confessions often include the promise of changed behavior. A good confession communicates to the injured party that the wrongdoer understands the victim's perspective and experience and credits this perspective. Theologian Geiko Müller-Fahrenholz writes,

> The German word *Entblossung* (literally, "denuding oneself") describes something the traditional word "repentance" no longer conveys. It identifies a process by which one returns to the point at which the original evil act was done. To revisit this moment implies admitting all the shameful implications of that act. It is painful to enter into this shame. It is more painful still to acknowledge this act in the face of those who suffered it. All confessions of guilt carry with them an element of self-humiliation which runs counter to our pride and seems to threaten our self-esteem. Nobody likes to be stripped of his or her defenses and to appear naked in front of others. (1997, p. 25)

Theologian Thomas Oden notes that our impulse is to cover up our transgressions. Confession reveals them. What wrongdoers attempted to cover up "becomes covered by forgiveness" (1992, p. 104). Müller-

Fahrenholz adds that confession and subsequent forgiveness release a corrective and restorative power. "It *corrects* the distortions which an act of evil establishes between two people or groups—the distortion of stolen power and enforced impotence. At the same time such correction *restores* the dignity of both sides. They recover their full height, as it were" (1997, p. 28).

Two variables play a role in confession. The first is the degree to which transgressors experience guilt and remorse about their action. The second is the degree to which they commit to change and then follow through with change. These variables form two axes to create a two-by-two grid from which we can examine different facets of confession (see figure 6.2).

No intent to change

Acknowledgment

Defensive posture (angry and hostile) toward accuser. May also denote shame-proneness. Or transgressor may not see that there was anything wrong with his or her action. Willing to lose relationship.

"I did it. So what?"

Account Giving

Defensive posture with explanation to minimize culpability; desires to keep connection but avoid consequences. Appeals to extenuating circumstances, misunderstandings or innocent intentions.

"I did it, but . . ."

No guilt or remorse

Guilt and remorse

Acquiescence

Gives into accusation of the other, even though believes self to be truly innocent. Changes behavior to appease partner and maintain relationship. May be a shame-based response.

"What did I do wrong? I'll change. Tell me how."

Authentic Apology

Acknowledgment of action with sincere sorrow. Ownership of impact on the injured party. Commitment to change in specific ways to restore trust and love to relationship. Desires to transform relationship.

"I did it. I'm sorry. Here is how I will change."

Committed to change

Figure 6.2. Confession grid

First, when transgressors feel no guilt or regret about their action and have no intent to change, confession takes the form of *acknowledgment*. Transgressors who merely acknowledge their offense may adopt a defensive attitude and express anger toward their accuser. Psychologist June Tangney (1995) suggests that this is one of two reactions that shame-prone individuals might display when they are confronted. The other shame-prone response is to hide. Acknowledgment says, "I did it. So what?" This form of confession does nothing to restore love and trust to a broken relationship.

Second, if transgressors experience guilt and remorse (perhaps from being confronted), but they have no intent to change their ways, their confession takes the form of *account giving* (Augsburger, 1996). Like acknowledgment, giving an account is a defensive stance. Accounts offer explanations that minimize the transgressor's culpability by appealing to extenuating circumstances, misunderstandings or innocent intentions gone awry. Account giving says, "I did it, but . . ." This attitude does little to restore love and trust.

It is important to underscore that the wrongdoer's perspective is not dismissed out of hand during reconciliation. Injured parties often want an explanation of why transgressors acted as they did. When injured parties are open to receiving this information, explanations can promote reconciliation. The difference is that they are offered to complete the picture of what happened rather than to escape accountability. Some counselors suggest that explanations can be offered very early in the process (DiBlasio, 1998), while others suggest delaying them (Holeman, 1997).

Third, if offenders commit themselves to change but feel no guilt or remorse, their confession takes the form of *acquiescence*. When wrongdoers acquiesce, they give themselves over to the accusations of another. Acquiescence agrees to change behavior in order to appease. The goal is peace at any price. When you acquiesce, you admit to a transgression you did not do (false or forced confession), or you own an offense that is not truly yours to own (agreeing that you "made" someone yell at you or hit you). Acquiescence says, "Tell me what I did wrong; I'll change.

Tell me how." Acquiescence can also include meeting demands or making changes only grudgingly. For example, Anne was doing all she could to stall or stop the sale of their home as part of Rick's preparations to divorce her. Her counselor convinced her to back off because her actions were alienating Rick. She *reluctantly* did so.

Finally, when wrongdoers feel guilt and remorse about their action, commit to change, and actually do change, confession takes the form of *authentic apology* (Augsburger, 1996). Authentic apology acknowledges the offense with sincere sorrow. Wrongdoers take responsibility for the impact that the offense had on injured parties. They commit to change in concrete ways that seek to restore trust and love. Authentic apology says, "I did it. I am sorry. Here is how I will change." This kind of confession vouches for repentance and nurtures reconciliation (see 2 Cor 7:10-13). One offender summed it up like this: *"Are you willing to take responsibility for what you've done?"*

Must confession be verbalized? Not necessarily. Wrongdoers may document their broken and contrite heart in many different ways. Sometimes symbols or rituals provide avenues through which confessions are offered and received. For example, church sacraments, such as Communion and baptism, or other rituals, such as foot washing, may convey confession's message.

Rick showed Anne his belief in her in an unusual way. They were living together once again and working diligently on their marriage in counseling. Rick's mother was disgusted with him for returning to Anne, and she wrote a letter to her son demanding that he repay twelve thousand dollars she had loaned him during the time of his separation from Anne. Anne reports, *"We went to the bank, and we borrowed the money against the equity of our house and gave her the whole amount at one time."* While this was not a ritual, it symbolized for both Anne and Rick that he was putting his money where his mouth was. Anne remarks, *"For the first time in his life he stood up to her [his mother]. In fact, just a few minutes ago he said, 'It feels pretty good to be a grown man now and be detached from her.'"*

A more significant event happened later along their journey to reconciliation. As a way to convince Rick that she was serious about changing, Anne suggested that they draw up a list of consequences she would experience should she fail to change. Anne continues the story.

> *Rick's attorney had drawn up a paper that said . . . I would basically give up everything if anything ever happened again. Rick went to our counselor that day. That night he came home from the counselor's office, and he took me over to the fireplace and burned the document, which had cost him over four hundred dollars for the lawyer to draw up. He said to me, "I'll forgive, and that means I give up the right to hurt you for hurting me." He said it. He said the exact words, and he said, "We're going to be okay now."*

How much information should a confession include? You will find a range of opinions in the therapeutic marketplace. I believe that confessions should be complete enough to disclose any secrets that could later damage the relationship. One offender "*told her everything . . . not every little detail . . . but I told her the full extent of the affair at that point.*" I agree that offenders do not need to share all the gory details. Injured parties can set the pace for how much specificity they want or need. However, paucity of confession creates pockets of secrecy that can contribute to emotional distance between confessing offenders and forgiving injured parties.

One offending husband recounted his full confession to his wife in this way: "*Telling my wife about the first affair was hard. Certainly telling her about the second one was even harder. I did that at the urging of my counselor, because I really didn't want to do this. I said, 'You know, she doesn't know about [the second affair]. She doesn't need to know about [it]. [It] is over and done with,' . . . but she [the counselor] said, 'Well, if you guys are going to reconcile, you can't have this between you, because it's always going to be there if you don't deal with it.'*"

Anne was aware of her need to ask for Rick's forgiveness. In her words, "*I would have been accountable for ruining our marriage; Rick didn't do it.*" But she struggled to offer an authentic apology to Rick that he would be willing to believe. He had "been here, done that" before, and look where they ended up. A friend gave Anne a book about codependency, and she took to heart the step of making amends. She made a list of the people whom she believed she had hurt by her unfaithfulness to Rick. She wrote a letter to them in which she confessed and asked their forgiveness. "*I wrote letters to all the people I had offended. I asked them to forgive me and pray for us. . . . [I told them] that I wanted to get the marriage back together and I was sorry for what I had done. I specifically stated what I had done. I sent letters to several people, eight or nine letters. The last thing I wanted to do was to admit to Rick's mother that I was wrong, but I did it. It felt good to tell the truth—that what I had done was wrong and I wanted them to forgive me.*"

What things do you need to confess to your mate? Write out your confession to be sure you are offering an authentic apology rather than saying things to appease your partner, or just making an acknowledgment or giving an account. If you are disclosing new information to your partner, you may want to think about his or her possible reactions. While you do not have any control over how he or she may respond, thinking about the impact of your words may help you develop empathy for him or her.

Anne's words were nice, but more was necessary. Rick needed to see changed behavior.

Rebuilding trustworthiness. The fourth station of repentance is the rebuilding of trustworthiness. Here is where the rubber meets the road. Transgressors can develop humility and empathy. They can confess. But if they do not demonstrate changed behavior over time, their actions do not match their words. It is impossible to go back and undo the past. The emphasis must not be on repairing the past but on preparing a better way forward.

Proving that one is loving and trustworthy takes time. It is not unusual for transgressors to become anxious and impatient when the offended mate seems to "take too long" to get over the offense (Holeman, 1997). Wrongdoers are likely to say either "Are you over this yet?" or "I'll never be able to live this down." Injured parties are likely to say, "You don't 'get it' yet," or "You don't understand how deeply you hurt me." Wrongdoers must be willing to sustain these efforts over the long haul. As Anne says, "*My counselor helped me to be more realistic about my expectations, because I wanted it to be instantly okay. You know, [get] him back—because that's the way he did it before.*"

Rick's next statement reflects the skepticism that many injured parties experience: "*She said she wanted to get back together, and it probably took two months for me to really believe that she was really trying. I mean, she obviously was trying. I could see that she was doing things differently. And I was able to see—well, not see but hear—if she was trying to talk to him or not.*"

Repair attempts must connect with the offense in ways that are meaningful to injured parties. For example, if trust was broken because an adulterous mate met with his or her lover during work hours (as Anne did), a logical act of compensation is to give a work schedule to the injured party so that the wounded mate could catch the repentant transgressor in any act of trustworthiness. Anne complied with Rick's demands in this regard:

> *I went back to a route that was far away from where [the other man] was. I made myself available [to Rick]; he knew where I was all the time. There was never any time that he couldn't [find me]. I was accountable to Rick. Rick rarely showed up and checked on me. But I made sure that at any time he could have. He had a map, and I told him where I would be. He knew where I was eating lunch. I had my radio in the truck so we could talk back and forth most of the time.*

Two additional changes meant a lot to Rick. Anne started to cook more meals for their family, and she obtained a license to operate a ham radio, a hobby Rick enjoyed but in which Anne had never had any interest. Rick says, "*It was another sign that she was trying, because a long time ago when I suggested she try to get her license . . . she didn't really express an interest in it whatsoever. But then she started it [wanting to study for her ham radio license]. She mentioned it on her own. I mean, without me. And I got the information for her, and I got the software so she could take computer tests and a study book for her and stuff."*

What things do you need to do to document that you are loving and trustworthy? Make a list. Share your list with your spouse in case she or he may want to add something or remove something. Follow through on your promises to act differently.

This one small act on Anne's part meant a world to Rick. It was a sign to him that she wanted to be with him in ways that were meaningful to him. Best of all, Anne had initiated their conversation about her ham radio license, which was a sign of her dedication to their marriage.

Encountering Mistrust

Rebuilding trustworthiness through acts of compensation and repair involves risk. Injured parties can reject repair attempts or continue to up the ante of what they require. Wrongdoers may work diligently to reestablish love and trustworthiness only to have a minor relapse (which is not "minor" to injured parties) take them back to the starting line. Mistrust is natural when couples begin to reconcile. Unfortunately it can develop into a major roadblock if trustworthy actions are not forthcoming or if injured parties do not permit demonstrations of trustworthiness to transform mistrust into trust. Retrusting may start out as a conscious choice that injured parties make, as is demonstrated in the following: *"For some time after this . . . I would have to determine to choose to trust. It would be the next deliberate exercise one did. One determined to choose to trust."*

Mistrust can deepen if wrongdoers become impatient with the injured party's healing process. You can see this at work in the following statements made by offenders:

- *It's taking awhile to rebuild the trust; [my mate] and I still don't have a relationship that is sexual at all, and it is something that we still struggle with. And sometimes I still feel hurt by that. It's different now. I'm not bitter and angry.*

- *Even in the last year and a half [the offense] pops up. [I am] trying to be understanding but sometimes questioning, "Well, are we over this? Are you sure you're not bitter?" "Are you sure you're not . . . ?" "Is there an issue still there then that's unresolved?"*

In early phases of reconciliation, partners are likely to be hypersensitive to one another's words and actions. This hypersensitivity flows two ways. First, wounded partners are on the alert for early warning signs of failure. This response may be intentional, but it also may be an automatic reaction. Wounded parties' antennae are up, scanning for suspicious behaviors, attitudes or emotions. Second, wrongdoers are on the alert for early warning signs of failure, although their concerns are different. Transgressors are more likely to be concerned about whether or not their efforts at repair will make a difference. Will they be able to "live this down," or will this hang over their head for the rest of their life (Holeman, 1997)?

Managing Mistrust

Mistrust can poison early repair attempts. It is important for couples to acknowledge the presence of mistrust but not let it call the shots. Mistrust must be managed.

Mistrust management is founded on several important assumptions. First, it assumes that the offender is fully committed to changed behavior over time. Second, it assumes that failures of some kind are inevitable. Obviously, among the interviewed couples these failures did not include another affair, nor did they include flagrant and inexcusable violations of pledges that had been made to one another (such as a promise to call home if leaving work later than usual). Even reconciling couples are vulnerable to the garden-variety failures that plague all couples. Remember my illustration in chapter three of the watershed boundary? Consistent and committed faithfulness to demonstrations of trustworthiness helps to create a cushion—a margin of error, if you please—that can soften the blow if you inadvertently slip up. Conversely, mistrust management does *not* ask injured parties to extend trust when manifestations of trustworthiness are not forthcoming, nor does it ask injured parties to deny the presence of their feelings of mistrust.

If all those assumptions are in place, then how we interpret our own actions and our partner's reactions may be a key to how well we manage mistrust. Social scientists refer to these interpretations as the attributions that we make about one another. One type of attribution is so common that it is called the "fundamental attribution error." This error says that when I do something well, I attribute my success to something about myself ("I am a hard worker"). When I do something poorly, I attribute my failure to unfortunate circumstances ("The test was unfair"). On the other hand, when *you* do something well, I am likely to look at the circumstances that may have contributed to your success ("You got a lucky break"), and when you do something poorly, I conclude that the fault resides with your character ("You are lazy").

Lack of attention to the fundamental attribution error can turn a small failure into a large one. For example, if I offer a repair attempt, I think that I am a forgiving or repentant person (internal motivation). If you offer a repair attempt, you are doing it because you have to (external motivation), not because you want to (internal motivation). If I am guilty of a failure of trustworthiness, I see the circumstances (external motivation) that got in my way ("I forgot to phone home because I am under so much pressure"). If you are guilty of a failure of trustworthiness, I see it as reflecting your attitude that you are not serious about reconciliation (internal motivation). While awareness of the fundamental attribution error can help to manage mistrust, dealing with mistrust may require the support of a counselor, especially when old habits interfere with the development of new ones.

Some Closing Thoughts

Thomas Oden considers repentance to be a "cleansing bath for the soul" (1992, p. 104). Repentance starts with transgressors experiencing new attitudes about the people they wounded (empathy) and about themselves (humility). Confession looks back at past deeds with deep sorrow and an intent to change. Acts of trustworthiness document confession's truthfulness and gradually shift the couple's focus to their future together.

Some final words from Anne are a fitting way to conclude this chapter:

> *I'm grateful that my husband gave me another chance. I don't know if humble is the word; I definitely don't take for granted the grace [chuckle]. I didn't understand what it meant until I've lived under it. It's a good feeling to be forgiven; it's freedom. It's freedom.*

7

EXTENDING FORGIVENESS

Each year I teach a graduate-level course on forgiveness and counseling. One semester a student told her mother that she was taking my class on forgiveness. Her mother responded, "Forgiveness? What is there to talk about for an entire semester?"

That's the dilemma with forgiveness. All of us have some idea of what forgiving another person is all about. Sometimes we agree, and sometimes we don't. *How* you conceptualize forgiveness makes a difference when you are trying to work your way through a difficult relationship issue. For example, the young-adult daughter of one of my clients told her mother that her father had fondled her when she was little. My client (the mother) felt paralyzed. She wanted to support her daughter. She also wanted to work on forgiving her husband. She couldn't see how she could do both, because *to her* "to forgive" meant "to forget"—literally. How could she forget what her husband had done to her daughter? When she developed a different understanding of forgiveness, the mother was able to create an action plan that both respected her daughter and responded to her husband's inappropriate action.

Holding a theoretical understanding of forgiveness is one thing. Living it out is quite another. The wideness of the gap between theory and practice depends on your definition of forgiveness. To make progress on this part of the trail, you must close the gap between your theory and your practice of forgiving transgressors.

You may recall that we began our list of essential items necessary to traverse the trail to reconciliation with the *commitments* that sustain reconciliation: commitment to Christ, commitment to the process of reconciliation and commitment to participation in a reconciliation-friendly community. With the previous two chapters we began adding the *tasks* of reconciliation to our supplies: growing up and repenting. This chapter presents forgiving the transgressor as another task of reconciliation.

What Does It Mean to Forgive?

What *does* it mean to forgive someone? Forgiving a transgressor is often confused with a number of closely related concepts. For example, forgiving is not condoning (to overlook), excusing (to remove blame), forbearing (to endure patiently), pardoning (to release from penalty) or forgetting an offense. These strategies do represent ways in which someone may deal with a transgression, but they usually work best when (1) the offense is minor, (2) the offense is the result of an innocent or infrequent misunderstanding or (3) the wrongdoer cannot be held morally accountable for his or her actions (such as a toddler's spilling juice on your white linen tablecloth).

However, if the wrongdoing is major and intentional, and if the culprit can bear moral responsibility for his or her actions, these strategies may preserve the relationship, but they do not restore the kind of love and trust on which reconciliation is built. Forgiving is also different from reconciling. I have said earlier that forgiving (and repenting) makes reconciling possible but not inevitable. Situations exist in which forgiving without reconciling is the wisest or only option. For example, if an offender has died prior to repenting or if a wrongdoer is unrepentant and does not change, then a wounded individual can forgive, but he or she cannot reconcile with the wrongdoer. This is not the biblical ideal, but it is reality for many people.

What, then, does it mean to forgive another person? The answer to that question is not as simple as we might think. Social scientists have been studying forgiveness in earnest since the mid-1990s, and so far they do not agree on a common definition. For example, Everett L. Worthington in *Five Steps to Forgiveness* describes forgiveness as a process that replaces "hot emotions of anger or fear that follow a perceived offense . . . with positive emotions like unselfish love, empathy, and compassion or even romantic love" (2001, p. 32). On the other hand, Robert Enright in *Forgiveness Is a Choice* writes, "When unjustly hurt by another, we forgive when we overcome the resentment toward the offender, not by denying our right to the resentment, but instead by trying to offer the wrongdoer compassion, benevolence, and love; as we give these, we as forgivers realize that the offender does not necessarily have a right to such gifts" (2001, p. 25).

If time allowed, I would continue to recite various definitions of forgiving proposed by social science researchers. In spite of the differences in definitions, all agree that forgiving involves some kind of change in your thoughts, feelings and actions toward someone who has hurt you.

In general, forgiving involves a *letting go* of some things and a *giving out* of other things. Given the emphasis of the biblical narrative on the reconciling work of Christ, I suggest that Christians add *a hope for bringing back* to these categories of change. Forgiving another involves a *letting go* of negative emotions such as anger, bitterness, grudges and the desire for revenge that we experience when a relationship has been wounded. While anger and resentment are among the normal feelings that immediately follow a perceived offense, they become destructive to our relationships when we nurture them over the course of time. The apostle Paul was keenly aware of this. In Ephesians, he spells out characteristics of the people of God after the cross of Christ destroys the "dividing wall of hostility" between groups who had formerly despised and distrusted one another—in this particular case, Jews and Gentiles—but who are now members of God's household (see Eph 2:11-14, 19). Paul writes, "Get rid of all bitterness, rage and anger, brawling and slander, along with every form of malice" (Eph 4:31). These emotions are unbecoming to those who are "created to be like God in true righteousness and holiness" (Eph 4:24). Everett Worthington (2003) observes that when these hot emotions remain with us over time, they eventually cool down and congeal into unforgiveness. Forgiving may start with a letting go of the negative emotions.

Forgiving can also involve a *giving out* of positive emotions. Worthington (2003) suggests that we replace the negative emotions identified in the preceding paragraph with positive ones like compassion, empathy, humility and love. We find this process of emotional replacement in the continuation of Paul's letter to the Ephesians. He writes, "Be kind and compassionate to one another, forgiving each other, just as in Christ God forgave you" (Eph 4:32). Theologically we would say that we are extending mercy, grace and agape love toward someone who does not deserve it and who in fact has forfeited all entitlement to these relationship-enhancing factors. For the secular person, forgiving may stop there. But for one who is a member of the people of God, there is more.

If we are to forgive "as in Christ God forgave you" and if we are to "live a life of love, just as Christ loved us and gave himself up for us as a fragrant offering and sacrifice to God" (Eph 5:2)—if we are to begin "letting go" and "giving out"—we need to add a longing for *bringing back,* that is, a hope for reconciliation. As I have already suggested, Christ did not die just so we might be forgiven by God and then distanced from God. Christ died so that we might be reconciled to God. This involves a transformed relationship with the one who wounded us: not a relationship based on lies, deceit, misuse of power, intimidation or whatever else eroded the commitment between us, but one built on truthfulness, loving-kindness and mutual regard, as is characteristic of the Trinity. And when this kind of relationship transformation is not possible—as many times in our interpersonal relationships it is not—we grieve, releasing the other into the hands of God.

Forgiving from the Heart

Forgiveness happens within the heart of the injured party. Injured parties can work on their side of the relationship, independent of any change on the part of transgressors. Is it easier to be forgiving when wrongdoers grovel, cringe, bow, stoop or fall at your feet and beg for your forgiveness? Probably. But my point is, that isn't necessary. Your forgiving another is not held hostage by their actions or lack of actions. You can extend forgiveness to another without her or his participation in the process. The majority of the studies on forgiving explore forgiveness from the perspective of the injured party, and most of the research-based models of forgiveness "house" forgiveness within the heart of the injured party (see, for example, Enright, 2001; Worthington, 2003). Forgiving without reconciling is especially appropriate when the transgressor is dangerous, unrepentant or not interested in doing his or her part to restore trust and love to the relationship. Extending forgiveness to another can lift a burden of pain from your shoulders. Be careful not to confuse it with reconciliation, however. Forgiving another can set your part of the stage for reconciling, but it is not the same thing as reconciling. Remember, reconciliation within marriage takes two people actively committed to the restoration of love and trustworthiness so that their relationship may be transformed.

Forgiveness researcher Everett Worthington and his colleagues have developed a process that they call REACHing for forgiveness, which injured parties can learn to help them forgive another.[1] Each letter in *reach* represents one step in Worthington's five-step model. To REACH for forgiveness, injured parties

> ***R****ecall the hurt.* Honestly and objectively recall what happened to you. The key in this step is to be as objective as you possibly can be.
>
> ***E****mpathize with the other.* Explore the hurtful event from the perspective of the wrongdoer. If possible, identify not only with that person's thoughts on the event but also with his or her emotions. This is very challenging, and I will say more about empathy later in this chapter.
>
> *Give the* ***A****ltruistic gift of forgiveness.* Make a choice about whether or not you are ready to forgive. Forgiveness is truly a gift that we give to another.
>
> *Make a public* ***C****ommitment to forgiving.* Tell someone about what you have done. Making a public commitment to forgiving helps

[1]If you would like to know more about REACHing for forgiveness, consider reading Everett Worthington's *Forgiving and Reconciling* (Downers Grove, Ill.: InterVarsity Press, 2003).

you to secure your action in your own heart and mind.

H*old on to forgiveness.* Many experience doubts about forgiving in the days to come. When doubts knock at your door, remind yourself that you have made a choice to forgive.

Forgiving and Reconciling

Worthington's model has helped many injured people forgive others with whom they will not reconcile. When the prospect of reconciliation is on the horizon, it opens other options for forgiving that not only require changes *within* the heart of the injured party but must also manifest themselves as work *between* forgiver and repenter. Family therapist Terry Hargrave (1994, 2001) presents such a model for forgiveness within families. He believes that restoring love and trust to intimate relationships requires activity on the part of the transgressor *and* the transgressed against, with the goal of relationship restoration clearly in mind. This demands resolution of the moral violation *within* the players involved as well as *between* them. In *Families and Forgiveness* Hargrave argues that this restoration process

> involves the victimized person's being given legitimate reason to believe that the wrongdoer accepts responsibility for the injustice. [This is] accomplished when the victimized person no longer has to hold the wrongdoer responsible for the injustice; the wrongdoer holds himself or herself responsible. . . . [It] demands that trust be reestablished between two people after a relational hurt. (1994, pp. 15, 16)

Can you hear echoes of our discussion about growing up (chapter five) and repentance (chapter six) in this passage? As you can see, Hargrave's understanding resonates with my picture of reconciliation.

Hargrave's Model and Reconciliation

Terry Hargrave (1994, 2001) believes that at the core of relational wounds within families is the violation of love and trust. He proposes that when members of our family injure us unjustly and unfairly, we doubt our family's love for us and their trustworthiness. When this goes on for years, we easily conclude that we are not lovable and our family is not safe. Forgiveness therefore acts as an antibiotic and an inoculation. It is the path by which we heal from relational wounds in our past and our present (antibiotic) and the way we stop ourselves from reenacting these harmful patterns in our future (inoculation).

Forgiveness therefore acts as an antibiotic and an inoculation. It is the path by which we heal from relational wounds in our past and our present (antibiotic) and the way we stop ourselves from reenacting these harmful patterns in our future (inoculation).

The work of forgiving is divided into four stations (Hargrave, 2001): insight, understanding, giving opportunity for compensation and the overt act of forgiving. The first two stations, insight and understanding, constitute *salvaging*. The last two stations, opportunity for compensation and the overt act of forgiving, encompass *restoration* (see figure 7.1). What is *salvage?* According to Hargrave, "Salvage is the use of forgiveness to gain insight into how to keep the damage done in the past from continuing to affect one's life, now and in the future. It means understanding the circumstances of the abused, and abuser, so that one does not carry the burden of pain alone" (p. 10). This happens through insight and understanding. Injured parties develop insight into the family dynamics that created environments in which the relational damage occurred. Insight allows wounded persons to track family ways of relating that are painful and to see how others in their family made sense of these transactions. Insight allows injured parties to name the pain from which they have suffered and to name the source of that pain. In the naming process, victims gain leverage to protect themselves and others from future suffering. Insight tells injured parties *how* something like this could happen in their family.

Understanding helps injured parties to comprehend the external circumstances (historic and current) and psychological processes (internal and relational) that influenced the wrongdoer. Victimized persons rediscover the transgressor's humanity and their own fallibility. Understanding helps wounded individuals see *why* the injustice occurred. Hargrave notes that if the wrongdoer is deceased, unavailable or unsafe, offended people can go no further in the process because they cannot change the future of the relationship single-handedly.

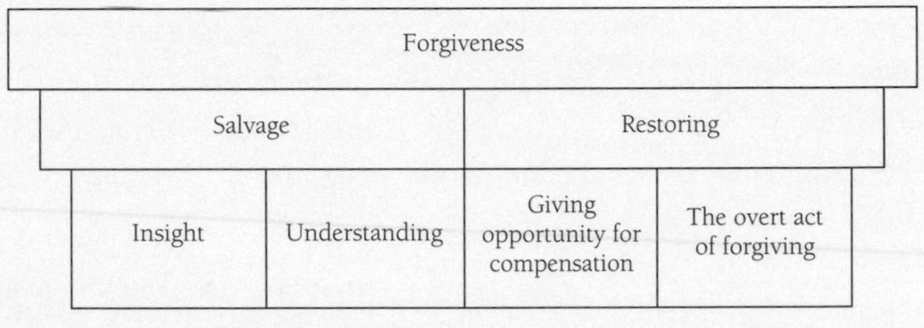

Figure 7.1. Hargrave's model of forgiveness

When hope for a new future is on the horizon, injured parties can engage in *restoration,* especially when offenders recognize their own culpability and resolve to become trustworthy. Hargrave explains the difference between salvage efforts and restoration in this way: "Restoration differs from salvage in that it requires the person who has been wronged in a relationship to put himself or herself in a position where love and trust can be rebuilt by the person who perpetuated the hurt" (p. 11). In other words, they repent. As the transgressor repents (that is, confesses and commits to changed behavior over time), the injured party can engage in *restoration* through the two stations of (1) giving opportunities for compensation and (2) the overt act of forgiving. Providing opportunities for compensation allows wrongdoers to demonstrate changed behavior in ways that restore love and trust. (We explored this aspect in chapter six.) In the overt act of forgiving, the injured party and wrongdoer clarify who was responsible for specific actions and commit to rebuilding their relationship. According to Hargrave, the overt act of forgiving catapults injured parties and wrongdoers into "an immediate alignment of love and trust. Instead of the victim prescribing a payment plan designed to gradually erase the indebtedness of the victimizer who caused the pain, the victim essentially cancels out any claim to the injustice" (1994, p. 90).

I am attracted to Hargrave's model for several reasons. First, his proposition that forgiveness is also a part of the relationship (rather than the private property of the wounded party) is consistent with a biblical worldview. In the ancient Near East of the Old Testament and in the Jewish and Greco-Roman world of the New Testament, people thought in terms of relationality rather than individuality. David Augsburger writes in *Helping People Forgive* that "the biblical world is clearly . . . a society of social solidarity, and its understanding of reconciliation and forgiveness are communal, not individual. Its primary focus is on the web of human covenants and commitments that enable just and loving relationships" (1996, p. 148). Theologian Joseph Sittler adds, "Of the great Christian or Jewish words—God, love, sin, guilt, forgiveness, reconciliation—none is a definition. They are all relational statements" (1986, p. 80). Sittler concludes that the definitions of these terms cannot be constructed in the abstract. Instead their meaning becomes "clear and recognizable only when you behold a relationship" (p. 80).

Second, recent scientific discoveries about extending forgiveness to a transgressor are consistent with Hargrave's model and parallel the processes that he describes as salvaging. Therefore we can add to our discussion the findings from psychological studies on how to forgive another person. Third, because Hargrave sheds light on ways in which forgiving contributes to reconciliation, his model is the "shoe that fits" the stories within this book.

The commitments of reconciliation—commitment to Christ, commitment to the hard work of reconciling and commitment to a reconciliation-friendly community—provide rich soil in which the seeds of reconciliation may germinate. Earlier chapters discussed growing up and repenting as two important tasks in the process of reconciliation. By now you have guessed that forgiving is another essential item as you travel toward reconciliation. The next chapter will add restoring truth and trustworthiness to our task list. You will see that when forgiving goes hand in hand with repenting, couples lay a strong foundation for reconciliation. After Chad and Gabriella's story, I will use Hargrave's model as a template for our discussion.

Gabriella and Chad's Story

Gabriella and Chad met during college. Chad was a big man on his Christian campus. Gabriella was the new, pretty freshman. No one was surprised when they married three and a half years later. After graduation, Chad enrolled in seminary and accepted a part-time position as a youth pastor in a church about forty minutes from campus. Later, when the senior pastor of that church resigned, Chad was invited to be the interim pastor.

Chad and Gabriella moved from campus housing into the church parsonage. The congregation grew under Chad's leadership, and before long the church asked him to be its full-time pastor. Being a preacher's kid, Chad knew what it took to grow a church. Being a military kid, Gabriella did not. She says of that time, *"I began struggling with feelings of 'the church is more important than me.' I began to feel distressed about this high level of commitment that a pastor makes to the church. You've got to be dedicated to your husband's career, and I heard it, but I hadn't experienced it."*

Chad adds, *"It was just an adjustment [for Gabriella]. It was like, 'Uhhhh, this is new territory for me,' and 'This is not as easy as I thought, and it's not as easy as you're making it out to be.'"*

Chad and Gabriella had five and a half years of ministry at that church. When Chad graduated from seminary, they accepted a call to another church. Under their ministry this church blossomed and flourished. During their fourth year there, Chad met a new couple at a worship service. He says, *"The chemistry was immediately apparent with these people."*

Gabriella adds, *"They befriended us, and we became very close friends. It was like we could talk about everything, even struggles we were having in the church. In other words, we weren't the professional pastor couple with them—*

we were actually ourselves with them. And that was so refreshing, because you don't always find people in the church that you can be yourself with. So we felt very blessed."

After a year and a half, Gabriella became uneasy when she watched her husband and her best friend interact. Gabriella reflects, *"I could sense there would be a connection between them. I would question him."*

Every time Gabriella questioned Chad, he replied, *"You're being jealous. There's nothing there."*

The more Gabriella asked him to back off, the more he resented it. Chad recalls thinking, *"It's just that [Gabriella's] reservations have been going on for a couple of years now. I really don't want to lose their friendship. They're a valuable asset to the ministry."* Chad was totally committed to his marriage. He said to Gabriella, *"This [an affair] would never happen to me, so why are you even talking about this? Even if you don't trust her, don't you trust me?"*

Finally Gabriella adopted a new attitude: *"You've got a man who was committed to the church before the marriage. So if you can't fight God and you can't fight the church, then join 'em. So I did with both feet. I got involved in heavy-duty women's ministries, Bible studies."* Things looked grand on the outside, but tension brewed below the surface.

Over time Gabriella's friend and Chad became more emotionally intimate, until one day they exchanged a hug that communicated more than brotherly or sisterly affection. Chad and Gabriella's best friend thus began an active sexual affair. He had no illusion about the sinfulness of his actions. *"There was a sense of guilt. 'Okay, I feel I was out of line,' but there was excitement in that. There was incredible titillation going on. I had never drunk, never smoked. Gabriella and I were just like model kids—straight-arrow kind of thing."*

Not surprisingly, Gabriella's concern about her husband's relationship with her best friend grew more intense. She tried to talk to her mother-in-law about her suspicions, but instead of supporting her, her mother-in-law cautioned Gabriella about spreading rumors that could ruin Chad's reputation. Twice Gabriella confronted her best friend. Her friend acted deeply hurt by these accusations, and each time Gabriella gave her the benefit of the doubt. Gabriella began to distrust herself. She says, "*I entered into this psychological maze of believing I couldn't even interpret reality correctly. You begin to think you're going to lose your mind.*"

Chad remarks, "*I would feel terrible about how she was feeling. I mean, I would see the turmoil in her, and that would kill me. The selfishness was stronger. It was like, 'I feel bad about this, but hey, you know, out of sight, out of mind.'*"

Two more years passed. Gabriella was caught on the horns of a dilemma. On one hand, she was convinced that something was going on between her husband and her friend. On the other hand, she questioned her ability to name reality. In desperation Gabriella went to the church elders. "*I laid it all out for them. I was begging them to talk to Chad. I was trying to protect my husband from this woman.*"

Gabriella recalls that at this meeting the elders told Chad, "'*Maybe none of what she says is true, but for her sake, you need to back off this friendship.*'" She adds, "*I remember my husband stoically going, 'Okay, okay, I can do that.' I even kind of felt patronized with this elder sitting in front of me saying, 'She may be totally wrong, but here's how you need to handle the situation, because you need a happy wife and she's not happy.'*"

The next day Chad, Gabriella and Gabriella's friend were at the church. At lunchtime Gabriella announced that she was heading home, then walked to her car. On impulse she returned to the church, and then she witnessed Chad touch her friend in an inappropriate manner. Chad saw Gabriella out of the corner of his eye and hurried back to his office, acting as if nothing had happened. Gabriella walked into his office and said, "*Buddy, you're in trouble. You can't get out of this one.*" Chad denied Gabriella's charges again, even when she talked with the elders.

The affair finally began to weigh on Chad. "*I would confess to God and say, 'Oh, I'm so sorry.' I would feel terrible and be [reading] Scripture and just pouring out my heart but never taking the next step necessary to cut it off. The last part of the affair got more stale, more obligatory. What devel-*

oped was then a real feeling of bondage for me."

Chad wanted to end the affair, but he didn't know how. He certainly wasn't going to tell the truth. He finally concluded that he would look for another church when the time was right. A geographical cure would do the trick.

But things came to a head a month later. One evening Chad was at home while Gabriella and two women, including her friend, were working at the church. Gabriella was in the church kitchen when the phone rang. She and her friend answered simultaneously. Gabriella says, *"I listened to the conversation. He said, 'Hello,' and my friend said, 'Hello,' and for the first time, I decided to deceive—not say hello and not reveal that I'm on the line too. I listened to them exchange 'I love you.' And I was hearing enough that I knew beyond a shadow of a doubt that he had made love with this woman."*

Gabriella stumbled out of the church in a state of shock and dismay. She prayed fervently as she drove to her sister's house. Gabriella did not want to confront Chad in their home, and she asked her sister's permission to do it at her home instead. Gabriella and her sister drove to Gabriella's house and told Chad he needed to come to the other home immediately. Thinking something had happened to one of his nephews, Chad followed the two women in his car. As he drove, he began to wonder if this involved his sister's children at all or if his number was up. When they were seated in Gabriella's sister's living room, Gabriella asked Chad, *"Do you have something to tell me?"*

Chad says, *"I think it was God's opportunity to spill, and the doors opened. I said, 'Yeah, I think it's worse than you can imagine.' I began to just spew the whole thing. It was like a bomb hit her."*

Chad told Gabriella about his three-and-a-half-year affair with her best friend. Then Gabriella let Chad have it.

> *I don't know what came over me. It was the most violent, ugly—I think I said the f-word a thousand times. I went on a five-minute machine-gun attack verbally about how he had ruined our lives, the church's life. I'm*

thinking that everything inside of me has died. Everything that you could ever hope and dream your life would be had died. I had an absolute mess of a marriage that was now living out its consequences. I watched my husband become a blubbering baby [who said to me], "I will do whatever it takes. I want a second chance. I've made the worst mistake I've ever made in my life."

Forgiving and Reconciliation

What, then, is forgiveness? You will recall that Hargrave's model includes two major parts: salvaging and restoration. His idea of salvaging is an *intra*personal process similar to how other researchers conceptualize forgiving. According to Hargrave (2001), one of the major distinctions between salvage efforts and restoration is their demand on the future relationship. You can think about it like this: Salvage gives injured parties a new way to look at the past and the perpetrator through insight and understanding. Salvage frees the wounded ones from the negative effects of broken love and trust, but provides *no expectation for reconciliation*. By contrast, restoration gives both parties the means to *rebuild their future* by giving opportunities for compensation and by the overt act of forgiving. Salvage is a change that happens *within* injured parties. Restoration is a change that happens *between* injured parties and wrongdoers to clear the path for reconciliation. We have already noted that many people do not cross over from salvaging to restoring, for justifiable reasons. They find peace and closure through salvaging. This is very similar to Worthington's REACHing for forgiveness concept (2003). This is a legitimate and biblically consistent action.

You cross a bridge when you move from salvaging to restoring. That bridge takes you to the shores of risk. According to Hargrave, "[Restoration with] people who have injured us unjustly sets us on a course that engages us into a relationship with the very people who have caused us so much pain. The decision to begin the process of [restoring] brings an unpredictable amount of risks as we expose ourselves to potential new damage" (1994, p. 60).[2]

He continues,

> This is what the process of [restoring] is about. It means that we return to the relational issues as they were when they caused us so much damage. When we arrive on the emotional scene where the love and trust were violated in our families, we open ourselves up to the possibility that whoever hurt us unjustly is now—at least in part—able to give us what we deserve. We build a bridge across the violation in order that our victimizer may address the damage in a trustworthy and loving manner. *In this way, the process of [restoring] is really a rebirth of the relationship.* [Restoring] provides a way for the entitlement of love and trust in a family to be restored, even if the love and trust have never been exhibited. [Salvaging] provides insight that gives us the power to stop future injustice, and understanding that gives identification that eases our pain, but it does not restore the relationship and reestablish the possibility of love and trust in the family. Restoring is a unique human possibility that has the potential of not only easing our pain from the past but also healing it. (1994, p. 64, emphasis added)

Restoration requires courage to risk trusting again. Excerpts from Gabriella and Chad's story will help us explore Hargrave's four stations of extending forgiveness. I will discuss each station in turn, using statements made by Gabriella and Chad. You will quickly note that I have added another station—hospitality (see figure 7.2). In the section that follows you will see how an attitude of welcome helps to bridge the gap between salvage and restoration. I have placed the entire process of extending forgiveness under the heading "Reconciliation." In figure 7.2 you can also see how I picture repentance and forgiveness working in tandem to foster reconciliation.

---

[2]Hargrave first published his model in 1994 in *Families and Forgiveness.* He has since modified the labels he uses, as presented in his 2001 book *Forgiving the Devil.* I have adjusted terms in this quote to avoid confusion and to be consistent with the current labels.

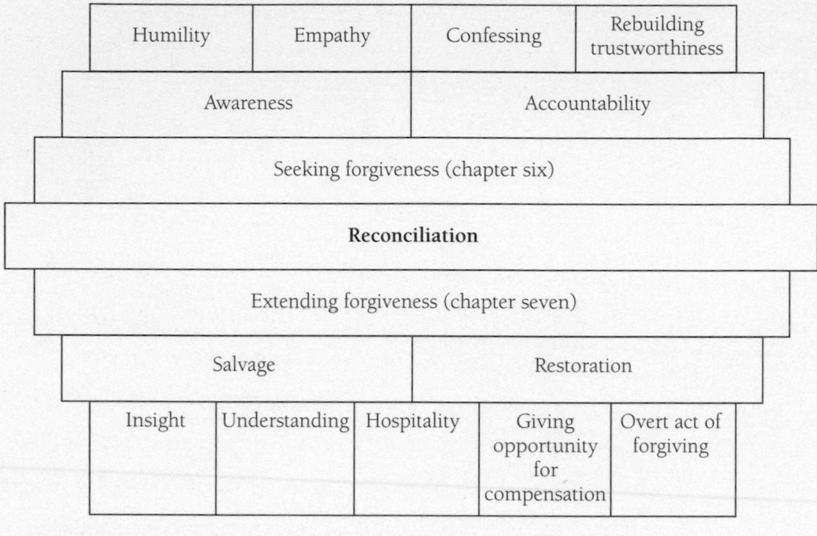

Figure 7.2. Forgiveness and repentance within a context of reconciliation

Station One: Insight

Insight accomplishes several things. First, it helps injured parties to assign responsibility to those who caused their pain. An injured party sees how his or her partner's past established habitual and damaging relationship habits. Insight is like a relational "aha!" You now understand how things worked in your or your mate's family of origin and how these patterns repeat in your marriage today. Insight often tracks dysfunctional habits over two or three generations. For example, an offended wife gained insight into her repentant husband when she realized he had been subjected to constant shaming and humiliation as a boy whenever his father had argued with him. Not surprisingly he had treated her similarly.

Gabriella saw how Chad's role as *"the spiritual hero"* in his family of origin had created an aura of invulnerability. Gabriella and Chad refer to this as *"the arrogance of our innocence."* The belief that they were "above it all" contributed to Chad's slide into relationally reckless behavior. Gabriella said during our interview, *"That, to me, is the weak link, the arrogance of the innocence that you just don't believe that would happen to you."*

To this Chad added, *"Obviously arrogance, lust, the things the Bible talks about that are selfishness were there. Some of those things were already in place in my life."*

Insight also helps you not pass the pain on to others. Gabriella and Chad have regular talks with their adolescent children about that time in their marriage and what their children thought about it and now think about it. Other couples intentionally change how they interact so that healthier patterns will be passed on to future generations.

Think about the circumstances and family environment in which your offender grew up. What can you learn about his or her life from this review? How might this review shed new light on your image of this person?

At first blush, insight doesn't sound very "forgiving." However, with further reflection, you can see that insight provides a measure of safety and security, because when we can name the pain from which we have suffered and name the source of that pain, we can take steps to protect ourselves from harm, and we can see in ourselves ways that perpetuate that pain in other relationships.

Station Two: Understanding

Understanding is the second station of forgiveness. First, understanding helps injured parties to gain perspective into *why* others acted the way they did. This is forgiveness's version of walking a mile in another person's shoes. Understanding helps wounded individuals to see the other as a fallible human being and not a monster. Second, understanding helps injured parties to see their own propensity to inflict harm. In other words, victims recognize they are capable of hurting others. When injured parties gain this kind of understanding, they may humbly conclude, "There but for the grace of God go I." Third, understanding changes wounded individuals' image of who they are and who the transgressor is. It reshapes identity. Let's discuss further each of these three outcomes of understanding.

Understanding why. To start with, we understand *why* others acted in the way they did. Understanding *why* involves crawling into the psyche of our transgressor and looking at our relationship through his or her eyes so that we can truly empathize. Empathy does not negate moral accountability. Instead it helps us to see the other's humanity. Numerous psychological studies have identified empathy as one of the most important factors in forgiving. Empathy usually takes the form of understanding the wrongdoer's perspective on life, coming to terms with his or her interpretation of the relationship. Gabriella believed that Chad loved her in spite of his actions. She knew the high esteem with which Chad's family held him and the legacy of being the fourth generation in his family to enter the ministry. She saw how this led Chad to invest more in the church than in his marriage.

Empathy is not necessarily easy to come to. If you want to work on empathizing with the other, you might try rewriting the event from the other person's perspective. You could also think about how they grew up and pay attention to the aspects of their family of origin that set the stage for their adult beliefs and behaviors. You could think about how your own way of relating to the other may have contributed to the relationship pain between you. This does *not* take the burden of responsibility off their shoulders! It does, however, help you see that their action didn't happen in a vacuum; it was part of a larger relationship story, in which you both play an active role.

Understanding our need for forgiveness. Then understanding helps us to see that we too have needed forgiveness because of our own propensity to inflict harm. Gabriella said, *"Would I do that if that was me? Could I be that way? It was coming to grips [with the fact] that any of us are capable of behaving and making choices—my own rage, the capacities we have to commit evil and the capacity we have of good."*

Understanding short-circuits Roy Baumeister's (1997) magnitude gap. He noticed how injured parties and wrongdoers entered cycles of increasingly harmful exchanges, due in part to differences in their perceptions of the aftermath from the wounding event. Compared to wrongdoers' beliefs about the impact of their transgression, injured parties believed they suffered *more* harm, *more* deeply and for *longer* periods of time than wrongdoers imagined them to have suffered. Victims retaliated to "even the score" as they saw it.

However, wrongdoers did not experience this as a tit-for-tat exchange. Offenders felt that injured parties had gone above what was necessary, leading transgressors to cry "foul ball" and claim the label of victim as their own. They retaliated against the formerly injured party to even the score as they calculated it. And the beat goes on.

Forgiveness demands that the buck stops here! Revenge is God's business, not ours (see Rom 12:17-21). And God doesn't even invite us to submit "revenge suggestions." Gabriella came to this insight:

> *I remember thinking, "Sin compounds upon sin compounds upon sin, and that's how we had so many problems. The sin is going to stop here. It's going to stop now. It's going to stop with me." I said it out loud to him. I wrote it in my journal, and I said it to my sister. And it was almost like, "I will not play by Satan's rules. I'm breaking the rules of his game." That's hard to do. It's like stopping a locomotive. It's like standing in front of an ongoing train and going, "Ka-BAM—I've just been hit, but I'm not going to get up and then get into the engine and do that to somebody else."*

Understanding who we are. Moreover, understanding changes our image of who we are and who the transgressor is. Moral violations misshape our view of our self and our transgressor by calling into question who we are. Gabriella experienced it like this: *"I remember looking at him and thinking, 'I don't know you. I don't know who you are anymore. I'm married to a stranger. I'm married to this evil stranger.'"*

Many times the pain of the offense is so intense that it becomes the only lens through which we can see. We are likely to see in the other the essence of pure evil (Baumeister, 1997). Who was Chad to Gabriella now? Was he her husband-lover or her enemy? As Gabriella posed this question to herself, she says,

> *One of the pivotal decisions I came to was that my husband is not the enemy, and my best friend is not my enemy. I remember verbalizing this to my sister, saying, "Satan is in this because his desire and his goal is to destroy everything, to destroy Chad's ministry, to destroy the marriage, to destroy everything." And I said to my sister, "I'm not going to let Satan do that." I was not going to pit me against my husband. We were going to have to work on this together, and I was going to have to be in it. I knew I had a choice. I could stay married legally, contractually, but empty inside for the sake of the kids. Or I could stay committed and make something of it. So coming to that was a pivotal decision for me, because if I had kept defining the lines of battle as "you're on that side and I'm on this side," there would have been no hope.*

This question cuts deep into the heart of reconciliation. Injured parties raise it in different ways. If they are angry, they are likely to say to transgressors, "Who do you think you are?"—revealing their sense of righteous indignation. Conversely, if they are filled with fear, they may ask, "How can you treat me like this?"—revealing their sense of powerlessness and vulnerability. The cross of Christ addresses both questions. On the cross Jesus represents both injured par-

Take time to vividly recall a time when you experienced being forgiven. Perhaps it was the moment when you understood the depth of God's forgiveness, or a time when someone else forgave you. Use this memory to help you recall your own humanity.

Make a list of the good qualities of the person who wounded you. This may take some effort if you are angry with her or him. Remember why you originally were attracted to this person and how this person has added to your life. This will help you recall the transgressor's humanity.

ties and wrongdoers, because both are in need of God's forgiveness.

In *Exclusion and Embrace,* theologian Miroslav Volf (1996) uses the metaphor of embrace to discuss the work of the cross. He argues that the central message of the cross is this: God seeks to embrace his enemies and transform them from enemies into God's friends (see Jn 15:15)—and even more than friends, into family (see 1 Jn 3:1). Gabriella came face to face with the fact that Jesus' forgiveness covered her husband's transgression as well as her own. She used a word picture to hang on to this biblical reality:

> *The pictures I began to have, Scriptures that began to come to my mind, were, "Cling to the cross, claiming the cross." Coming to the decision of the cross and what Christ accomplished on the cross up to that point for me had been only one-dimensional. It had been for the sins of the world, and cognitively I understood that it covered my sins too, but [I had been] feeling like I didn't have any biggies, never had experienced any other biggie sins, not from my parents, sexual abuse or anything. This was the first big sin that required me to realize, "The cross covered that too." Oh, my! Then I came to the conclusion at the same time that the cross is bearing everybody's sin; [Jesus is] hanging on the cross, covering my best friend's and my husband's sin; he is hanging for my pain too. [I] saw myself wrapped around the cross, with my legs wrapped around the bottom of the pole, clinging.*

Station Three: Forgiving as Hospitality

Earlier in this section, we noted that injured parties cross a bridge when they move from salvaging to restoring. What makes up that bridge? My conversations with our reconciling couples suggest that as they committed to reconciliation, injured parties adopted a softer stance toward their transgressors. This softer stance is an invitation of welcome that is manifested in words, actions and attitudes directed toward wrongdoers. It mirrors the open arms of someone waiting to embrace another. It is the welcome of hospitality. By this I do not mean the kind of hospitality modeled by the restaurant and hotel industry. Instead I refer to biblical hospitality, an ancient practice in which gracious hosts offer friendship, nourishment and shelter to strangers. As a bridge between salvaging and restoring, I propose that hospitality is a third station of forgiveness.

Hallmarks of biblical hospitality include offering food, shelter and protection. Christine Pohl, author of *Making Room: Recovering Hospitality as a Christian Tradition,* notes that the distinctive of Christian hospitality was the "emphasis on including the poor and neglected, the ones who could not return the favor" (1999, p. 6). The practice of biblical hospitality reflected the host's commitment to and participation in God's reconciled community. For example, in the Old Testament Abraham and Sarah invited into their home three strangers who turned out to be God's messengers. In the New Testament, believers were instructed to pursue hospitality (see Rom 12:13), cautioned not to neglect hospitality (see Heb 13:2) and challenged to offer hospitality ungrudgingly (see 1 Pet 4:9). God extended his ultimate and most lavish invitation of hospitality to us through Jesus Christ. Through his death on the cross, Christ opened the door into God's family for us. Through his resurrection, he stands at the door and bids us welcome. We, who were enemies of God, are ushered into God's kingdom when we accept Jesus' invitation.

Strangers are those who do not belong to the people who surround them. They lack a place in the community in which they find themselves. In biblical hospitality, hosts invite those who have no place into the community of those who belong. Unless someone who currently belongs to the community welcomes the stranger and escorts the stranger in, community members will think of the stranger as an intruder or an invader. Similarly, through acts of betrayal, wrongdoers forfeit their right to a place in the relationship. When injured parties extend hospitality, they offer the intangible gift of place to the one who has lost her or his place in the relationship. If transgressors try to make a relationship place for themselves without this invitation, they will seem like intruders or invaders to injured parties. The transgressed-against must crack open the doors of their heart before acts of compensation can be seen as olive branches of peace and not battering rams of war.

Consider the example of the younger son in the parable of the prodigal son (see Lk 15:11-32). He lost his place in his family when he liquidated his inheritance and left home for a distant country. The repentant son returned home, hoping to find a place as a servant, not a son. Instead the loving father embraced him, identified him as "son" and gave him signs of sonship: shoes, a ring and a robe. Like the younger son in Luke's parable, Chad had "unhusbanded" himself. His contrite and repentant heart waited to see whether or not Gabriella would welcome him home.

Gabriella's welcome was typical of those interviewed. First, she committed to reconciliation and clearly verbalized that to Chad. For the three weeks after his confession, they lay in bed weeping for what they had lost. Gabriella's choice to reconcile was strengthened by Chad's response to her pain. She says, *"If he hadn't been like that, if his response had been 'Sorry, honey, I can't handle this emotional stuff. I'm gonna hit the bar,' I would have felt more alienated and more detached. I mean, choices he made supported my commitment to restoring."*

Second, Gabriella embraced the hardships and heartaches that came with Chad's resignation and their immediate relocation to another city. They went into debt. Their family of four lived in a small basement apartment in a relative's home for a year until they could afford a house of their own. Gabriella entered the work force and left her cherished role as a stay-at-home mom. She was willing to absorb this pain for the sake of their reconciliation. She describes it like this:

> *I was learning to redefine my expectations of what life was going to be for me now. My life was not going to be the way it was before. I had to accept that and even voiced my frustration to him: "I have to forgive you, not just for the affair, but I have to forgive you because now you've thrown me into the work force full time. And my house is really a mess, and my kids don't have me at home to make cookies for them after school." . . . All of those issues are the aftermath and consequences of an affair. If I'm not committed to that, then it won't restore. I mean, I could*

blow up two years later and say, "I've had it. This is enough. I'm divorcing you."

Moreover Gabriella immersed herself in their relationship while retaining the right to grieve and to be angry. She never minimized the sense of betrayal that she experienced, nor did she hide her outrage at what had happened. But even with these intense expressions, she reaffirmed her commitment to reconciliation.

Finally, she and Chad restored their pattern of praying together. Spiritual reconciliation was as important to her as marital reunion. Supporting all these activities was her desire to remain emotionally open to Chad. She knew that she could not do this on her own. *"I continually prayed, 'God, soften my heart. You're going to have to soften me for this,' because it's so easy to stop loving. I was watching, observing, experiencing God softening my heart over and over again to forgive Chad every morning when I woke up."* As Gabriella looked at Chad through the eyes of the crucified Christ, she saw him as one who needed welcome, and she gradually opened the door of her heart to him.

Actions of hospitality may be small or large, commonplace or remarkable. If you are the injured party, review how you may have already shown an attitude of biblical hospitality to the transgressor. What can you do to continue this practice? If you are the transgressor, how has the person you offended been hospitable toward you?

How might hospitality look in your relationship? Perhaps it begins with a determination to pay attention to how you launch into conversations about the offense. Marriage researcher John Gottman (1994) notes that men are most receptive to difficult conversations when their wives use a "soft" start-up instead of a "hard" start-up. A soft start-up may go like this: "I'm having a real hard time today, and I need to talk to you." A hard start-up may go like this: "You have ruined my life. The least you can do is sit here and take it like a man." Hospitable actions may include declaring a temporary moratorium on hard conversations in order to carve out space for some fun.

Family psychologists Howard Markman, Scott Stanley and Susan Blumberg (1994) observe how small events in a couple's day can trigger major arguments. They suggest that couples take control of this type of guerilla warfare by making specific time to talk about hard things. They also advise couples to take a breather from hard discussions and intentionally impose a "no talk" rule for a limited period of time. During this moratorium they recommend that couples do things to enhance their intimacy, such as doing something fun together. Hospitality might also mean that one mate intentionally does things for his or her spouse that makes the spouse feel cared about. This is particularly effective if both mates participate in these "caring days" (Stuart, 1980).

Station Four: Giving Opportunity for Compensation

When injured parties give repentant wrongdoers the opportunity for compensation, they recognize and credit perpetrators' actions that rebuild love and trust in the relationship. This station includes establishing specific avenues of trustworthiness. As trustworthy behaviors are extended by wrongdoers and credited by injured parties, a foundation of safety and love is reestablished.

As we have already discussed in the chapters on commitment and repentance, reconciliation takes two and demands the transgressor's dedication to consistent changed behavior over time. This rebuilding happens incrementally and is not without temporary setbacks. Nevertheless the overall movement is forward toward restoration. For example, Chad had a change in attitude about how he had prioritized his ministry over his marriage. He explained, *"It doesn't matter how successful I am [in ministry] with these hundreds of people, if I blow it here [in my marriage], I've blown it. I'm not successful. And so I want to be successful in my marriage. When I say success, I want to be the kind of husband and father God wants me to be."*

This change was important to Gabriella. As she saw Chad put it into action, she observed, *"The church was not number one anymore, but his family became number one. And our marriage became more important to him than it ever had to me, and I could see that being demonstrated on a daily basis."*

Giving opportunity for compensation may mean injured parties are on the lookout for ways in which their partners are offering repair attempts. While it is most powerful when acts of compensation are directly related to the offense, tangentially related acts can contribute to the overall sense of reconciling. However, when injured parties are still smarting from the wound, they may close their eyes to offers of repair or dismiss them out of hand. When injured parties credit repair attempts, they affirm their commitment to reconciling. Early repair attempts will not result in an immediate swell of warm fuzzy feelings for the wrongdoer, and transgressors would do well to readjust their expectations of sweeping their mate off his or her feet. However, as time passes and injured parties catalog these attempts, appreciation, gratitude and respect can emerge.

Earlier in this chapter I brought to your attention a "small" difference between how Hargrave uses the term *forgiving* to refer to an *inter*personal process and how other researchers use it to refer to an *intra*personal process. Innovative research by Michael McCullough, Frank Fincham and Jo-Ann Tsang (2003) may actually help us bridge this gap. This team defines forgiveness in terms of the degree to which injured parties avoid, seek revenge or extend benevolence to transgressors (consistent with *intra*personal definitions). Using a survey based on this definition, they measured changes in study participants' scores over time and compared these changes with a number of other factors. McCullough, Fincham and Tsang discovered that forgiving another is not a linear process; that is, you don't become consistently more and more forgiving as time passes. Instead, fluctuations in levels of forgiveness were observed over time. They noticed that empathy helped injured parties initially to forbear with their wrongdoer but not necessarily forgive that person over time. Surprisingly, injured parties who *held transgressors responsible* for their actions became more forgiving over time. The research team speculated that this might lead injured parties to confront their offenders, giving offenders opportunities to repent. I want to be sure to clarify that their study is not intended to explore forgiving as an *inter*personal process. Nevertheless, I find it fascinating that this research report is relatively congruent with the claims Hargrave makes in his model.

Station Five: Overt Act of Forgiving

Hargrave thinks of the overt act of forgiving as "relational rebirthing" (2001, p. 83). Injured party and wrongdoer confront the relational violation directly. Wrongdoers accept responsibility for their actions. The promise of restoration is exchanged. Hargrave identifies three elements that must be present. First, injured parties and wrongdoers agree on some of the specifics about the violation. In other words, they reach a common story about what happened that preserves the dignity and moral accountability of each person. Second, wrongdoers acknowledge their responsibility for the hurt and pain they caused, as we discussed in the chapter on repentance. Third, victimizers offer an apology for the damage, and victims accept the apology. This is the point where Hargrave's fourth station reflects my ideas of reconciliation most clearly. For the ensuing discussion, I will continue to use Hargrave's nomenclature (overt act of forgiving) to designate this station. I realize that the risk of confusion increases as I do this. Remember that other forgiveness researchers (see for example, Enright, 2001; Worthington, 2001, 2003) limit "forgiving" to processes internal to the injured party. This contrasts with how Hargrave uses the term *forgiving*. When he writes about the "overt act of forgiving," he refers to an interpersonal (in contrast to an intrapersonal) process enacted between injured party and transgressor.

The overt act of forgiving catapults injured parties and wrongdoers into "an immediate alignment of love and trust. Instead of the victim prescribing a payment plan designed to gradually erase the indebtedness of the victimizer who caused the pain, the victim essentially cancels out any claim to the injustice" (Hargrave, 1994, p. 90). This description may remind you of the actions of the merciful king in Jesus' parable in Matthew 18; he forgives his servant of an unrepayable debt. The overt act of forgiving launches the reconciling couple on a new trajectory. To borrow a phrase from 2 Corinthians 5:17, "the old has gone, the new has come!"

Sometimes a distinct event marks this station. Such was the case for Gabriella and Chad. It was one thing for Gabriella to welcome him back into their marriage. It was another thing altogether to welcome him into her bed. Gabriella said, *"In the process of talking about when did you have this affair and where did you sleep, I discovered that he had been in my bed in my bedroom once. So the bedroom, the holy of holies, the sanctity of the marriage bed, had been defiled."*

Gabriella knew that she had forgiven him on one level, but how was she going to cleanse this sacred space? She gave that serious thought and prayer. She wanted her forgiving to be bone-marrow deep, and this included finding a way to restore the purity of their sexual life together. Gabriella believed that *"reclaiming that marriage bed was a symbolic spiritual act. I did it and it was hard. And when I described for you the whole cross scene and me clinging to that, it was a reclaiming of what Jesus had done for him on the cross. I was saying to Chad, 'You don't deserve this, but I'm giving it to you free. It's grace.'"*

A few days after Chad's confession, Gabriella called him into the bedroom. Chad describes their experience this way:

> *She laid herself across the bed, and she was completely naked and she had her arms . . . it was like she was in the shape of a cross. She said, "Come, come here. Lie on me," and she said, "I forgive you." And it was almost like . . . it was almost like a parallel to Jesus dying on the cross. Because I knew it killed her, really, in some ways it really killed her. And yet there was this hope of life after death, resurrection and restoration and renewal. And so I always knew . . . I was assured of her forgiveness. I knew that trust wouldn't be there, and that would have to be rebuilt and continues to be rebuilt.*

Gabriella adds, *"It was a sacred moment. It was an intentional moment. It was a recovenanting moment. It was telling him once again, 'I am going down the aisle with you.'"*

I include Gabriella's extravagant act not as a prescription of what you should do but as a description of how one person embodied the message of the cross in her context and offered the overt act of forgiving. Other reconciled couples accomplished this station in equally dramatic moments in ways that were consistent with their characters and their circumstances. One injured mate burned the divorce papers that had been drawn up by his lawyer. Another couple decided that their home held too many painful memories; they chose to build a new home as an outward and visible sign of the emotional rebuilding in which they were engaged.

How do you know that you are ready to reconcile? Hargrave (1994) raises this same concern and offers three questions by which you can evaluate your readiness to move from salvaging to restoring.

- How willing are you to have the injustice addressed and your pain healed? If you are enraged over the unjust act, you may be unwilling to accept the offers of love and trust by a repentant offender.
- How important to you is the continuation of the relationship with the offender? You will be more willing to test the trustworthiness of the relationship if it is important to you.
- How ready is the offender to treat you in a loving and trustworthy manner? If the offender is truly repentant, as we discussed in chapter six, forgiving can move forward.

You may want to draw up a list of what restored trust will look like. Let the transgressor know what he or she can do to demonstrate his or her trustworthiness. Make a list of the things he or she has already done to be faithful to your relationship. This will help you to credit acts of repair. Also be alert to ways in which you and your partner can symbolically remember your act of forgiving. Perhaps you would like to take communion together or renew your wedding vows. Whatever you do, be sure the ritual is consistent with who you are and reflects your faith commitments.

Wrapping Up

The dilemma with any model is its step-by-step appearance. Extending forgiveness is too messy a process to be that straightforward. For example, Gabriella stopped at each station of forgiveness, but not necessarily in the order in which I have presented them, and she returned to some of the stations more than one time. Let me encourage you to use this model as a map that can help you locate work that you accomplished or work that is yet to be done. Remember that moving from salvaging to restoring includes risk and therefore requires courage. This will change you and your wounded relationship.

8

REBUILDING TRUTH, TRUST AND TRUSTWORTHINESS

The saying goes, "Honesty is the best policy." But have you noticed how nervous we get when our honesty is likely to upset someone we care about? I can easily recall times when friends have asked my opinion about something important to them. "What do you think?" they ask me. My moment of truth (interesting turn of a phrase) has arrived. If I don't like it, my mental computer whirls as I evaluate the cost of being totally honest. Usually the processing time is short. My friends know that I will speak truthfully to them, even when I know that they may not be particularly happy with what I have to say. I desire no less from them. I trust them when I know that they speak truthfully to me, and I like to think that my truthfulness is evidence of my trustworthiness.

Voicing a dissenting opinion ("I don't like it") has some risks *(will I be rejected?)*, and we weigh those risks even as we begin to speak. But what about when we have *done* something that we know is wrong or that we suspect falls into the gray areas of life? How forthright are we when others question us about those occasions? Many marital problems develop as deceptive speech covers up questionable actions, and trust is destroyed when the treachery is revealed. If the couple decides to reconcile, injured parties not only struggle to forgive, they also struggle to trust.

Forgiving and trusting are oriented toward different points in time. Forgiveness and repentance look backward. This helps you bring closure to a past event. Trust, on the other hand, looks forward to the future. Trustworthy actions help you lay claim to a new future together.

And the present? Well, that's where the rubber meets the road. Forgiving and repenting make trusting possible, but not inevitable. One mate put it like this, *"We didn't really know how to be a couple because . . . we still had trust issues. We didn't know if we really could trust each other for the long haul. We wanted to, we really wanted to at that point, but we didn't know if we could. We didn't know how to jump over that breach of trust."*

Rebuilding trust takes time. You had a foretaste of this in our chapters on repentance and forgiveness. In chapter six (repentance) the focus was on transgressors demonstrating consistent changed behavior over time as a vehicle to reestablish trustworthiness. In chapter seven (forgiveness) the emphasis was on injured parties' receptivity to these acts of compensation. Repenting and forgiving do not automatically lead to trusting. An offender astutely remarked, *"Trust isn't automatically rebuilt. Your credibility is not built back overnight."* Another statement from an offended party supports this: *"I also learned through counseling and the books that we read that there's a difference between forgiveness and trust. Many people who don't understand the difference between forgiveness and trust would flippantly say, 'Well, how can you stay married to him? You don't trust him.' Well, I don't trust him, but I forgave him."*

Reconcilers sense that trustworthiness is linked to truthfulness. Therapists Barbara Krasner and Austin Joyce write, "Without a stance in which truth is disclosed and invited, trust becomes a fantasy or a longing, but never a reliable reality" (1995, p. xxi). No truth, no trust. Certainly demonstrations of changed behavior contribute to trusting again. After all, "seeing is believing." But what happens when injured parties *cannot* observe these deeds, such as when wrongdoers are at work or out of town, or when the change is more intangible, like a change in attitude or thought? That is when the connection between truth and trust tightens. When injured parties believe that the one who wounded them speaks truthfully, they can trust more fully. Confidence in truthfulness increases confidence in trustworthiness.

The first part of this book unpacked the commitments that nurture reconciliation (commitment to Christ, to the process of reconciling and to a reconciliation-friendly community). This chapter concludes our discussion on tasks of reconciling (growing up, repenting, forgiving, restoring truth and trustworthiness). As we explore the relationship between truth and trust, I hope you will see how essential the link between truthfulness and trustworthiness is for reconciliation. Let's hear Peter and Noelle's story before I dive into the core concepts of this chapter: trust and truth. I'll conclude this chapter with an exploration of how Noelle and Peter restored truthfulness and trustworthiness to their relationship.

Noelle and Peter's Story

Noelle and Peter met through their participation in a coffeehouse ministry during college. Each one thought they had discovered their soul mate. They married one year later. Trouble soon appeared on the horizon of their relationship. According to Noelle, *"I seem to have gotten lost in our early marriage. I think that revolved around the issue of becoming one. Being twenty-one years old, I didn't know what 'one' would mean, and somehow I thought it meant losing my own identity. Life revolved around Peter and what he needed to accomplish his goals. And everything I did just supported his goals; I had none of my own."*

Peter remembers their early years differently. *"Almost immediately, from our first night of marriage, we started having difficulties with our situation—specifically in the way we now related to each other."* Instead of dealing with the issues directly, Peter busied himself with life and withdrew from the relationship.

> *I buried myself in my work and went to school and got a master's degree. At that time I did a lot of blaming of Noelle for why something was wrong or why we were not relating. I went down the whole list of why we were just incompatible. A lot of it came down to the issue of physical intimacy not being there, in my perception. I frequently accused her of being so practical and pious and not spontaneous. I saw her as the more spiritual, and I resented that. I responded to her stoic affect with overly emotional responses and cycles of depression, which I blamed on her lack*

of responsiveness. This quickly brought me from a position of "She's righteous. She's a good person for me. She is who God brought to me," to "This isn't working. We're wrong for each other. This can't be God's plan"—that sort of thing.

Peter entertained thoughts of divorce but dismissed them because he didn't want to let his family of origin down.

Relationship challenges continued when they decided to start a family. Noelle had difficulty getting pregnant, and five years of fertility counseling followed. The resulting pregnancy and delivery were filled with stress and anxiety. This stress continued to drive a wedge between Peter and Noelle. Their marriage hit rock bottom after the births of their two children, who were sixteen months apart. Peter and Noelle had very different lives for the next four years. Peter buried himself in seventy- and eighty-hour workweeks, which led to emotional closeness with several women coworkers and a sexual affair. Peter thought, *"Noelle isn't like all these people that I feel so compatible with. God couldn't have wanted me to be with a person that I can't communicate with, and obviously these people understand me so well."*

On the other hand, Noelle says, *"I didn't have time to take care of myself. Or I should say I chose not to take the time to take care of myself. I took care of babies instead. I didn't feel good about my own body, and Peter constantly reminded [me] of that and told me about the wonderful women at the office and how they did it all."* Noelle felt buried by the burden of childcare. The distance and hostility between them grew. Peter was now talking about divorce, and Noelle was not objecting.

Shortly thereafter Peter and Noelle entered a period of personal discovery. Peter's crisis began when the woman with whom he was having an affair ended their relationship. He began to see a counselor and to take medication for depression. The therapist challenged Peter to stick with his marriage for the sake of the children. Peter also became involved in Promise Keepers and an ongoing men's Bible study. He experienced personal spiritual growth as he learned about who he was in

Christ through Neil Anderson's Freedom in Christ ministry (Anderson & Mylander, 1997). Peter discovered that these four things helped him to have *"a new focus for self-responsibility and personal and spiritual development that was structured around a set of tools that I could use right at that time."*

Noelle began a sixteen-month degree program related to her profession. Her studies helped her come to grips with events in her childhood that she now labeled childhood sexual abuse. With the support of her counselor, she confronted her perpetrator. Noelle says, *"I felt by confronting my perpetrator that there was potential of helping my relationship with Peter; it certainly wouldn't hurt it."* Noelle found her voice and began to use it. She no longer would tolerate Peter's verbal belittling of her or the children. *"So when Peter started complaining [and talking about divorce], I was no longer scared about what that would be like, because I figured I could handle it."*

Although God was working in Noelle and Peter's individual lives, their marital life remained in turmoil. They couldn't break out of a cycle of fighting and bickering. Noelle explains,

> *I had very little trust for Peter, and when he would tell me that he was changing, that he was trying to change, I would watch him closely. And I was very guarded. I didn't know if I could trust him or not. He hadn't changed enough at that point to have earned my trust. I still believed in a covenant marriage relationship, and I still wanted it to work. I wanted to be able to be okay, but I also knew that I wasn't going to put up with verbal abuse or ask my children to do that. So . . . he had a lot at stake. And he knew it. For the first time, I felt like he had a lot to lose and I didn't.*

Noelle realized that she was still furious with Peter and this anger was controlling her life. She sought the help of another individual counselor. *"That's where forgiveness began. I didn't know how to do it."* Help in forgiving came to Noelle from several spiritual resources. The most significant was when she took to heart lessons on forgiving that she learned through a study of Hosea in Bible Study Fellowship.

God spoke to me through that study. God loves me even though I am imperfect, and he asks me to love my husband in the same way, even though he is imperfect. I had essentially lied to my husband in that I hadn't told him for many years about what had happened to me as a child when I was molested. He would question me and I would deny it. As I recognized that God had forgiven me, I realized that I needed to forgive Peter also.

Peter and Noelle were still not experiencing the transformation in their marriage for which they longed. Noelle says, "*We were progressing through our own stuff and, I think, getting more healthy individually. But that wasn't particularly affecting our marriage. It was helping us have a better understanding of who we were as individuals.*"

Peter says, "*I [went] from saying, 'I'm totally incompatible with this woman' to 'I want this marriage to work for my children. I want to honor God. I want to be a good dad. I don't know why God has got us in this relationship with this pain, but I'm going to do what he asks me to do.' So it was kind of this stiff upper lip, damn the torpedoes and move ahead sort of thing. The healing was all on an individual level and a relationship to the Lord and the desire for a relationship with Noelle but no sense of an ability to have one.*"

At some point in their individual journeys, Peter told Noelle about his affair. He explains, "*I don't know that I expected it to accomplish anything. I think it was more of just seeing it as something on a path of my own development to say, 'I need to have this out in the open. I need to be honest about this.' Questioning, is this maybe something that's keeping us from being what we need to be for each other?*"

Noelle says, "*I had a lot of anger about the affair because that was the ultimate betrayal. Along with the acknowledgment from Peter about the affair came the confession that before we were married, he had had multiple sexual partners, which I had never known. I thought that he had come into our marriage as a virgin, and I was almost more angry about that initial betrayal.*" Fortunately Noelle and Peter had grown enough as individuals that it did not undo the progress they had made. Nevertheless, the marital transformation they wanted eluded them, and divorce was still an option.

Peter and Noelle's pastor invited them to attend a marriage retreat based on Anderson's Freedom in Christ material. Peter says, *"At that stage our relationship was still painful to us, but both of us had such a desire for it to not be painful. We both desired to have a good relationship. We just didn't know how to do it."*

Noelle adds, *"We went there seeking restoration, knowing if it didn't happen, it would probably be the end of our marriage."* During the retreat, the pastor would present a session. Then couples would go to their hotel rooms and discuss their marriage in light of the focal topic. Noelle says, *"That finally allowed us a safe place to talk. We had private time when we were given assignments to pray through and process the material."*

Peter says, *"Times of tears, time of confession . . . not so much confession of anything new but just seeking forgiveness for the pain that had been caused. I don't think anything new was confessed, but it was the act of confessing and seeking forgiveness during that time in both the painful memories and the sins committed against the marriage."*

It was during this weekend that *"a miracle happened,"* and their marriage was transformed. Peter says, *"At that time we didn't trust one another, even though we were working on the relationship. We had been so wounded by one another. We were so hurt, and literally God worked what felt like physical healing in both of us on that weekend. We were facing our twentieth anniversary that next summer. Before the retreat, we had been looking at it with a sense of resignation. After the retreat, we planned a rededication of vows ceremony. It was just an absolute miracle."* The couple still had work to do. Could they use this divine jump-start to transform distrust into trust and to continue speaking the truth in love?

Trust and Truth in Families

Fair and trustworthy family relationships are expressed through how well or poorly people manage their relationship *obligations* (what they give) and *entitlements* (what they receive or take). According to family therapist

Terry Hargrave, "The give-and-take in a relationship should be balanced so that the relationship is fair. The interdependence of a spousal relationship requires us to assume responsibility for our actions, to accept the consequences of how we carry out the relationship, and to strive for fairness and balance in the relationship's give-and-take" (2000, p. 16).

Relationship problems emerge when the balance between giving and receiving is askew in ways that allow members to shun their obligations or to take more than they are entitled to receive. Consider how this perspective sheds new light on the animosity that was so evident between the sons of Jacob (see Gen 37). The ten oldest brothers felt that Joseph received more benefits in this family than he was entitled to, while they were left with more burdens than they thought they deserved. This perceived imbalance of give-and-take led to family violence and deception (see Gen 37:19-35). This same lens helps us understand the elder brother's negative response to his father's embrace of his prodigal son (see Lk 15:25-32). Moral violations, such as the ones we have seen in our reconciling couples, bankrupt trust when wrongdoers take from the relationship unfairly and neglect their marital or familial obligations. As you read Noelle and Peter's story, did you sense their frustration about the perceived imbalance between their obligations and entitlements? Partners who feel short-changed experience resentment rather than trust.

Hargrave defines trust as "the ability to give to another freely because you believe that person will responsibly give to you what you need" (2000, p. 38). Trust is the result of mutual and reliable giving and taking. Hargrave writes, "Trust serves as the basis of intimacy in that responsible and reliable behavior on the part of the spouses allow them to predict that the other will be committed . . . and will behave in such a way that each can fit his or her life to the other's" (p. 107).

In healthy families, past acts of care are like deposits in the family's trust bank, while present acts of care earn mates credit on which requests for giving and taking are based. For example, say you assume additional responsibility at work or church. You and your mate must now renegotiate how household chores and childcare are managed between you. Based on your past trustworthiness, your partner can give to you in this way because he or she anticipates that you will give to him or her in the future in a way that balances the distribution of burdens and benefits. Your giving may be concrete ("I'll do this job that has normally been your responsibility") or intangible (frequent words of gratitude and recognition of your partner's labors on your behalf). Many times we cannot "repay," and in these cases due recognition by others of the investment of one family member becomes an important way to maintain equitable give-and-take. Trust is an essential relational resource in healthy, secure, intimate relationships (Boszormenyi-Nagy & Krasner, 1986).

Truth can also be defined within a relational context. Relational truth is many sided. In other words, two or more sides characterize relationship stories and exchanges. Minimally there is "your truth" and "my truth." Krasner and Joyce observe that "at one time in our lives, each of us has learned that our truths are inconvenient, that they are likely to cause trouble, that they tend to burden the very people whom we truly want to please" (1995, p. xxii). When we believe that our truth will "cause trouble," we may be tempted not to speak it or to speak it in ways that are manipulative. This undermines relationship trust. One solution is to speak our truth clearly and to listen to the truth of others respectfully. This truthful speaking and respectful listening describes a dialogic process called *direct address*. Krasner and Joyce write, "The choice for direct address, to surface one's truth and to elicit the truth of another, results in vital association between people who have a legacy of give-and-take in common. . . . Movement toward vital association signals a willingness to own my contribution to injustice and estrangement—in desperate hope that you will be willing to own your part" (p. xxiv).

Notice how direct address invites conversations about forgiving and repenting, that is, "a willingness to own my contribution to injustice and estrangement" and a hope that "you will be willing to own your part." It also captures much of our discussion in chapter five, where we explored the dimensions of differentiation of self and self-responsibility. Direct address is one way to speak the truth about our relationship in love (see

Eph 4:15). You can imagine that courage is regularly required for truthful speaking and respectful listening when a relationship had been wounded. Hearing another's truth and speaking your own creates anxiety (which requires self-soothing), opens opportunities to go on to maturity *and* increases trustworthiness. Within the context of reconciliation, truth and trust are restored through three processes: residual trust, direct address and merited trust.

Residual Trust

The earlier discussion of trust alluded to a reservoir of trust that builds over time as a result of one person's actual care for another (giving). Krasner and Joyce (1995) call this *residual trust*. All relationships, no matter how dysfunctional they are, contain *some* elements of trust. Every act of kindness, every compliment, every sacrifice for the sake of the relationship—no matter how small—becomes a deposit in the relationship trust account. When couples think about the balance of giving and taking in their relationship, they conduct an imaginary audit that acts like a "summation of a 'ledger sheet' that records the merit *between* people" (Krasner & Joyce, 1995, p. 12).

All couples have a sense of the balance in their trust account. Marriage expert John Gottman (1994) has discovered that couples that maintain a balance of five "deposits" to every "withdrawal" sustain stable marriages over time. When couples make too few deposits (give) relative to the number of withdrawals (take) over time, Gottman suggests that they may be set on a trajectory toward divorce. Krasner and Joyce (1995) propose that "family disappointments blind people to the residual trust that *still* exists between them" (p. 10, emphasis added).

Residual trust becomes the launching pad from which wounded partners begin to establish trustworthiness when the blinders are removed. Residual trust serves as a down payment toward future acts of trustworthiness by laying a historic foundation on which couples can begin to rebuild. First, partners tap into this residue of trust whenever they credit their partner's past actions on behalf of the relationship. You can see this at work in the following reflection from Noelle:

> *[For a time] all I could see were the warts and bumps and flaws and the pain that he had caused me. Then slowly I started seeing how he was a good father. He was a wonderful provider for us. I have more material things than I ever dreamed possible as a little girl. Not that that's important, but Peter has made it happen. He is a very tender person. When he was in the business world, he was told by several people, "You're never going to make it to the top of the corporate ladder because you're too nice." Well, you know what? That nice part of him is the part that I love, and I don't want it to become hardened so that he can climb the corporate ladder. We began doing recreational things together that we both enjoy and found we enjoyed our time together. There was no big profound "aha," but we were able to start seeing the potentiality, that we're never, ever a finished product here, and God sees all the potential.*

Second, partners draw on residual trust when they think about other family members who have been and will be affected by their decisions. Peter was seriously thinking about divorce when one wise counselor challenged him to consider the investment his children have made in their family. Peter says, *"For me, the children were a real important part of that process. When I bitterly related to my counselor that I didn't just want to do it for the children, he immediately shot back with 'That's the best reason to make your marriage work.' I think that that continued to be a motivating factor through the time—to save the children, not because I had to, but because they were part of the process."*

This emphasizes the responsibility that parents bear for the well-being of their children. Efforts that are made on the behalf of future generations are powerful and carry considerable weight.

A third source of residual trust deserves to be mentioned, even though Noelle and Peter did not highlight it. Hope for the future is sustained when mates think about their history. It is as if partners do not want to jettison their entire marital life. Positive exchanges in the past suggest the possibility of harmony and peace in the future. This benefits both transgressor and victim. Wrongdoers are encouraged to work to reclaim what was lost. Injured parties are encouraged to persevere in the face of doubts. The impact of "historical constraints" is seen in the following statements:

- *We started dating when we were seniors in high school. We grew up together. We came to the Lord a week apart. [There is] so much invested that certainly I couldn't just throw that away. I just couldn't and I didn't want to. But it was a choice I had to keep making over and over again.*
- *Even when it was crazy, there were a few things there to hang on to. We were very traditional. Birthdays were special. Thanksgiving was special. Easter. Christmas. . . . We had a lot of things that we just kept going.*
- *She knew me. She knew who I was in the failings and faults that I had. She accepted that . . . and that's hard to give up when you find that.*
- *My wife reminded me of all the good that I had tried to do for [her] and for the children, because I couldn't think of anything good that I had done. All I could think of were negative thoughts. I needed to hear that the wrong that I had done was not all that I have done. That gave me some of the hope that I was looking for to keep on looking for more hope.*

How does residual trust work to nurture reconciliation? Residual trust is the foundation from which partners begin the process of truth telling. Peter's decision to tell Noelle about his affair grew out of their residual trust fund *and* contributed to future trustworthiness. When reconciling efforts are in their infancy, residual trust is the platform from which couples say hard things to one another with the glimmer of hope that their disclosures will not demolish them. Residual trust is also the thread on which the future of the relationship may hang until a couple has accumulated a minimum number of demonstrations of changed behavior.

Direct Address

If residual trust helps couples to jump-start rebuilding by recalling trustworthy interactions from the past, direct address sustains the process. Direct address is one avenue for speaking truthfully and establishing trustworthiness in the present. It is characterized by "a willingness to know one's own truth and to risk it in the service of building fairness and trust. The choice to delineate one's truth and to elicit the truth of another can energize, catalyze, and magnify the intrinsic vitality" that lies between people who are connected (Krasner & Joyce, 1995, p. 217). Direct address requires one to have his or her voice. Noelle struggled to find her voice. *"A huge part of my problem was to find my own voice. I began to realize that God could give me strength through my relationship with him, and regardless of what Peter did or didn't do, God would be what I needed and God would be my refuge."*

Make a balance sheet of how you and your partner have experienced the give-and-take in your marriage. Because you are more likely to remember hurtful exchanges, you want to be sure to think carefully about ways in which you have exchanged acts of care over the course of your marital life. Look closely for those things you may now take for granted or even discredit, but that are actually ways your partner contributes to your family life.

Look through a family album. What stories of trustworthiness can you find in those pictures?

What do you know about who your mate "really" is that forgiving and repenting may help bring to light once again?

Direct address contributes to reconciliation in three important ways. First, it supports mutual truth telling in the form of honest dialogue between intimate partners. Second, it facilitates differentiation of self. Third, it undermines the destructive power of secrets.

Direct address and dialogue. Direct address is fundamental to dialogue. And dialogue is fundamental to trust. Dialogue unfolds in two movements. First, you must speak *truthfully* from your experience. Second, you must listen *respectfully* and *nonjudgmentally* when your partner risks speaking his or her truth (Krasner & Joyce, 1995). Krasner and Joyce propose that "people's willingness to disclose their ground and to offer consideration to the truths of another can invariably be linked to the in-built human longing to hold and be held accountable for justice owed and deserved" (p. 5). This dynamic exchange contributes to restoring the ethical dimensions of damaged relationships. Dialogue is *not* a "proclamation of what *I* feel and what *I* want, with massive disregard for the terms of another person; or my compliance with what *you* want, with massive disregard for my terms" (p. 47). Instead dialogue through direct address gives due consideration to what you owe the relationship and what you believe you are entitled to in a given context, with equal regard for your mate's terms and your own terms. You will see in the following quotations that Noelle and Peter had an opportunity for dialogue through the structure of the church's marriage retreat:

> *What it did was give us permission to go into the "no-talk rule" areas in our relationship. There were things we needed and wanted to talk about but didn't know how or where to begin. The format of the retreat provided a safe and respectful forum to discuss the difficult things. When we went to our room, there were written prayers that we had to read together. We just prayed that God would help us to be honest with each other and that there would be healing in our marriage, and God honored those prayers.*
>
> *It was real important to have personal time and privacy in our room to be able to step through those things. Those were very sad times of processing. A lot of tears, a lot of pain in working through, but it was truly cathartic and miraculous, the outcome that happened through that.*

Dialogue through direct address is not about techniques—although structured exercises that teach good speaking and listening skills may help some couples (Markman et al., 1994). Direct address is about heart-to-heart revelation. During our conversation, Peter and Noelle emphasized that standard communication techniques, the bread and butter of many marital counseling sessions, were not helpful to them. Peter said, *"Everything we were confronted with before had been skill based—how do you communicate, how do you do dates, how do you do this? None of it was from the heart. That weekend got to our hearts, and then we could move on to the other things."*

For one thing, their individual secrets robbed these tried-and-true methods of their power to create dialogue. Noelle commented, *"It just didn't work, no matter what kind of skills we were being taught, when we had these underlying secrets that we weren't willing to talk about. And of course, at that point it was easy to say it was the fault of an unskilled therapist, and so we just quit therapy [laughs]. We wouldn't own our own problems."*

Do you need help with your communication skills? Special techniques were helpful to most of the reconciling couples. If you need to learn better ways to speak and listen, seek the help of a counselor or one of the many good marriage books that are available in bookstores.

Perhaps your everyday life is filled with too many distractions for dialogue. Plan a time with your partner to put aside the phone, television, newspaper, radio and so on for a face-to-face conversation.

Peter and Noelle might have benefited from these strategies if they had been released from secret keeping earlier in their journey toward reconciliation. (I will say more about secrets and direct address in an upcoming section.) On the other hand, couples who had a "good enough" trust base discovered that these common communication strategies supported dialogue. For example, a structured communication process taught one reconciling couple how to have *"deep conversations."* Since learning how to share more profoundly, one husband can claim, *"In the past three years, my wife has never said to me, 'We can't have deep conversation.'"* Every couple with whom I talked emphasized the difference that honest communication made to their relationship. If you were to ask for before-and-after photos of these couples, one caption would read, "Before, we had guarded and insincere conversations. Sometimes we even lied to one another. Now we have honest communication, even when it hurts."

Direct address and differentiation of self. Direct address also helps to develop differentiation of self. You will recall that differentiation of self is defined as the ability to be an "I" while you are connected to someone who is important to you. For example, while they were dating, Noelle and Peter focused on their many similar interests. However, on their honeymoon, they discovered that their basic personalities were quite different. Peter interpreted these differences as "incompatibilities," a perception that contributed to his intense marital discontent. Through direct address, Noelle and Peter learned to appreciate their differences rather than degrade them. Noelle says:

> *I think that a huge key for our reconciliation was to recognize how different we are. For years we had focused on our similarities. People would look at us and call us the Bobbsey Twins because we looked the same on the outside. Yet we knew we were very different on the inside, which meant we experienced things differently emotionally. I think we felt a lot of freedom in acknowledging our differences and realizing we didn't have to be the same all the time. We were free to truly complement each other in the sense of completing each other to become whole or one.*

For Peter, personal responsibility, self-differentiation and direct address went hand in hand. As he became a "self," he recognized what he owed his marriage in addition to what he wanted out of it. This opened up a new way to interpret conflict between Noelle and him, a way that incorporates direct address. Peter says, *"Before we started personal healing, it seemed like if we disagreed about what was for dinner, that was reason, literally, for divorce. I mean, it would degrade into that sort of discussion. Since then, it is truly that the wound is now not a wound against me. It's a pain to the relationship that means it isn't whole, and I want it to be whole, where before the response was, 'This doesn't feel good. I want out.'"*

Noelle also observed how differentiation helped her deal with conflict. She is now willing to own only her relationship obligations, rather than take on both her obligations and Peter's. She says, *"I used to own all our problems. It was always my fault. Now I'm learning to stop and think when something happens, 'Well, what's this about? Is it about me or us or just Peter?' If it's about Peter, I let it go and he can process it alone, unless he asks for my input. Otherwise it's his problem to solve."*

Direct address and secrets. Family therapist Edwin Friedman called family secrets "the plaque in the arteries of communication; they cause stoppage in the general flow and not just at the point of their existence" (1985, p. 52). As Noelle observes, *"How can you have open communication if you still have secrets from each other? It just didn't work no matter what kind of skills we were being taught when we had these underlying secrets that we weren't willing to talk about."*

Friedman describes the specific and predictable impact of secrets. Secrets divide families between those who "know" and those who "don't know." Secrets create unholy alliances when those who "know" collude to hide the obvious from those who "don't know." Secrets also distort perceptions. Those who "don't know" create inaccurate explanations to account for what is going on (or not going on). Peter and Noelle felt this tension. Noelle says, *"It was also a relief when Peter acknowledged his unfaithfulness; I had suspected it for so long that the confession took away the craziness of what I was experiencing. So in that sense, it almost empowered me more too, because it affirmed what I was believing must be the truth."*

Most people keep secrets to protect themselves or somebody else. Family therapist Evan Imber-Black (1998) advises individuals to think through the ramifications of disclosing a family secret. Noelle and Peter's story suggests that repairing the damage of marital betrayal creates a unique opportunity to disclose marital secrets. Noelle put it this way: *"When the secrets came out, then there was hope for rebuilding, but prior to that, my sense was that we were just kind of standing around. [After the secrets were exposed], I felt like we were able to engage not only with our individual issues but also in our future."*

Direct address is one way that couples can expose secrets to the light.

Noelle says, *"I remember being very intentional about that. I reached a point where I told myself, 'You just need to give up everything you have and lay everything out there and have no more secrets.' It was an intentional all-or-nothing choice. If it failed, then at least I'd know I'd given it my all."*

One couple was so adamant about the damage that secrets can do to marital unity during reconciliation that the husband repeatedly said, *"No more secrets!"*

Peter and Noelle committed themselves to open and honest communication. Noelle says, *"Because our secrets were about sexuality, we committed to open communication in that area of our relationship. We acknowledged that God says sexuality is sacred in marriage and we could talk about it openly and without shame."*

Are there secrets blocking your dialogue? If so, consider the costs and benefits of disclosing those secrets to your partner. You may find it helpful to do this with a trustworthy pastor or counselor.

Merited Trust

Residual trust draws on past trustworthiness. Direct address promotes present truthfulness. Merited trust aims for the future. Merited trust is "gained through contributions, care, and direct address offered to another" (Krasner & Joyce, 1995, p. 217). Merited trust rebalances the ledgers of give-and-take because "entitlement is gained and indebtedness is balanced" (p. 217).

In healthy relationships, unacknowledged giving and receiving will still contribute to intimacy. In broken relationships, it is imperative that injured parties and transgressors *recognize* efforts of fair giving and taking. This acknowledgment is a form of merited trust, and it elicits hope for the future. Peter and Noelle's individual counseling was a kind of merited trust. Peter says, *"We were both processing through things and saw the other processing. I think the Lord brought us to a point where we both chose to do it individually as an open process."*

This type of earned trust was important, but their marriage required more. At the marriage retreat, Peter and Noelle developed a plan. In Noelle's comment you can see the importance of merited trust and recognition: "*The final step [in the marriage retreat] was developing a plan for future growth and continued commitment to each other. We took the plan very seriously, and that was where trust started rebuilding in really meaningful ways. The plan we developed addressed weak areas we wanted to strengthen as well as strengths we wanted to continue building on. Every night we read our plan together, and my trust began to grow because every night I heard Peter recommit to building our marriage.*"

According to Terry Hargrave, an experienced family therapist, "Trustworthiness is neither a promise nor a guarantee. Victims can never be sure that their spouses won't be unfaithful again, just as infidels can never be sure that their spouses will forgive them. Trustworthiness is a resource that accumulates over time to allow people to deal with each other based on realistic and valid assumptions and demonstrations of reliability" (2000, p. 171).

Trusting is a choice that transgressors and injured parties make on a daily basis during their journey on reconciliation road. Initially, great anxiety partners with tentative trust. Will he do what he says? Will she follow through? As merited trust accumulates, anxiety dissipates and trust becomes robust once again. An injured wife said it like this: "*This difficulty evaporated. And you can't really watch evaporation happen. You just*

How are you demonstrating your trustworthiness? Would it be helpful for you and your partner to create a "covenant" of trustworthiness that identifies important ways in which you will be faithful to one another?

Pay close attention to your partner during the coming week. Make a list of everything your mate does that contributes to your relationship. Tell your mate how this impacted you.

If you have pledged to be faithful to some behavioral change, how well are you doing? It is important to maintain this change whether or not your mate acknowledges it. Affirmation is nice but not necessary for you to continue to be trustworthy.

know when things are soggy wet, and you're aware when they're dry. It's not easy to identify the gradual dissipation of this wrenching experience. I very much remember saying to myself, 'Do I trust him to do this? Do I trust him to go there? Do I trust him to be somewhere else?' And I could see myself feeling more trust until I was able to say, 'Yeah, I trust him. I trust him completely.'"

Threats to Merited Trust

I grew up in northeastern Pennsylvania, where the winters are long and the springs come late. This is a perfect climate for the development of healthy potholes. This activates "pothole defensive driving" strategies. You cannot assume that a puddle is merely a puddle; puddles may be potholes in disguise. Cautious drivers approach suspicious puddles with care. In addition, drivers mark in their memory the locations of potholes that have developed along their regular routes and carefully maneuver around them. Potholes interfere with your travels only when you fail to take them seriously.

Any relationship can develop potholes. Potholes start as small relationship glitches, or lack of couple attunement, if you will. They emerge as a result of fluctuations in closeness and distance, and as a result of rebuilding setbacks. In healthy relationships, potholes are quickly repaired. Imagine that your spouse normally comes home from work in a good mood, but tonight he or she came home in a grumpy mood, and you ended up in an argument. You hit a pothole. Later in the evening or the next day, one of you might begin a brief conversation about the exchange to achieve relationship repair (saying, for example, "I'm sorry I snapped at you last night").

However, when your relationship is "under construction," that same scenario could easily escalate into something nasty. A grumpy mood may be (mis)interpreted as a sign that the person is not interested in working on the relationship and a harsh discussion may follow ("I knew you didn't care about me") rather than a sympathetic exploration ("You don't seem to be yourself tonight. Did you have a rough day?").

Relationship potholes are things you can do something about. However, they threaten to undermine merited trust because they drain trust from the account in the same way that service charges reduce the balance in your bank account. When your relationship is under construction, inattention to the presence of potholes can transform shallow ones into axle-bending ones.

Marriage researchers Howard Markman, Scott Stanley and Susan Blumberg (1994) identify four kinds of relationship potholes: (1) misunderstanding, (2) rapid escalation of a difficult discussion into a full-blown fight, (3) invalidation of your partner's experience ("How can you feel that way?") and (4) negative interpretation of the meaning behind your partner's words ("What do you mean, 'what's for dinner'?"). Misinterpretation, rapid escalation, invalidation and negative interpretation threaten merited trust because they run counter to the principles of direct address.

Markman and his colleagues recommend that couples activate their best speaking and listening skills when these threats to merited trust appear. They also suggest that couples think carefully about when might be the best time to have hard conversations. One suggestion is to create a time free of distractions (I realize that is very challenging if you have small children at home) and bring all of your communication skills with you to this session. If you sense that the discussion you need to have will take more than one session, Markman and colleagues advocate making several appointments so that this issue does not control your relationship by leaping out at you when least expected. You control when, where and how you talk about it.

Another threat to merited trust is the failure to recognize the activation of old interaction patterns. Our couples worked diligently to establish new ways to relate to one another. But old habits die hard. Most of us have experienced the difficulty of totally shaking off an old habit. You might think of ex-smokers who experience the urge for a cigarette when under unexpected and intense stress. The reconciling couples discovered the importance of being alert for this kind of relapse and for stopping its escalation. One way they did this was by creating different ways to respond if one of them slipped into an old relationship habit.

Several years after his marriage was on solid ground, one offending husband realized that he and his wife had stumbled into an old destructive pattern. The couple chuckled as they shared their experience with me. He said,

> *Last night we went into this stupid discussion. I got into "that" mode. I just started snorting and clawing the ground, and I'm just ready to go. "I'll take you on; try and hold up against my logic. See if you can stand it." And I was able to recognize that I was gearing up for the battle and my motivation to try and convince her that I was right. I sensed that it had the potential to bring forth tears, and I said [to myself], "This is crazy; I have to stop. I can't even talk to her right now." I had to actually go completely silent. I picked up my Bible. I began to read the Bible and read her to sleep. It was the only way to stop myself. It was hard to walk away from it.*

His wife added, *"Last night comes closest to the stuff that we used to do on a regular basis. I could see the humor in it, because I could see so clearly. I felt sorry for [him] a little bit. Not in a demeaning way but in a 'Oh, he's hurting' way: 'Why is he doing this? Bless his heart. He's going to feel so bad about it later.'"*

Prior to their reconciliation, this type of conversation would have escalated into a full-blown verbal assault by the husband. Fortunately he had grown enough in his level of self-differentiation that he took full responsibility for stopping his part of the exchange. His wife also recognized what was developing, but instead of becoming frozen with fear or responsible for her partner's actions, she became curious to see what he would do *about himself* and extended grace to him instead of judgment.

So remember, potholes are relationship concerns that are under your control. Just as you can drive carefully and avoid potholes in the pavement, you can act and respond in ways that will keep relationship potholes as shallow as possible and thus avoid draining your merited trust account dry. Relationship defensive driving strategies include developing awareness of when former harmful ways are reappearing and creating new healthy ways to change how the pattern unfolds. You may use good listening skills to avoid misinterpretations (Markman, Stanley & Blumberg, 1994). You may decide to take a time-out to regain self-control if you sense your temperature rising too rapidly. You may employ appropriate humor to defuse the tension. However, if you encounter too many potholes too regularly, you may want to consult with a counselor to help you repair the road before you decide that the road is too dangerous for safe travel.

Closing Thoughts

This chapter has focused on the importance of truth and trust to reconciliation. Trust is restored as couples remember ways in which each has cared for the other over the course of their lives together. Residual trust provides a foundation for direct address. Direct address cultivates truth telling, which deepens trustworthiness. Merited trust builds on that foundation to secure the relationship's future. The couples I interviewed emphasized that rebuilding trust and learning to speak truthfully takes time. Sometimes transgressors backslide and then couples have to repair the relationship pothole. I can sum up this chapter this way: No truth, no trust. Know truth, know trust.

9

CONCLUSION

We've a Story to Tell

If left to my own devices, I would read nothing but fiction. When I lose myself in a good story, I am refreshed and able to face the decisions and tasks that await me. Fiction is only one source of stories that revive me though. My family history provides another resource. For example, I come from a long line of strong women. My maternal great-grandmother was a force to be reckoned with, even though clubfeet confined her to a wheelchair. My paternal grandmother raised three children alone during an era when divorce was unseemly for respectable women. Women in my family don't swoon. They get on with life. My third source of life-affirming, hope-generating stories is the community of faith. These stories are written in the biblical text, recounted throughout church history and lived by my contemporaries within the body of Christ, such as the reconciled couples who have shared their faith journeys with us. My story is part of the larger story of the reconciling God. It is ultimately God's story that gives me the broadest interpretive horizon for my life. Fiction is nice. Family history is enlightening. The biblical story is transforming.

Stories help us make sense of life. We tell our stories to one another to share our joys and our sorrows. Our stories highlight some aspects and minimize others. They give our life a sense of coherence. Stories also help us make sense of adversity. According to trauma expert Ronnie Janoff-Bulman (1992), people talk about trauma in ways that help them strain meaning out of senseless situations. What sense we make out of life is often determined by the stories we use to interpret our experiences.

I write this book from my narrative as a white American woman who practices orthodox Christianity with Wesleyan theological roots. These narratives shape how I think about the work of God's hand in my life, especially my troubles. Earlier I suggested that the divine love story as told through the life, death and resurrection of Jesus Christ can provide the ultimate narrative horizon for our stories of betrayal. How do reconcilers talk about the "facts" of their marriage? How do these stories move them toward reconciliation?

With this chapter we add a final essential item to our list of things that are needed to travel along reconciliation road: rewriting the story of the relationship in a way that affirms reconciliation. The first part of this work focused on the commitments that sustain reconciliation. You saw how commitment to Christ, commitment to the work of reconciling and commitment to a reconciliation-friendly community nurtured the process of reconciling for the couples who shared their stories with me. The second part of this book discussed tasks that move couples toward reconciling. As mates grow up, repent, forgive, and restore truth and trustworthiness, they find that they are able to restore love and trust to their marriage.

I could have included this final chapter in the "tasks" section, but obviously I didn't! It seemed to me that, as couples became more secure in their reconciled state, a new story of their marriage emerged. For many of these couples, this process took about two to three years after their decision to work on reclaiming their relationship. The new narratives that emerged were not something these couples sat down and intentionally created, but instead they were the fruit of the couples' labors—fruit that produced more good relationship fruit.

Alicia and Mitch's story will show us how reconcilers "re-storied" their lives in ways that continued the transformation process. We will explore how the process of creative remembering and "forgetting" helped reconcilers to transform a "guilt story" into a "grace story" (Augsburger, 1996, p. 120). In addition, you will see how noteworthy episodes became benchmarks that represent important turning points in the couple's journey toward reconciliation. Moreover, we will explore how they renewed the oneness of their relationship through the emergence of a new "us." Finally, we will discuss how successful reconcilers envision their future.

Mitch and Alicia's Story

Alicia and Mitch, committed followers of Jesus Christ, married when they were young adults. During their early years of marriage, the couple joined an exciting ministry team. While church members admired the close friendship that existed between Mitch and Alicia and another pastoral couple on the team, in reality Alicia and Mitch were caught in a relationship vortex. Over time Mitch and the other pastor's wife began spending large blocks of time together. Mitch says, *"Alicia went along with my going on dates [with the other pastor's wife]—my spending several days away with this person. Initially it was the understanding between Alicia and myself [that] 'there's nothing sexual about this. We're really good friends. This is a really important friendship to me.' That was the truth initially. It slowly became untrue, but I still stood with the story 'there's nothing sexual.'"*

This pattern continued for six years. Mitch rationalized, *"I'm committed to Alicia. I do not plan to leave Alicia. This is having your cake and eating it too."*

Eventually Alicia's discontent grew. She says, *"I spent more nights than I can count on my face before God, because Mitch would be out. I just said, 'God, I don't know what to do here. I don't have a relationship with my husband, I caretake.' Yeah, we have some relationship. We do certain things together. We have roles, but we don't have a friendship. There are huge, bigger and bigger areas that we don't talk about."*

Gradually Alicia's eyes opened to the inappropriate nature of their relationship with the other couple and to how her silence had contributed to it. Alicia stopped believing that what transpired between Mitch and this woman was private. She now called it secret. Alicia confronted them both. She said, "*This has got to stop.*" Mitch had assumed that this would happen one day, and he had resolved to end the other relationship when Alicia demanded it.

Alicia and Mitch entered a period of profound personal, marital and spiritual growth. Their relationship with the Lord deepened as they responded to God's call in their lives. They began individual counseling. They developed ways to protect their marital boundaries. New ministry opportunities accelerated their individual, relational and spiritual maturation. They celebrated the births of their children. Time passed. Their marriage was secure.

Yet unfinished business lurked in the shadowy corners of their relationship. Mitch had never told Alicia the full account of his relationship with the other woman. He and Alicia did agree that he was guilty of infidelity; Alicia says, "*We came out of this with a definition of infidelity that is not physically based.*"

But he continued to deny any physical sexual misconduct. That the relationship had not become physical was a lie. Mitch says, "*I guess I carried a lot of anxiety in this little pocket. . . . 'Things are really going well, but how would they go if my wife knew, or if I disclosed in this area?'*" Mitch wondered whether it was more loving to bear his secret alone or to make a full disclosure to Alicia. Did his desire to confess arise from selfish motives to assuage his guilt or because confession was the truly loving thing to do? Mitch decided that he would confess the next time Alicia asked him if his relationship with this other woman had been sexual. That time never came, because Alicia chose to trust Mitch's word, even if she harbored doubts about his truthfulness in this one matter.

Time passed. The pressure of the secret began to wear on Mitch, and he finally told Alicia the whole truth. Mitch says, "*I do not know what all it was that I was expecting. I had rehearsed or imagined or dreaded it or feared that moment for years and years and years. I'd probably gone through all sorts of things.*"

Alicia was angry. She felt "*set up,*" because it seemed as if Mitch had waited until he knew she would not leave him because of their children.

However, she was more infuriated that Mitch had let her believe a lie than she was about the physicality of the affair. Alicia says,

> *The best sense for me was not so much he finally admitted it as I knew I was right and he's finally saying I was right. And it had more to do with me and affirming myself because I knew this already. Mitch has always encouraged [me] in most areas, but this was an area in which he kept saying, "Oh no, no, no," and all the rest of me said, "Ah, yes, yes, yes." For me the biggest disclosure had been when we decided that what had gone on—regardless of whether or not we were going to agree on the physical involvement—was infidelity.*

Fortunately Alicia was more forgiving than she was angry. Mitch says,

> *With Alicia's knowing and forgiving, I experienced a depth of God's forgiveness that touched me to the soles of my feet and to the core of my being. [It] was a part of the healing and transformation and maturing and moving forward of who I am as a person. There's a sense in which, for me, Alicia is the hero of this relationship. It's not a matter of our forgiving each other. She forgave me. It wasn't reciprocal. She's really the hero—a hero of forgiveness and acceptance. I became the recipient of the grace and the power of the forgiveness that she extended to me, which then strengthened our relationship and brought a degree of intimacy and closeness that had been absent, and closed some of the gap.*

Remembering and Forgetting

"Forgive and forget," says the old proverb. Is this true? How can Alicia forget Mitch's long-term affair? Is God's practice of forgetting our sin (Ps 103:12; Jer 31:34) one that Alicia must follow? Must she develop some form of "sanctified amnesia" before we can say she has truly forgiven Mitch? And what about Mitch? Do we want him to forget the turmoil that his actions created for his wife? Shouldn't he remember his sin so that he does not take her forgiveness for granted?

In this section we will explore the relationships between remembering, forgetting and reconciling. The path is by no means straightforward. It takes some unexpected twists and other paradoxical turns. To deal with this conundrum (should we remember or forget?), we will explore three lines of thought. The first is physiological. The second is theoretical. The third is theological. Each one uniquely contributes to our discussion. After this somewhat lengthy exploration, we will look at the outcomes of good remembering and appropriate forgetting, that is, the restoration of oneness and a vision for the future.

Before launching into our discussion, I want to make a few comments about timing and sequence. I chose the metaphor of essential items for wilderness trekking because it avoids any hint of linearity. What items you pack depends on where you are going and how long you intend to travel. A ten-minute stroll through the woods may require nothing more than sunscreen, whereas a full-blown wilderness expedition includes everything on our starter list, and then some. Nevertheless, timing and sequence do factor into this chapter. Just as I might argue that commitment to Christ surfaced among the *first things* that reconcilers packed, this chapter represents items that emerge further along on the journey; they are among the *latter things* tucked into a reconciliation backpack. Couples do not begin their journey toward reconciliation with a new story of who they are in hand, but a new story develops as they travel.

Perhaps it might be more accurate to say that this chapter features factors that are most clearly recognized in hindsight. As couples practiced repenting and forgiving, as they committed to truth and trustworthiness, as they made reconciliation a central organizing principle of their relationship and as they participated in reconciliation-friendly communities, they developed new ways to think about their relationship, recognized significant turning points in their journey, created a vision for their future—all things that addressed the question of how they should remember and forget. With that said, let's turn our attention to the first line of thought, that is, how our created nature influences the degrees to which we remember and forget.

The Physiological Stream: Wired to Remember

The physiological stream reflects our body's response to trauma. We know that highly emotional events are more deeply encoded in our brain than less emotive ones. Furthermore, negative events are more deeply encoded than positive ones. This means that negative events are very resistant to being forgotten, and they become associated with other environmental and relationship cues (Cozolino, 2002; Seigel, 1999). In other words, our memory retrieves highly charged negative events quickly, especially if they have been repeated. All reconcilers in this book would place their experience of marital upheaval as a highly charged negative event—the kind that is resistant to being forgotten.

This does not negate that some traumatic events so overwhelm us that our brain fails to encode many facets of the event, such as when accident victims cannot remember their accident. However, the types of negative exchanges that our reconcilers experienced do not fall into this category. Instead many of our couples experienced what marriage researcher John Gottman (1994) identifies as the distance and isolation cycle. This cycle develops after partners experience repeated episodes of intense, negative emotional exchanges. This emotional flooding activates the fight-or-flight mechanisms of the autonomic nervous system (for example, rapid heart rate). Over time, the brain associates these unpleasant physiological reactions and the resulting painful emotional responses with the spouse. Gottman concludes that to avoid pain, we back away from our partner, because our partner triggers these unpleasant reactions. In sum, we are physiologically wired to remember painful events and to reexperience their intensity.

Consider Joseph's response to his first sighting of his brothers in Genesis 42: "As soon as Joseph saw his brothers, he recognized them, but he pretended to be a stranger and spoke harshly to them. 'Where do you come from?' he asked. . . . 'You are spies! You have come to see where our land is unprotected'" (vv. 7, 9). Joseph repeats this accusation two more times. The ten brothers are in a tight spot. They can't seem to convince this powerful stranger of their innocence. This ruler could have them executed. Instead of death, Joseph gives them a test to prove that they are honest men: One of the ten brothers will go back to Canaan and then return to Egypt with their youngest brother, Benjamin. Meanwhile the other nine will cool their heels in Pharaoh's prison.

Joseph's apparent reactivity is consistent with the kind of reaction a person might expect when intense, negative feelings catch him or her off-guard. I find it of interest that three days pass before Joseph holds a second audience with his siblings. "Do this and you will live, for I fear God," says Joseph (Gen 42:18). Joseph's revised decree reverses the number of brothers who are to go and stay. One (instead of nine) will experience Pharaoh's "hospitality" and nine (instead of one) will collect Benjamin. I wonder what God said to Joseph during that three-day cooling-off period? Is it possible that during this time the emotional flooding that Joseph may have experienced was replaced by more clear and calm thinking? Did Joseph's concern for the welfare of the families in Canaan replace his personal need for reparation?

Mates cannot delete their memories of repeated painful exchanges as I can delete paragraphs from a manuscript. These memories and their associated emotional content surface whenever they are triggered by circumstances. I talked with several couples who affirmed the value of this interview project yet declined to participate. Consistently their reason was that they were fearful of dredging up pain. During the process of reconciliation, negative affect is gradually replaced by positive affect through the process of forgiveness (McCullough et al., 2003; Worthington, 2001). As a result, partners can recall past memories with ever *decreasing* degrees of pain. The couples who declined may indeed have been on their way toward reconciling, but they had not yet reached the point where they were secure enough in their recovery that they could remain relatively calm while discussing the things that had happened. Couples who did share their stories were not afraid of the feelings that might surface. Many husbands and wives shed tears as they reviewed particularly painful points, but they were equally likely to weep with gratitude when they talked about the joy of their reconciliation. These tears of joy by far outnumbered the tears of sadness.

Forgiveness researcher Michael McCullough (1997) suggests that forgiveness reverses the negative cascade that Gottman (1994) identified. Psychologist and forgiveness expert Everett L. Worthington (2001) proposes that after the hot emotions of anger and rage dissipate, we are likely to ruminate about the offense. *Unforgiveness* is the cold stew of resentment and bitterness that results from this process. He suggests that when people forgive they replace bitterness and resentment with empathy, humility and compassion. They do not "forget." Instead they can remember without being overwhelmed by paralyzing pain. I am suggesting that the repenting/forgiving/reconciling process follows a similar path. (Future research will verify whether or not my hunch is accurate.) As couples journey toward reconciliation, they do not "forget" what has happened; instead they discover that they are able to remember with less pain. In sum, although our brains resist forgetting, the acts of repenting and forgiving change the emotional content of what we remember. Here is how one partner voiced this aspect of remembering:

> *I think God has replaced all that. The anger. The bitterness. Whatever those yucky feelings were. I feel like he's replaced that with his love. There is so much hurt and there's so much pain that went into our relationship for so many years. But honestly, it's even hard to remember that today. Truly, I mean it really is. We can go back and we can dredge it up, and we can remember this event and that event, and you know, we could bring it all up again if we want to. But for the most part, today I just feel we're such a contented little couple.*

The new story that grows out of forgiving and repenting ushers in new patterns of interaction. In many ways this is similar to how the story of the cross of Christ invites us to leave the "old story" of our life behind (that is, to put off the old self) and to inhabit the new story as God's reconciled people (that is, to put on the new self), which is manifested by life practices consistent with membership in the community of believers (see Col 3:9-10). When old behavior patterns threaten to sneak into the picture, the apostle Paul challenges the community to remember that who they now "are" is incompatible with those "former" ways of living (Eph 2:19-22; 4:21—5:20). Reconcilers also discover that they can draw on their new story when they somehow reactivate "forgotten" harmful interaction patterns.

The Theoretical Stream: Creative Remembering

Let's plunge into the theoretical stream. A counseling movement has developed around how the stories we tell about our lives shape our identities, define our realities and affect our prospects (Freedman & Combs, 1996; White & Epstein, 1990). Our personal stories coalesce into a plot with a past, a present and an anticipated future. Narrative therapies suggest that we select some stories to remember and others not to remember. These "not remembered" stories are not necessarily forgotten, but they play a less important role in shaping who we are. The *specific* memories we use to build this plot determine the contour of the story. Clinicians from these schools propose that clients "reauthor" or "rewrite" their lives by highlighting stories of strength and growth that have been neglected and by diminishing stories of weakness and helplessness that have been accentuated.

Other lines of research explore how the accounts of painful interpersonal exchanges change, depending on who is telling the tale (injured party or wrongdoer) and the perspective they adopt (unrepentant, forgiving and so on) (Baumeister et al., 1990; Stillwell & Baumeister, 1997). For example, perpetrators tend to expand on mitigating circumstances and their own good intentions while omitting statements about responsibility, whereas victims accentuate the severity of the event and omit the perpetrator's positive actions. When couples reconcile, they also find ways to reconcile their stories by challenging the kinds of biases that I mention above. While the following quotations do not provide lengthy explanations, they do give the flavor of how some of our couples now think about their marriage. Consider these statements as reconciliation sound bites.

- *We say that we've been married thirty-one happy years and one awful year.*
- *We will be married twenty-six years. And I had one year off for bad behavior. That's what we kid each other about now.*
- *Well, out of twenty-one years, there's not been very many bad years. There were a couple of real bad times, but overall it was good.*

Memory plays a central role in how we cast our stories. Many assume that memory provides an accurate and detailed account of what happened. The scientific study of memory refutes this common assumption. We do not tap into our brain cells for an "objective report." Instead we construct our memories from the thoughts, feelings, images, smells and sensations that we experienced at the time of the event. When we "remember" something, we activate neural pathways that bring to our consciousness a reconstructed and sometimes revised version of the event (Siegel, 1999).

I remember my father's hospitalization when I was thirteen, and I remember not going to the hospital to see him. When I looked back as an adult, this puzzled me. I loved my father, so I assumed that I was somehow prohibited from going to the hospital, perhaps because of my age. When I asked my mother about this, she said that she *had* asked me if I wanted to go to the hospital every time she went to visit my father (which was daily) and I had refused to go.

Hmmm. Notice how my memory helped me to maintain a picture of myself as a dutiful daughter rather than a frightened adolescent. This is not to suggest that we make things up (although it may have seemed so to my mother). It is to say that we reconstruct our remembrance of what happened so that life makes sense to us. This is particularly important when we think about recovering from relationship betrayals. *How* we remember will affect the future of the relationship too.

In sharing our memories with one another we arrive at a common interpretation of what happened and what it means. Ross and Buehler (1994) refer to this meaning-making process as "creative remembering." Edwards and Middleton (1988) call it "conjoint remembering." In effect, our reconciling couples engaged in this process as they told me their stories. They did not talk about "just the facts." Instead they recounted a shared narrative about their experiences of betrayal and restoration. Psychologists Benjamin Karney and Nancy Frye studied the ways couples talk about the development of their relationship. These researchers found that spouses who believed their present relationship was better than it had been in the past were optimistic about their future. Karney and Frye write, "These results support the idea that partners can maintain confidence in the future of their relationship even if they acknowledge that their relationships have been less than satisfying, as long as they believe that the relationship has been improving over time" (2002, p. 234).

As reconcilers practiced the restorative factors I have described in this book, they could testify to improvement over time. The following words of Mitch illustrate this: *"I see our relationship as a continuing process [of] our love and care for each other. The need to nurture. The need to build. The need to make an investment in the relationship as ongoing. But there's a sense of security that has come out of this experience and others that says, 'We can handle anything.'"*

If you have taken an introduction to psychology class, you have probably seen pictures that play tricks on your vision. For example, there is the picture that looks either like a young woman or an old hag, or the illustration of the vase that becomes the profile of two persons facing one another. What accounts for these optical illusions? Obviously the lines on the paper never change. What changes is where you focus your attention. This dictates how your mind organizes and then attributes meaning to the image. Your focus provides an interpretive frame for your mind. Reconcilers experience a similar thing. They take the "facts" of what happened and then shift their focus so that they see an interpretation of those "facts" in ways that support reconciliation. This requires mental flexibility, a willingness to entertain alternative ways to interpret an event and a readiness to have this new interpretation change how you see yourself and your mate.

Consider the example of Joseph, son of Jacob, again. Joseph could have spent his entire life fuming about how his brothers had ostracized him from his family in a most extreme manner. He could have become a bitter man. Instead we discover evidence that he journeyed toward forgiveness. Genesis 41:51-52 records the meaning of the names of Joseph's sons. He named his first son Manasseh, saying, "It is because God has made me forget all my trouble and all my father's household," and he named his second son Ephraim, saying, "It is because God has made me fruitful in the land of my suffering." Obviously Joseph did not "forget" his brothers (he had no trouble recognizing them when they asked for grain) or his father, but he "forgot" his trouble because it receded into the background as God's blessings advanced to the foreground of his life (Volf, 1996). Joseph focused on God's blessings rather than on his suffering.

Genesis 50:19-20 provides another outstanding example of Joseph's focus. The ten sons of Jacob feared that Joseph would now take his revenge and kill them because Jacob, their father, had died. To their plea for forgiveness Joseph replied, "Don't be afraid. Am I in the place of God? You intended to harm me, but God intended it for good to accomplish what is now being done, the saving of many lives." Joseph did not diminish what had happened to him. He never *forgot* the evil that they had perpetrated against him. But he saw that event in terms of how God transformed an evil event by filling it with new meaning (the saving of many lives).

Psychologist and forgiveness researcher Steve Sandage calls this process "extending the narrative horizon" (Shults & Sandage, 2003). When reconcilers rewrite the story of their relationship, the nature of their revision depends on where they place their focus. For example, when Mitch and Alicia look back over their early years, they do not see a "transgressor" and an "injured party"; they see "two kids." This perspective opens new possibilities for their future. Mitch says, *"Alicia talks about 'when we were kids.' That's it. We see that as something before. We've changed through a variety of different things, and we've changed together. We've changed for each other. We've changed on behalf of ourselves and also on behalf of the relationship. And we're committed to continue to do that so that there's never any point of saying, 'This is who you are and so this won't work.' Or 'You are a problem here.' If we have a problem then we work on it. We change."*

Alicia says, "*It's not an experience that defines 'now he is the one who sins' and 'I am the one who forgave' and we are going to be that for the next thirty years. Oh, what a power trip! [laughs] Honestly! What a power trip. Noooo.*"

Here are some examples of how other couples attributed new meaning to their betrayal stories:

- *I honestly feel we had to go through as a family what we went through to get us to where we're at today. And I'm just pretty darn tickled [with] where we're at today.*
- *It's making these wise decisions now. This is the second half of our lives. Let's do it up right. And in our thinking, doing it right was whatever God called us to do. Let's be obedient to him. So it was a wonderful time of just communicating and looking forward to everything.*
- *My husband and I both feel that everything that ever happened to us brought us to this point [of being reconciled].*

The Theological Stream: God's Memory

Our third stream is theological. What role does remembering or forgetting play in our relationship with God? The biblical narrative emphasizes that God remembers his covenant with us even as he forgets our sins. Theologian Gregory Jones comments:

> When God promises to "blot out [Israel's] transgressions" and "not remember [Israel's] sins" (Isaiah 43:25; see also Jeremiah 31:34), God is not simply letting bygones be bygones. Rather, God is testifying to God's own gracious faithfulness. Moreover, such forgiveness provides a way to narrate the history of Israel's sinfulness

> within the context of God's covenant of grace. To be sure, such a narration makes it possible, and even necessary, to forget the sin. But the past itself, the history, is and needs to be remembered so that a new and renewed future becomes possible. (1995, p. 147)

Theologian Miroslav Volf argues that God engages in "redemptive forgetting" (1996, p. 136) or the "grace of nonremembering" (p. 138). Volf proposes that at the point that God makes "all things new," "all things old" (including our pain and suffering) will pass into oblivion and will cease to exist (Rev 21:1). How else could heaven be free from tears and sadness (see Rev 21:4)? On the other hand, the crucified Lamb of God (see Rev 5:6-14) is an ever-present reminder of the cost of our reconciliation with God. Volf writes,

> How can God forget the wrongdoings of human beings? Because at the center of God's all-embracing memory there is a paradoxical monument to forgetting. It is the cross of Christ. God forgets humanity's sins in the same way God forgives humanity's sins: by taking sins away from humanity and placing them upon Godself. How will human beings be able to forget the horrors of history? Because at the center of the new world that will emerge after "the first things have passed away" there will stand a throne, and on the throne there will sit the Lamb who has "taken away the sin of the world" and erased their memory (Revelation 22:1-4; John 1:29). (1996, pp. 139-40)

God remembers and God forgets. God remembers who we are as he sees the face of Christ reflected on our face. He forgets our sins because they will "pass away." Yet while we anticipate Christ's return, when the new will supersede the old, we must live in the now. The now includes our imperfect and hurtful ways of relating to one another. While calling us to a certain kind of forgetting, Volf also calls us to *remember* injustice until justice is restored. We are not called on to subject ourselves to abusive behavior at the hands of our mate or to condone repeatedly untrustworthy actions. These call for confrontation. However, when repenting and forgiving lead to reconciling, then Volf (1996) and fellow theologian Gregory Jones (1995) challenge us to remember. We remember so that we do not repeat our sinful interactions. One offending wife put it like this: *"I haven't forgotten that it happened, and I'm not in fantasyland, thinking that everything is going to be wonderful from now on and that that didn't really happen; we know that it did really happen. I don't want to forget that it happened because I don't want to repeat the past. I don't want to sweep it under the rug."*

Are there times when images of the past sabotage your present efforts by bleeding into your exchanges? Can you find a way to say, "That was then and this is now," so that past pain does not distort present realities?

We remember so that we can celebrate the goodness of God and rejoice in the progress that has been made. Another spouse said, *"There's times when it's very necessary, I think, to recall [the betraying event]. Just remember well. I think it's good to remember where we came from and to see where we are today."*

We remember so that we can distinguish between "then" and "now" when past pain seeps into present situations. You can see this in the following statement: *"Now when we're faced with [relationship pain], we can truly say, 'That was then and this is now, and we're on this side.'"*

Benchmark Events

Another way couples write a new story about their relationship is through the identification of episodes that become benchmarks on their journey toward reconciliation. Surveyors create benchmarks to mark a point of known elevation. The benchmark is usually cut into some durable object, such as stone, and it serves as a reference point for determining elevations. Benchmark events remind couples of important turning points in their rebuilding history, or they serve as reference points that help couples to see how far they have come. These are events to be remembered!

In the Old Testament, the Israelites followed a similar practice. For example, after successfully crossing the Jordan River with the children of

Israel, Joshua set up at Gilgal twelve stones that the priests had taken out of the Jordan. Joshua explained,

> In the future when your descendants ask their fathers, "What do these stones mean?" tell them, "Israel crossed the Jordan on dry ground." For the LORD your God dried up the Jordan before you until you had crossed over. . . . He did this so that all the peoples of the earth might know that the hand of the LORD is powerful and so that you might always fear the LORD your God. (Josh 4:21-23, 24)

The priest Samuel constructed a reminder after God helped the Israelites subdue the Philistines: "Then Samuel took a stone and set it up between Mizpah and Shen. He named it Ebenezer, saying, 'Thus far has the LORD helped us'" (1 Sam 7:12). When we "raise our Ebenezers," as we are encouraged to do in the hymn "Come Thou Font of Every Blessing," we mark the special places in our lives where God has helped us.

Alicia and Mitch raised at least three Ebenezer stones. The first was when they ended their enmeshed relationship with the other ministry couple. Alicia says, *"This whole situation back then is one of those slightly larger than normal piles of rock that is a place that God worked. He changed me. He gave us the strength to change ourselves."*

The second Ebenezer involved Alicia's seeking advanced training for her chosen vocation. To pursue this, the couple had to relocate for six months. Mitch says, *"This was again a step and a commitment that we don't just do what I want to do. This is something for you."*

The third Ebenezer revolved around medical complications that threatened their child's life. Alicia says, *"We've had confirmation of God's grace under fire and also confirmation from our viewpoint as a couple that we can stand up to some pretty tough things that [might make] other people crumble. So it gives you a little more confidence, I think."*

Mitch adds, *"[It came] after our child had been born, which was a very traumatic and miraculous experience in which we both felt deeply touched by the hand of God and given to by God. We both lived in a certain sense of grat-*

itude. And when you are feeling grateful, it's hard not to be forgiving."

Why is it important to note Ebenezer events? First, couples tend to evaluate their current degree of recovery with an ideal image of the future. They could resort to thinking, *If we are not* all *better then we are not better* at all. This perspective is not particularly helpful, especially during early phases of rebuilding. Couples are likely to say, "We have so much further to go" and become discouraged. Conversely, if they make note of where they *have* been as compared to where they *are*, they are likely to say, "We have come a long way" and be encouraged. Ebenezer stones mark important moments when progress became evident.

Try drawing a reconciliation timeline. On one end mark your "start" date, month or moment. Then recall in chronological order the significant turning points that you and your partner have experienced. Stop when you come to "today." What relationship differences exist between when you started and where you are now? What would be the next small step you and your mate can take to help you continue your journey?

Second, Ebenezers help couples reauthor their relationship by becoming "chapters" in their reconciliation story. These chapters of hope encourage couples to persevere. According to psychologist Kenneth Gergen,

> People carry with them many stories and within this repertoire they can typically locate stories of value, wonderment, and joy. . . . These stories are valuable resources, almost like money in the bank. To draw them out and place them in motion . . . is to invest in new visions for the future. In sharing these stories confidence is stimulated that indeed the vision can be realized. In effect, appreciative narratives unleash the powers of creative change. (1999, p. 177)

Third, Ebenezer stones draw couples closer to God and remind them that their marital story is embedded in God's reconciliation story. Here we remember our own state as God's forgiven ones, who display his

How are you remembering what happened? Do your Ebenezer moments stand out, or have they been overshadowed by moments of shame and betrayal? What difference would it make if you wrote down every positive episode that you have shared since you started to rebuild and posted this list so that you could review it daily and add to it?

character when we reconcile with one another (see Mt 18; 2 Cor 5). We have already noted that recalling times when we have been forgiven elicits gratitude and humility, emotions that facilitate repenting and forgiving. Psychologist David Augsburger says it like this: "A gift story replaces the old guilt story, a grace story now includes injuries and losses, lifting them out of a truncated resentment story and setting them in an open-ended story of forgiveness" (1996, p. 120).

One offended wife was delighted to tell me the story of a gift she had commissioned especially for her husband. It was her way of telling him that he meant something special to her—he was worth her effort to commission this beautiful gift.

Renewed Oneness

As couples journey toward reconciliation, they develop a renewed sense of oneness. Marriage therapist Terry Hargrave defines oneness this way: "'Us' is what we are together. 'Us' is created by two individuals in a committed relationship; it takes on a personality with characteristics of its own. It is not just two individuals who share, it is two individuals who give up part of themselves to create a oneness, an 'us'" (2000, p. 6).

Marital researcher Scott Stanley considers oneness a factor that lies at the heart of commitment. "The identities of two mates are joined together to form a new, third identity of 'us,' where 'we' becomes a crucial element of life together" (1998, p. 161). I suspect that you too thought of the biblical description of marriage as two becoming one (Gen 2:24). You will want to also keep in mind that this "one" includes two differentiated and whole persons (see chapter five) who commit to a relationship that can reflect self-giving love, mutuality, reciprocity and grace—as in the Trinity. Marital betrayals damage or destroy this sense of oneness (Hargrave, 2000). Reconciliation restores it.

A sense of coupleness—or "we-ness"—develops as each mate becomes as concerned about what happens to "us" as he or she is about what happens to "me." Marriage experts Hargrave (2000) and Stanley (1998) observe that couples with a strong sense of "us" are as aware of their responsibilities to their relationship as they are of their individual rights. But they do not let their sense of personal entitlement destroy their oneness. Nor do they let their oneness destroy their individuality. You can see this expressed in the following statements:

- *We've dealt with some things differently since then [the offense]—gradually changed our approach to our marriage, to our decision making. We've begun to join forces in things. . . . It's much more of a relationship now than it was. It's much more the two of us building something together.*
- *I certainly think another layer of the rebuilding is to feed each other's strengths and realize what these strengths can contribute to life in general and to our relationship.*
- *We look back on that as partners at that time. We went through this together. Not only did we go through that together, we went through this forgiveness and reconciliation together.*

Notice how the above quotations highlight "us" or "we-ness." This sense of bonding is not bondage but belonging. This belonging is not possessive ownership but a nonpossessive love that values the individuality of the other as it does the identity of the self. This sense of "us" emerges as couples participate in shared activities, prioritize their marriage above other relationships and engage in the everyday talk that promotes intimate conversations (Duck, 1994).

You may recall from chapter three that marital reconciliation takes two people who are committed to the hard work of relationship transformation. But can we call this "teamwork"? In the movie *Remember the*

Titans an African American football coach tries to bring a sense of "us" to his racially mixed team. Football practices are a disaster because the players do not play as a team, even though they are playing for the same team. As the story unfolds, the coach creates ways for these players to get to know one another. Respect grows among them and true teamwork emerges.

A similar process happens in marital reconciliation. A husband and wife first join forces to save their marriage. True teamwork emerges as constraint commitment changes to dedication (chapter three), and the sense of "us" is reborn. Teamwork not only becomes apparent as a result of reconciling, but it also serves to maintain the benefits of reconciliation when trouble comes.

Roadblocks and detours are troubling external circumstances that impinge on all relationships. You do not create them, but you must deal with them. You lose your job because your company is downsizing. You and your mate must now adjust to these new circumstances. An accident or illness disables one spouse. The marital team must redistribute family roles and responsibilities to accommodate this unfortunate situation. Decisions must be made about caring for elders in the extended family. Do you invite your aging relative to live with you or not? Roadblocks and detours may emerge during any phase in the family life cycle.

Reconciling relationships face these normal types of roadblocks and detours as well as some that are particular to reconciliation (such as your counselor moving away). The choices couples make regarding roadblocks and detours will influence their journey of reconciliation. Our reconcilers decided to manage them as a team.

One couple moved across the country to be closer to the wife's father, who was in failing health. They had made substantial and dramatic changes in their formerly wounded relationship, and each felt that the decision to relocate was the right one to make. However, the cost of living prohibited them from immediately buying a home of their own, so they moved in with the wife's father. The couple quickly discovered that three people in a trailer gave them little marital privacy. At the time of our conversations, they were in the process of thinking through their options. They sensed that the closeness they had worked so hard to achieve before the move was becoming ragged around the edges. This alarmed them. The husband said, *"We keep saying to one another, 'Talk to me, talk to me.'"* They were as determined to maintain their marriage as they were to fulfill their care for her father. They were dealing with the situation as a team. This detour was becoming a place of grace.

A New Identity

The above elements—creative remembering, benchmark events and renewed oneness—help reconcilers develop a new sense of who they are. They not only have a sense of "we-ness," but the "us" who they have become is something new. Their couple identity is not created merely from the facts of their lives (wedding date, age, addresses, occupations) or from a catalog of their comings and goings. It requires an interpretive lens or frame through which they make sense of the facts and the events. Chapter two established that these reconcilers interpret the facts of their lives through the interpretive horizon of the cross of Christ. Theologians Stanley Grenz and John Franke write, "To be a Christian entails coming to see the story of God's action in Christ as the paradigm for our stories. As Christians we share an identity-constituting narrative" (2001, p. 48).

What cultural or community stories frame how you think about your wounded relationship? Do these stories give you hope for your future? If not, how might alternative stories give you hope? What role does God's story play in your interpretation of your relationship?

Notice how the stories of reconciliation mirror the grand story of our redemption. In Colossians 3:9-10 we read, "Do not lie to each other, since you have taken off your old self with its practices and have put on the new self, which is being renewed in knowledge in the image of its Creator." According to Grenz (2001), these verses bring two distinct, biblical narratives into sight. The first is the story of creation and sinful humankind (the old self). The second is the story of salvation and reconciliation, centered in the cross of Christ (the new self). Grenz continues, "In believers these two narratives coalesce into a composite story—namely, the story of being transferred from the narrative of sin into the narrative of grace" (p. 255).

Reconcilers experience this transfer not only in their relationship with God but, equally important, in their relationship with one another. The process of "re-author-ization" tells the story of their being transferred from a narrative of transgression to a narrative of reconciliation. Here is how Alicia and Mitch express this:

> Mitch: *We are committed to growth and change. Therefore we are committed to the fact that we are different people now than we used to be; that this is understood—that we're different now than we used to be. That may be me who did that, but I'm different now. And we acknowledge that in each other. We're not bringing up stuff from the past because that was a part of a different person.*
>
> Alicia: *Throughout all of this mess [we were] feeling more and more like we were admitted to the human condition. . . . It's just the way it is.*
>
> Mitch: *I guess we really engineered it together and built together to bring closure to that period of our lives and to give us more freedom to relate in the present and in the future as well.*

A Vision for the Future

"Stories give us *vision*" (Augsburger, 1996, p. 118). Much has been written these days about vision and mission statements for companies, families, marriages and individuals. A vision statement sets the direction for the future. At one point the only vision statement our reconcilers had on their plate was "to do whatever it takes to restore our marriage" (chapter three). As their pilgrimage toward reconciliation took shape, these couples began to imagine what a reconciled future would look like. One couple had their counselor witness their "marriage covenant." This public commitment (Worthington, 2001) to reconciliation fortified their efforts. Another couple wrote their own vision statement and reviewed it *together* each evening. The new story of their relationship included a new plot and a new ending. For example, Mitch said, "*[Alicia says], 'We were kids then. Let's leave that. And we don't have to keep dragging it forward.' So it was permission to leave it behind that she gave me. And I guess to some degree gave us a freer future because I didn't have this thing hanging over my head about what might blow up along the way.*"

Other reconcilers saw their future in more concrete terms. One mate expressed it this way: "*[We're] talking about retiring now—sharing in dreams together of the future and what it's going to be like when the kids have left home and having that freedom. . . . We're looking forward to spending the future together.*"

One couple's journey of reconciliation inspired them to rethink their life direction. Neither one was enamored with their current occupation, even though they were respected and successful in their chosen fields. Both wanted to invest the rest of their lives in something more meaningful. After a heart-searching discussion, they decided to pursue master's degrees in counseling. Here is what one of them said about that transition:

> *When we started talking about going to graduate school and sharing a vision of doing therapy together, that was a real bonding experience for me. We sat down and started just talking about the frustrations of the career track, how it's just kind of a job and where do we find our passion in life, what's fulfilling for us, and for both of us, it was dealing with heart issues, not business. So it was just kind of a gradual building-block process.*

Another couple had doubted that their marriage would survive the betraying event so that they could celebrate their twenty-fifth anniversary. Now they are dreaming of their marital future after that anniversary. Here is what they say:

[Our dream is] to grow old together. . . . We've got this thing about being able to spend retirement time at the ocean. We think about that. I don't know if that will ever happen, but it's out there.

We haven't put any plans to it at this point. It's a dream. We're wanting to be involved grandparents. . . . We really want to love on our grandkids when it's time for us to do that. That's a neat dream.

Visions of new futures *together* developed as couples gained increasing measures of love and trust in their marriage. It was as if they said, "Now that we are confident that there will be an 'us' in our future, what do *we* want to do?" All couples emphasized that they were dedicated to protecting their relationship. And all agreed that what they now have is superior to what they had. Many speak at churches or retreats about their marital transformation. While they would not want to repeat the process, they certainly could offer this paraphrase of Joseph's words: "This evil nearly destroyed us, but God has redeemed our situation so that now we have a story to tell that may bring hope to others who are traveling along reconciliation road" (see Gen 50:20).

What vision do you have for your future? Perhaps a marital vision or mission statement would help you make your vision visible. If you have such a vision statement you might want to review it. How might you update it to reflect your current journey?

WRAPPING UP

The stories of our reconciling couples affirm that morally—even mortally—wounded marriages can find new life. This new life begins when couples embed their story of transgression and betrayal within God's larger story of redemption and reconciliation. Couples engage the process of creative remembering, the collaborative activity of "rewriting" their love story. This re-vision does not diminish the fact that betrayal nearly doomed their marriage to destruction. It does not call evil by any other name. Nevertheless the new revised version includes accounts of forgiveness and repentance, as evidenced by Ebenezer moments in the couples' rebuilding histories. Couples declare, "This is *our* story." They now face a future *together* with a sober realization of what they almost lost, a deep appreciation for what they have restored and a bright hope for the future. If you have successfully traveled along reconciliation road, think about the story you tell yourselves about your relationship. How might your story bring hope to others? Do you too have a story to tell?

APPENDIX A

Resources for Reconciliation

The reconciling couples who were interviewed for this study often mentioned particular resources that helped them. These resources are listed below, with bibliographic or contact information as appropriate.[1] Descriptive information is drawn from respective websites.

Books

Al-Anon Family Group. (1976). *Blueprint for progress: Al-Anon's fourth-step inventory for Al-Anon and Alateen groups*. New York: Al-Anon Family Group Headquarters.

Allendar, D. B., & Longman, T. (1995). *Intimate allies*. Wheaton: Tyndale.

Blackaby, H. T., & King, C. V. (1994). *Experiencing God: How to live the full adventure of knowing and doing the will of God*. Nashville: Broadman & Holman.

Carmichael, A. (1999). *Mountain breezes: The collected poems of Amy Carmichael*. Fort Washington, PA: Christian Literature Crusade.

Carter, D., & Jaenicke, D. (1992). *Torn asunder: Recovering from extramarital affairs*. Chicago: Moody.

Crabb, L. (1988). *Inside out*. Colorado Springs: NavPress.

Harley, W. F. (1986). *His needs, her needs*. Old Tappan, NJ: Revell.

MacDonald, G. (1988). *Rebuilding your broken world*. Nashville: Oliver-Nelson Books.

---

[1]This list does not represent my endorsement of these resources. Readers will need to determine which items may be of help to them. Additional resources may be found in the reference list.

Markman, H., Stanley, S., & Blumberg, S. (1994). *Fighting for your marriage: Positive steps for preventing divorce and preserving a lasting love.* San Francisco: Jossey-Bass.

Shostrom, E. L., & Montgomery, D. (1978). *Healing love: How God works within the personality.* Nashville: Abingdon.

Swindoll, C. (1988). *Laugh again.* Dallas: Word.

Wheat, E. (1980). *Love life for every married couple: How to fall in love, stay in love, rekindle your love.* Grand Rapids: Zondervan.

Yalom, I. (1992). *When Nietzsche wept.* New York: Basic Books.

Centers or Programs

Alcoholics Anonymous. Alcoholics Anonymous is a fellowship of men and women who share their experience, strength and hope with each other that they may solve their common problem and help others to recover from alcoholism. The only requirement for membership is a desire to stop drinking. There are no dues or fees for AA membership; the organization is self-supporting through contributions. AA is not allied with any sect, denomination, politics, organization or institution; does not wish to engage in any controversy; and neither endorses nor opposes any causes. Its members' primary purpose is to stay sober and help other alcoholics to achieve sobriety.

Telephone numbers for Alcoholics Anonymous are often listed in local telephone directories. Outside the United States and Canada, you may contact the international General Service Office nearest you, or visit the website <www.alcoholics-anonymous.org>.

Bible Study Fellowship. BSF International is an interdenominational, not-for-profit, international, lay Christian organization not affiliated with any church or group of individuals or underwritten in any way.
www.bsfinternational.org
877-273-3228

Freedom in Christ Ministries. The mission of Freedom in Christ is to equip the body of Christ to be alive and free in him. Its vision is to boldly

and strategically supply resources to leaders worldwide to establish the church free in Christ.
9051 Executive Park Drive, Suite 503
Knoxville, TN 37923
865-342-4000
www.ficm.org

Link Care Foundation. Link Care began in 1965 and exists to help educate, train and counsel missionaries and pastors in order to help them be more effective in life and ministry. Link Care has worked with more than one hundred different denominations and mission boards.
1734 W. Shaw Avenue
Fresno, CA 93711-3416
Counseling Center phone: 559-439-2647
www.linkcare.org

Marble Retreat. Marble Retreat is an interdenominational psychotherapy center serving Christian ministers in crisis. It offers a blend of spiritual and emotional approaches to touch the whole person. Its mission is "helping to bring healing and restore hope to those in vocational Christian ministry through Christ-centered, brief, intensive psychotherapy."
139 Bannockburn
Marble, CO 81623
888-216-2725
www.marbleretreat.org

Overcomers Outreach. Overcomers Outreach is a ministry that was born out of the deep need for a support system for individuals and families within evangelical Christian churches. Overcomers Outreach support groups use the Bible and the twelve steps of Alcoholics Anonymous to minister to individuals who are affected by alcohol, mind-altering drugs, sexual addiction, gambling, food and other compulsive behaviors or dependencies. Family members are welcome at meetings. The message is based on the Bible, and the ministry is motivated by the love of

God. Overcomers Outreach's mission is to bring the gospel of Jesus Christ to the hurting and to meet human needs in his name without discrimination. Overcomers Outreach is a bridge between the church and the traditional twelve-step programs.
P.O. Box 2208
Oakhurst, CA 93644
800-310-3001
www.overcomersoutreach.org

The Walk to Emmaus. The Walk to Emmaus is a spiritual renewal program intended to strengthen the local church through the development of Christian disciples and leaders. The program's approach seriously considers the model of Christ's servanthood and encourages Christ's disciples to act in ways appropriate to being "a servant of all."
Upper Room/Walk to Emmaus
1908 Grand Avenue
P.O. Box 340004
Nashville, TN 37203-0004
877-899-2780
www.upperroom.org/emmaus/

APPENDIX B

Advice About Reconciliation

The following excerpts are reconcilers' responses to the question, "What advice would you pass on to others as a result of your experience?"

An Attitude of Prevention

People who take their spouses for granted, thinking they're always going to be there, [assume], "They'll never divorce me because they're committed to marriage." That's when you have to watch out [and] to not take it for granted that your spouse is getting everything that they want just because they don't tell you what's wrong.

I guess for young marrieds I would say that it is insidious to get into a routine, or drifting apart. It happens real subtly a lot of times and before you know it, you're not in touch with each other. We always thought we were doing a good job of guarding our relationship, and somehow or another we let that slide. . . . A relationship takes tending.

I think the other thing would be that trust isn't a given. And when it's lost, it's very difficult to rebuild. . . . The relationship builds over time, and that trust grows over time. You make a commitment and you get married and you can't just rest on it and think, "Well, it's always going to be there." It [trust] can still be fragile in a marriage. So you have to guard that trust.

Talking about pornography or something: don't think you're not vulnerable. Marriages can be vulnerable at any point, and if this is a prob-

lem before you get married, don't think it's going to go away after you get married. . . . You can be vulnerable to it at any point. It's not always something that happens because of early childhood trauma. It's something that can erupt at a time of stress. So you just have to guard your heart.

God's Role

I really would like to let people know that God's preparing you for the things that you're going through. This is not something that is outside of his hand that he can't take care of. He's not going to just give you the package the day that everything happens and say, "Okay, here's what you need to handle this situation." He's been walking you and building you all the way along. And that's what I see when I look back over my life.

I don't know how most of the marriages make it without putting Christ in the center. Whenever a relative gets married and I know that they aren't Christians, I think to myself, "You know, you've got a fifty/fifty chance." I just don't think you can do it without putting him in the center and without asking him into the marriage every day. I don't know how marriages last that don't do that. It's so vital now, so incredibly vital.

Don't be afraid to learn about Jesus. Just to have an open mind and to know that there is nothing wrong with accepting him. Life would be a lot easier with him than it is without him.

Watch for what God's going to do, because if you invite God into that process [reconciliation], he'll do above and beyond what you'll ever imagine. He's not going to be happy just putting the pieces back together the way they were. He is going to make a whole new, beautiful thing. It's not just putting you back where you were. When God's involved, it's making it better. So let him fix what he wants to fix.

Understanding from Others

I think it would be so helpful to have a pastor at that particular point in some form or fashion sharing your marriage. I just think that it's such a time when pastors can . . . surround that couple with so much love that it will foster growth. But then, at the same time I think God will send people if you do not have a pastor there. And I think that's what happened to us.

I just wish people understood suffering more clearly. I think what happens is when someone is suffering, we attribute all kinds of things to their personality and character that are misnamed, mislabeled. Let the person just rest with you in their suffering, help them name it, help them see it, help them know that it's not always going to be like this. There is more to them than their suffering. There was a prehistory, there was a post-history, and it's okay, and when life smacks you in the face, it is personal. It is happening to you and no one else will ever feel it to the depth that you feel it. And it's okay to sense the deep personalness of this. And no one will ever carry that burden in the same way that you do. And however far you fall, you're not falling farther than any other human being. But, you know, it's just . . . it's happening and you're in the middle of it. And it is all right to be a person in a period of suffering.

Managing the Crisis

I thought the really important thing . . . is just not to beat up on the other person. Don't let the weeds grow up.

The four people who need to be there to do it [reconciliation]: the two spouses, the competent counselor and God.

I like the word intentional. *It's real easy to guard a relationship, but still I think it's important to be real intentional about doing things that build one another up and that put us in the place to share. That's different for a lot of different people, but when you find those things that help you to connect, be intentional about doing that—be intentional to show your spouse that you cherish them.*

Look for those areas where you can have some hope. Maybe sometimes it's biting off a little bit at a time. Look for that hope for the next two weeks instead of thinking about the long road. Sometimes it may be only getting through the day and not leaving. And that's okay. If that's what you can accomplish, then that's what you can accomplish. And try to rejoice in the small steps. And rejoice for one another in the small steps. Celebrate those. Instead of looking at the ten million things you didn't do, I see the one thing, and I'm really glad, and I'm really grateful. Express that gratitude or appreciation. . . . "I know this is really hard on you. It's risky for you to do and I appreciate that."

I think there are two broad areas that I want to suggest. The first one has to do with self-understanding and responsibility. If you need to grow in self-understanding and to work at developing perspective, [do it]. I guess my lesson was that I needed to work harder at knowing who I was and then taking responsibility for that and taking action as I understood that. And the second piece would be that I think there are times when it's unrealistic for a couple to expect to work everything out just on their own, and they need to look for a wise, objective third party, whether that be a counselor, a pastor or objective friend, who can really give some outside perspective. You really begin chasing your tail in a circle after a while with some things, and somebody else needs to get you back on the path. So looking for some constructive help would be another piece that I think would be helpful.

I think a lot of it was talking a lot. Spending a lot of time together. Figuring out what was really important. Majoring on the major things. Deeper dependence on God than ever before and suffering through that. Daily grieving of just being in a fallen world is important. Just realizing that the place of emptiness isn't going to go away and that's not [your spouse's] fault. And realizing that because she's my wife and because I love her and because I'm vulnerable, she will hurt me incredibly, again, even if she doesn't mean to, she will. And knowing that's going to happen. Knowing that we don't live in a perfect world. Realizing that on a way deeper level. It's really owning that—the pain that comes with that.

I think to have true restoration, there had to be a willingness for both of us to truly be vulnerable and just to trust that process.

jured parties. They commit to change in concrete ways that seek to restore trust and love. Authentic apology says, "I did it. I am sorry. Here is how I will change."

awareness. Part of the process of repentance. When transgressors develop awareness, they change how they think about themselves, the injured party and the event. They can view the event through the eyes of the wounded person. Humility and empathy facilitate awareness.

confession. Involves admission of guilt and sorrow about what happened and about what is happening. Confessions often include the promise of changed behavior. A good confession communicates to the injured party that the wrongdoer understands the victim's perspective and experience, and credits this perspective.

dialogue. Unfolds in two movements. First, you must speak *truthfully* from your experience. Second, you must listen *respectfully* and *nonjudgmentally* when your partner risks speaking his or her truth.

differentiation of self. "The capacity to be an 'I' while remaining connected" to significant others (Friedman, 1985, p. 27). When you are an "I," you are clear about what you think, feel, want and desire, and you are able to let others have their own thoughts, feelings, wants and desires without you feeling threatened or diminished. You value yourself for your own made-in-the-image-of-God uniqueness and you value others for theirs. You can differentiate between your thinking and feeling, and you can decide which of these functions takes the lead during intense (that is, anxious) interpersonal exchanges. You fear neither engulfment nor abandonment by significant others. You tolerate pain for the sake of growth.

direct address. Truthful speaking and respectful listening that happens in a dialogic process.

empathy. The ability to adopt another person's perspective. Includes cognitive perspective-taking ("I see what you are saying," or "I can understand how you feel that way") and empathic concern for the feelings of another person.

entitlement. A sense of what others owe us relationally.

forbearance. Postponement of enforcing one's rights, privileges and assertions. Includes refraining from avoiding the wrongdoer or seeking revenge. Also includes a continuance of benevolent and kind actions and attitudes toward the transgressor.
forgiveness. The process of replacing negative emotions such as anger, rage, resentment and bitterness with positive emotions such as empathy, compassion, humility and love. For members of God's reconciled kingdom, gratitude for our own forgiveness can motivate our desire to forgive one another.
fundamental attribution error. A common way for people to account for their own or another's actions. The self is credited when the action is desired, while the actor cites circumstances if the action is undesired. The observer blames the other if the action is undesired but cites circumstances if the action is desired.
guilt. Evokes negative evaluation of specific actions without becoming enmeshed with a negative evaluation of the self. Guilt concludes, "I did something wrong, and there is a way to fix it."
humility. Includes looking at one's self soberly (see Rom 12:3) and having a modest sense of one's own importance. Involves *realistically* acknowledging both strengths and shortcomings.
magnitude gap. A condition in which injured parties and wrongdoers view the transgression and its impact diferently. Injured parties see the consequences of the offense in a more serious light than transgressors do.
merited trust. Gained through contributions, care and direct address offered to another.
obligations. Actions and/or attitudes that we "owe" to another. These are our relationship debts.
rebuilding trustworthiness. Demonstrations of consistent changed behavior over time by wrongdoers. The behavioral changes relate to the offense in ways that are meaningful to the injured party.
reconciliation. An active commitment to the restoration of love and trustworthiness by both injured party and transgressor so that their relationship may be transformed.

repentance. A decisive *turning away* from thoughts, words and deeds that have betrayed love and trust, and a wholehearted *turning toward* attitudes and activities that can restore love and trust to the relationship. Includes confession and a commitment to consistent changed behavior over time.

residual trust. A reservoir of trust that builds over time as a result of one person's actual care for another.

restoration. One phase in Terry Hargrave's model of forgiveness within families (Hargrave, 1994, 2001). Helps transgressors and injured parties rebuild love and trust through giving opportunities for compensation and through the overt act of forgiving. An interpersonal process.

salvaging. One phase in Terry Hargrave's model of forgiveness within families (Hargrave, 1994, 2001). Helps injured parties to understand "the circumstances of the abused and abuser, so that one does not carry the burden of pain alone" (Hargrave, 2001, p. 10). This happens through insight and understanding. An intrapersonal process.

self-responsibility. Allows us "to work at seeing the parts of ourselves that contribute significantly to our own pain and our relationship discomfort. . . . [It] is the ability to see a relationship problem as a result not only of the other person's limitation but also of one's own" (Guerin, Fogarty, Fay & Kautto, 1996, p. 43).

self-soothing. The ability to regulate intense feelings when significant relationships get loaded with anxiety. A behavior (reducing your own anxiety) and an attitude (your *self* as responsible for reducing your own anxiety).

shame. Experienced as an extraordinarily painful, negative evaluation of the global self in response to an interpersonal transaction. Shame concludes, "*I* am defective, and there is *no way* to fix what is wrong."

trust. The ability to give to another freely because you believe that person will responsibly give to you what you need. The result of mutual and reliable giving and taking.

truth. Relational truth is many sided. Two or more sides characterize relationship stories and exchanges. Minimally there is "your truth" and "my truth."

understanding. One station in Terry Hargrave's model of forgiveness within families (Hargrave, 1994, 2001). Helps injured parties to comprehend the external circumstances (historic and current) and psychological processes (internal and relational) that influenced the wrongdoer. Helps wounded individuals see *why* the injustice occurred.

REFERENCES

Adams, M. M. (1999). *Horrendous evils and the goodness of God.* Ithaca, NY: Cornell University Press.

Anderson, N., & Mylander, C. (1997). *The Christ-centered marriage: Discovering and enjoying your freedom in Christ together.* Ventura, CA: Regal.

Arriaga, X. B., & Rusbult, C. E. (1998). Standing in my partner's shoes: Partner perspective taking and reactions to accommodative dilemmas. *Personality and Social Psychology Bulletin, 24,* 927-48.

Augsburger, D. W. (1996). *Helping people forgive.* Louisville, KY: Westminster John Knox Press.

Baumeister, R. F. (1997). *Evil: Inside human violence and cruelty.* New York: W. H. Freeman and Company.

Baumeister, R. F., Stillwell, A., & Heatherton, T. F. (1994). Guilt: An interpersonal approach. *Psychological Bulletin, 115* (2), 243-67.

Baumeister, R. F., Stillwell, A., & Heatherton, T. F. (1995). Personal narratives about guilt: Role in action control and interpersonal relationships. *Basic and Applied Social Psychology, 17* (1 & 2), 173-98.

Baumeister, R. F., Stillwell, A., & Wotman, S. R. (1990). Victim and perpetrator accounts of interpersonal conflict: Autobiographical narratives about anger. *Journal of Personality and Social Psychology, 59* (5), 994-1005.

Boszormenyi-Nagy, I., & Krasner, B. R. (1986). *Between give & take: A clinical guide to contextual therapy.* New York: Brunner/Mazel.

Bråkenhielm, C. (1993). *Forgiveness.* (T. Hall, Trans.). Minneapolis: Augsburg Fortress.

Cohen, S., & Willis, T. A. (1985). Stress, social support, and the buffering hypothesis. *Psychological Bulletin, 98,* 310-57.

Cozolino, L. (2002). *The neuroscience of psychotherapy: Building and rebuilding the human brain.* New York: Norton.

DiBlasio, F. (1998). The use of a decision-based forgiveness intervention within intergenerational family therapy. *Journal of Family Therapy, 20,* 77-94.

Duck, S. (1994). Steady as (s)he goes: Relational maintenance as a shared meaning system. In D. J. Canary & L. Stafford (Eds.), *Communication and relational maintenance* (pp. 45-60). San Diego: Academic Press.

Edwards, D., & Middleton, D. (1988). Conversational remembering and family relationships: How children learn to remember. *Journal of Social and Personal Relationships, 1,* 3-25.

Emmons, R. A. (2000). Personality and forgiveness. In M. E. McCullough, K. I. Pargament, & C. E. Thoresen (Eds.), *Forgiveness: Theory, research, & practice* (pp. 156-75). New York: Guilford Press.

Enright, R. D. (2001). *Forgiveness is a choice: A step-by-step process for resolving anger and restoring hope.* Washington, DC: American Psychological Association.

Enright, R. D., & Fitzgibbons, R. P. (2000). *Helping clients forgive.* Washington, DC: American Psychological Association.

Exline, J. J., & Baumeister, R. F. (2000). Expressing forgiveness and repentance: Benefits and barriers. In M. E. McCullough, K. I. Pargament, & C. E. Thoresen (Eds.), *Forgiveness: Theory, research, & practice* (pp. 133-55). New York: Guilford Press.

Finkel, E. J., Rusbult, C. E., Kumashiro, M., & Hannon, P. A. (2002). Dealing with betrayal in close relationships: Does commitment promote forgiveness? *Journal of Personality and Social Psychology, 82,* 956-74.

Freedman, J., & Combs, G. (1996). *Narrative therapy: The social construction of preferred realities.* New York: Norton.

Friedman, E. H. (1985). *Generation to generation: Family process in church and synagogue.* New York: Guilford Press.

Gergen, K. J. (1999). *An invitation to social construction.* Thousand Oaks, CA: Sage Publications.

Gorman, M. J. (2002). *Cruciformity.* Grand Rapids: Eerdmans.

Gottman, J. M. (1994). *Why marriages succeed or fail and how you can make yours last.* New York: Fireside/Simon & Schuster.

Gottman, J. M. (1999). *Seven principles for making marriage work.* New York: Three Rivers Press.

Green, J. B. (1997). *The gospel of Luke.* In G. D. Fee (Series Ed.), The New International Commentary on the New Testament. Grand Rapids: Eerdmans.

Green, J. B., & Baker, M. D. (2000). *Recovering the scandal of the cross.* Downers Grove, IL: InterVarsity Press.

Green, J. B., McKnight S., & Marshall, I. H. (Eds.). (1992). *Dictionary of Jesus and the gospels.* Downers Grove, IL: InterVarsity Press.

Grenz, S. J. (2001). *The social God and the relational self: A trinitarian theology of the imago dei.* Louisville, KY: John Knox Press.

Grenz, S. J., & Franke, J. R. (2001). *Beyond foundationalism: Shaping theology in a postmodern context.* Louisville, KY: John Knox Press.

Guerin, P. J., Jr., Fogarty, T. F., Fay, L. F., & Kautto, J. G. (1996). *Working with relationship triangles.* New York: Guilford Press.

Hargrave, T. D. (1994). *Families and forgiveness: Healing wounds in the intergenerational family.* New York: Bruner/Mazel.

Hargrave, T. D. (2000). *The essential humility of marriage: Honoring the third identity in couple therapy.* Phoenix: Zeig, Tucker & Theisen.

Hargrave, T. D. (2001). *Forgiving the devil: Coming to terms with damaged relationships.* Phoenix: Zeig, Tucker & Theisen.

Holeman, V. T. (1997). Couples forgiveness exercise. *The Family Journal: Counseling and Therapy for Couples and Families, 5,* 263-66.

Holeman, V. T. (2000). Thinking about reconciliation. *Marriage and Family: A Christian Journal, 3,* 369-82.

Holeman, V. T. (2003). Marital reconciliation: A long and winding road. *Journal of Psychology and Christianity,* 22 (1), 30-42.

Imber-Black, E. (1998). *The secret life of families: Truth telling, privacy, and reconciliation in a tell-all society.* New York: Bantam.

Jacobson, N. S., & Christensen, A. (1996). *Integrative couple therapy: Pro-*

moting acceptance and change. New York: Norton.

Janoff-Bulman, R. (1992). *Shattered assumptions*. New York: The Free Press.

Jones, L. G. (1995). *Embodying forgiveness: A theological analysis*. Grand Rapids: Eerdmans.

Jory, B., Anderson, D., & Greer, C. (1997). Intimate justice: Confronting issues of accountability, respect, and freedom in treatment for abuse and violence. *Journal of Marital and Family Therapy, 23* (4), 399-419.

Karney, B. R., & Frye, N. E. (2002). "But we've been getting better lately": Comparing prospective and retrospective views of relationship development. *Journal of Personality and Social Psychology, 82* (2), 222-38.

Kelley, D. L., & Waldron, V. R. (2003, February). *Forgiving communication as a response to relational transgression*. Manuscript submitted to National Communication Association, Interpersonal Division. Washington, DC.

Kerr, M. E., & Bowen, M. (1988). *Family evaluation*. New York: Norton.

Krasner, B. R., & Joyce, A. J. (1995). *Truth, trust, and relationships: Healing interventions in contextual therapy*. New York: Brunner/Mazel.

Lamb, S. (2002). Women, abuse, and forgiveness: A special case. In S. Lamb & J. G. Murphy (Eds.), *Before forgiving: Cautionary views of forgiveness in psychotherapy* (pp. 155-71). New York: Oxford University Press.

Lerner, H. G. (1989). *The dance of intimacy*. New York: Harper & Row.

Markman, H., Stanley, S., & Blumberg, S. L. (1994). *Fighting for your marriage*. San Francisco: Jossey-Bass.

Martin, R. (1981). *Reconciliation: A study of Paul's theology*. London: Marshall, Morgan & Scott.

Marty, M. (1998). The ethos of Christian forgiveness. In E. L. Worthington, Jr. (Ed.), *Dimensions of forgiveness: Psychological research and theological perspectives* (pp. 9-28). Radnor, PA: Templeton Foundation Press.

McCullough, M. (1997). Theoretical foundations and an approach to prevention. *Marriage and Family: A Christian Journal, 1* (1), 81-96.

McCullough, M. E., Fincham, F. D., & Tsang, J. (2003). Forgiveness, forbearance, and time: The temporal unfolding of transgression-related interpersonal motivations. *Journal of Personality and Social Psychology, 84*, 540-57.

McCullough, M. E., Pargament, K. I., & Thoresen, C. E. (Eds.). (2000). *Forgiveness: Theory, research, and practice*. New York: Guilford Press.

McCullough, M. E., & Worthington, E. L., Jr. (1999). Religion and the forgiving personality. *Journal of Personality, 67*, 1141-64.

Moltmann, J. (1981). *God in creation: A new theology of creation and the spirit of God.* (M. Kohl, Trans.). San Francisco: Harper & Row.

Müller-Fahrenholz, G. (1997). *The art of forgiveness: Theological reflections on healing and reconciliation*. Geneva, Switzerland: World Council of Churches Press (WCC Publications).

Nouwen, H. J. M. (1992). *The return of the prodigal son.* New York: Doubleday.

Oden, T. (1992). *Life in the Spirit.* San Francisco: HarperSanFrancisco.

Ortberg, J. (1997). *The life you've always wanted.* Grand Rapids: Zondervan.

Pannenberg, W. (1991). *Systematic theology.* (G. W. Bromily, Trans.). (Vol. 1). Grand Rapids: Eerdmans.

Pargament, K. I. (1997). *The psychology of religion and coping: Theory, research, and practice.* New York: Guilford Press.

Pargament, K. I., & Rye, M. S. (1998). Forgiveness as a method of religious coping. In E. L. Worthington, Jr. (Ed.), *Dimensions of forgiveness* (pp. 59-78). Radnor, PA: Templeton Foundation Press.

Piper, W. (1954). *The little engine that could.* New York: Platt and Munk.

Pohl, C. D. (1999). *Making room: Recovering hospitality as a Christian tradition.* Grand Rapids: Eerdmans.

Ross, M., & Buehler, R. (1994). Creative remembering. In U. Neisser & R. Fivush (Eds.), *The remembered self: Construction and accuracy in the self-narrative* (pp. 205-35). New York: Cambridge University Press.

Rusbult, C. E., Bissonnette, V. L., Arriaga, X. B., & Cox, C. L. (1998). Accommodation processes during the early years of marriage. In T. N. Bradbury (Ed.), *The developmental course of marital dysfunction* (pp. 74-113). New York: Cambridge University Press.

Sandage, S. J. (1999). Meaning, morality, and community: An interview with William J. Doherty. *Marriage and Family: A Christian Journal, 2* (4), 355-66.

Sandage, S. J., Aubrey, C. J., & Ohland, T. K. (1999). Weaving the fabric of community: A model for counselors and therapists. *Marriage and Family: A Christian Journal, 2* (4), 381-98.

Sandage, S. J., Worthington, E. L., Jr., Hight, T. L., & Berry, J. W. (2000). Seeking forgiveness: Theoretical context and an initial empirical study. *Journal of Psychology and Theology, 28,* 21-34.

Schnarch, D. (1997). *Passionate marriage.* New York: Norton.

Schnarch, D. (2002). *Resurrecting sex.* New York: HarperCollins.

Shults, F. L., & Sandage, S. J. (2003). *The faces of forgiveness: Searching for wholeness and salvation.* Grand Rapids: Baker.

Siegel, D. J. (1999). *The developing mind.* New York: Guilford Press.

Sittler, J. (1986). *Gravity and grace.* Minneapolis: Augsburg.

Snyder, C. R. (2000). The past and possible futures of hope. *Journal of Social and Clinical Psychology, 19* (1), 11-28.

Snyder, C. R., Michael, S. T., & Cheavens, J. S. (1999). Hope as a psychotherapeutic foundation of common factors, placebos, and expectancies. In M. A. Hubble, B. L. Duncan, & S. D. Miller (Eds.), *The heart and soul of change: What works in therapy* (pp. 179-200). Washington, DC: American Psychological Association.

Snyder, C. R., Rand, K. L., & Sigmon, D. R. (2002). Hope theory: A member of the positive psychology family. In C. R. Snyder & S. J. Lopez (Eds.), *Handbook of positive psychology* (pp. 257-76). New York: Oxford University Press.

Stanley, S. (1998). *The heart of commitment.* Nashville: Thomas Nelson.

Stanley, S. M., & Markman, H. J. (1992). Assessing commitment in personal relationships. *Journal of Marriage and the Family, 54,* 595-608.

Stillwell, A. M., & Baumeister, R. F. (1997). The construction of victim and perpetrator memories: Accuracy and distortion in role-based accounts. *Personality and Social Psychology Bulletin, 23* (11), 1157-73.

Stuart, R. (1980). *Helping couples change: A social learning approach to marital therapy.* New York: Guilford Press.

Tangney, J. P. (1995). Shame and guilt in interpersonal relationships. In J. P. Tangney & K. W. Fischer (Eds.), *Self-conscious emotions: The psychology of shame, guilt, embarrassment, and pride* (pp. 114-39). New York: Guilford Press.

Tangney, J. P. (2002). Humility. In C. R. Snyder and S. J. Lopez (Eds.), *Handbook of positive psychology* (pp. 411-19). New York: Oxford University Press.

Tangney, J. P., & Fischer, K. W. (Eds.). (1995). *Self-conscious emotions: The psychology of shame, guilt, embarrassment, and pride.* New York: Guilford Press.

Volf, M. (1996). *Exclusion and embrace.* Nashville: Abingdon.

Walsh, F. (1998). *Strengthening family resilience.* New York: Guilford Press.

White, M., & Epstein, D. (1990). *Narrative means to therapeutic ends.* New York: Norton.

Williams, C. (1956). *The forgiveness of sins.* London: Faber and Faber.

Witvliet, C. V., Ludwig, T. E., & Bauer, D. J. (2002). Please forgive me: Transgressors' emotions and physiology during imagery of seeking forgiveness and victim responses. *Journal of Psychology and Christianity, 21* (3), 219-33.

Worthington, E. L., Jr. (1998a). An empathy-humility-commitment model of forgiveness applied within family dyads. *Journal of Family Therapy, 20,* 59-76.

Worthington, E. L., Jr. (Ed.). (1998b). *Dimensions of forgiveness: Psychological research and theological perspectives.* Radnor, PA: Templeton Foundation Press.

Worthington, E. L., Jr. (2001). *Five steps to forgiveness: The art and science of forgiving.* New York: Crown Publishers.

Worthington, E. L., Jr. (2003). *Forgiving and reconciling.* Downers Grove,

IL: InterVarsity Press.

Worthington, E. L., Jr., & Drinkard, D. T. (2000). Promoting reconciliation through psychoeducation and therapeutic interventions. *Journal of Marital and Family Therapy, 26,* 93-101.

Worthington, E. L., Jr., Kurusu, T. A., Collins, W., Berry, J. W., Ripley, J. S., & Baier, S. N. (2000). Forgiving usually takes time: A lesson learned from studying interventions to promote forgiveness. *Journal of Psychology and Theology, 28,* 3-21.

Worthington, E. L., Jr., & Wade, N. G. (1999). The psychology of unforgiveness and forgiveness and implications for clinical practice. *Journal of Social and Clinical Psychology, 18,* 385-418.

Yalom, I. D. (1985). *Theory and practice of group psychotherapy* (3rd ed.). New York: Basic Books.

ACKNOWLEDGMENTS

I am blessed to belong to a wonderful community of friends who willingly read various renditions of this book. Many thanks to Lise, Joel and RuthAnne for your many helpful comments along the way.

Without my sabbatical from Asbury Theological Seminary and a grant from the Wabash Center for Teaching and Learning in Theological Education, this manuscript would not have seen the light of day.

Finally, to the men and women who talked with me about your deepest pain, my deepest thanks. My fingers may have typed the words, but you have lived the story. It is to you that I dedicate this work.

Subject and Names Index

acceptance, 13, 236
accommodation, 13, 235
account giving, 137, 138, 236
accountability, 127, 129, 135-43, 235
acknowledgment, 137, 138, 235
acquiescence, 137, 138-39, 235
agency thinking, 84
Alcoholics Anonymous, 63, 228
anxiety, 96-120, 141
attributions, 145
Augsburger, David, 76, 81, 87, 135, 155, 218
authentic apology, 129, 137, 139, 173, 236
awareness, 127, 130-35, 237
Baumeister, Roy, 130, 133, 164
benchmark events, 215-18
Bible Study Fellowship, 228
biblical culture, 75, 155
Blumberg, Susan, 171, 197
Bowen, Murray, 96, 115
Bråkenhielm, Carl Reinhold, 87
Buehler, Roger, 211
commitment, 14, 33-51, 53-57, 59-64, 66-71, 155
communication, 63-64, 69, 191-92, 197
community, 72-92, 155
of believers, 24, 75, 77, 87, 111, 200
confession, 37, 121, 123, 131, 136-41, 236
conflict management, 13, 96
conjoint remembering, 211
coping strategies, 45
couples' stories
adultery, 14-16, 35-36, 57-58, 64-65, 78-81
alcoholism, 8-9, 97-100
emotional abuse, 35-36, 37-38, 43
Internet pornography, 46-49
Crandall, Bonnie, 111-12
creative remembering, 211
dialogue, 189-92, 237
differentiation of self, 96, 100-114, 119, 132, 152, 192-93, 236
direct address, 185-86, 189-94, 236
divorce, 19-20, 98
Dobbins, Richard, 107-8
Doherty, William, 74-75
Drinkard, Dewitt, 12
Ebenezer, 216-18
Edwards, Derek, 211
emotions, 105-6
empathy, 26, 128-29, 130, 133-35, 164, 236
Enright, Robert D., 149
entitlement, 183, 236
essential items for reconciliation, 28-29, 34, 53, 74, 96-97
family of origin, 162
Fincham, Frank, 172
forbearance, 13, 238
forgetting, 204-15
forgiveness, 14, 25-26, 37-38, 42, 44, 45, 147-76, 178, 237
Franke, John, 221
Freedom in Christ Ministries, 227-28
Friedman, Edwin, 96, 107, 114, 115, 193
Frye, Nancy, 211
fundamental attribution error, 145, 237
future, 222
Gergen, Kenneth, 217
God, 23, 38-41, 50-51, 213-15, 231
Gorman, Michael, 82, 112
Gottman, John, 19, 68, 95, 170, 186, 206, 208
grace, 45-49, 218
gratitude, 42-43, 44, 45
Green, Joel B., 44, 110-11
Grenz, Stanley, 38, 108, 221
growing up. *See* differentiation of self
Guerin, Philip, 114, 117
guilt, 26, 128, 132-33, 137, 138, 139, 218, 237
Hargrave, Terry, 128, 129, 131, 152-56, 160, 173, 175, 184, 195, 218, 219
hope, 22, 56, 82-84, 187
hospitality, 161, 167-71
humility, 26, 124, 128, 130-33, 237
identity, 101-6, 111-14, 221-22
Imber-Black, Evan, 193
insight, 153, 154, 162-63
Janoff-Bulman, Ronnie, 200
Jesus Christ, 10, 19, 24, 37, 39-40, 44, 46, 48, 50,

109-14, 150, 166-67, 222
Jones, Gregory, 44, 45, 213, 215
Joyce, Austin, 185, 190
Karney, Benjamin, 211
Krasner, Barbara, 185, 186, 190
Lerner, Harriet, 96, 113, 115, 117
Link Care Foundation, 228
magnitude gap, 130, 134, 164-65, 237
Marble Retreat, 229
Markman, Howard, 171, 197
Martin, Marty, 24, 75
Martin, Ralph, 40
McCullough, Michael, 13, 19, 172, 208
memories, 206-8, 210
merited trust, 194-99, 237
Middleton, David, 211
mistrust, 143-45
Moltmann, Jürgen, 108
Mount Rainier, 27-28
Müller-Fahrenholz, Geiko, 136, 137
narrative, 200-24
  biblical, 22, 23-25, 37, 38-41, 77, 201, 213-15, 222
  community stories, 76
  narrative horizons, 37, 212
neural encoding, 206
nonanxious presence, 114, 116
obligations, 183, 237
Oden, Thomas, 130, 136, 145
oneness, 218-21
opportunity for compensation, 153, 154, 171-73
optical illusions, 211
Ortberg, John, 66
Overcomers Outreach, 63, 229
Pannenberg, Wolfhart, 108
Pargament, Ken, 45, 72
pathway thinking, 83
perseverance, 70-71, 234
Pohl, Christine D., 168
prevenient grace, 130
prevention, 231-32
professional counseling, 69-70, 89-91
REACHing for forgiveness, 151-52, 160
rebuilding trust, 141-43, 178, 237
reconciliation
  aspects of, 10-11, 13-14, 16
  biblical pattern of, 23
  bridge to, 18
  cautions against, 16-18
  cheap reconciliation, 12
  community, 76-78
  definition, 12, 237
  detours, 220-21
  failure to, 17, 18, 25, 49-50, 86-88, 144
  model of, 162
  readiness for, 175
  roadblocks, 220-21
  training for, 66-70
  with God, 19, 23, 40, 41
  with one another, 41-42
reframing, 26, 211-12
relationship
  history, 187-88
  maintenance, 52
  potholes, 196-99
  preservation, 12
  transformation, 12-14, 25, 40, 61
remembering, 204-15
repair attempts, 142-43
repentance, 14, 26, 28, 121, 122-24, 127, 128, 132, 134, 152, 177, 178, 238
research method, 20-22
residual trust, 186-88, 238
restoration, 153, 154, 160-61, 238
revenge, 165
risk, 18, 143, 160-61, 169
Rocky Mountains, 27
Ross, Michael, 211
Rye, Mark, 72
salvaging, 153, 154, 160, 162-67, 238
Sandage, Steven, 134, 212
Schnarch, David, 96, 106, 114, 115, 116
secrets, 69, 191, 193-94
self-responsibility, 117-20, 173, 238
self-soothing, 114-17, 119, 132, 238
shame, 26, 131, 132, 238
sin(s), 24
Sittler, Joseph, 155
Snyder, C. R., 82, 90
social facilitation, 72
social support, 46, 84-85, 232-33
Stanley, Scott, 59, 62, 171, 197, 218, 219
stories. *See* narrative
support groups, 85-86
Tangney, June, 132, 138
teamwork, 219-20
trauma, 200, 206-7, 232-33

Trinity, 22, 23, 38, 108-9, 218-19
trust, trustworthiness, 14, 63, 112, 137, 143, 144, 152, 171, 175, 177, 178, 184-85, 188, 189, 195, 196-99, 238
Tsang, Jo-Ann, 172
understanding, 153-54, 163-67, 239
unforgiveness, 44, 108
vision, 222-24
Volf, Miroslav, 167, 214, 215
Walk to Emmaus, 229
Walsh, Froma, 12
Williams, Charles, 49
Worthington, Everett, 12, 18, 148, 149-50, 151-52, 160, 208

Scripture Index

Genesis
1:1, *38*
1—3, *39*
2:24, *218*
3, *122*
4, *122*
27:36-46, *8, 122*
27—50, *76*
37, *184*
41:51-52, *212*
42:7, 9, *206-7*
42:18, *207*
50:19-20, *212, 224*

Joshua
4:21-23, *216*
4:24, *216*

1 Samuel
7:12, *216*

2 Samuel
12, *122*

Psalms
55:12-14, *7*
103:12, *204*

Isaiah
35, *3, 73*
43:25, *213*
53:3-6, *48-49*

Jeremiah
31:34, *213*

Matthew
4:17, *122*
5:23-24, *124*
6:10, *113*
7:3-5, *101, 117*
18, *218*
18:15-17, *124*
18:23-35, *44-45, 77, 173*

Mark
1:4, *122*

Luke
5:32, *123*
9:23-25, *10*
11:4, *44*
15:11-32, *8, 76-77, 124, 132, 169, 184*
22:22, *113*

John
1:29, *214*
10:18, *113*
13:1, *113*
15:15, *167*

Romans
5:8, *40*
5:10-11, *24*
12:3, *131*
12:13, *168*
12:17-21, *165*
12:18, *119*

1 Corinthians
12:12-26, *75*

2 Corinthians
2:5-11, *41*
2:14—7:2, *41*
5, *218*
5:17, *40, 75, 174*
5:18—6:2, *24, 25, 40*
7:10-13, *139*
7:12, *41*

Galatians
5:6, *82*
6:2, *73*

Ephesians
2:11-22, *24*
2:11-14, *149*
2:19, *149*
2:19-22, *209*
4:15, *186*
4:21—5:20, *209*
4:24, *149*
4:31, *149*
4:32, *150*
5:2, *150*

Philippians
2:5-7, *110, 112-14*

Colossians
1:19-23, *24*
3:9-10, *208-9, 221*

Philemon
24, *77*

Hebrews
5:14, *101*
6:1, *101*
12:1-3, *70*
13:2, *168*

1 Peter
2:9, *75*
4:9, *168*

1 John
3:1-3, *75, 167*

Revelation
5:6-14, *214*
21:1, *214*
21:4, *214*
22:1-4, *214*